# Lightning Strikes Once

*All-Phase Electric:*
*The First*
*Thirty Years*

*By* RONALD F. KINNEY

*Dedicated to my wife, Eva, and my
six children: Lisa, Marla, Ron Jr.,
Richard, Stephen and Maureen,
without whose support I would not
be where I am today.*

Copyright ©1989 by All-Phase Publishing Company
P.O. Box 67
Benton Harbor, Michigan 49022.

Library of Congress Catalog Card Number:
89-81811
ISBN 0-9625022-0-0 (hardbound)
ISBN 0-9625022-1-9 (paperback)

# Table of Contents

I.  BRANCHING OUT: HISTORY AND GROWTH .... 1
New Life for the Old A&P ..................... 2
"Seven by Seventy" and Beyond ................ 10
Heading East and South ...................... 17
Lessons Learned ............................. 23
Four in One ................................. 31
I Was Nearly Mortally Wounded ................ 36
One New Branch per Month ................... 41
More New Territory .......................... 47
Westward Ho! ............................... 54
Strange Circumstances Lead to
    More Florida Acquisitions .................. 56
Timely Opportunities ......................... 63
On the Wild Side............................. 68
Service Centers: A New Concept ............... 70
An Instantaneous Reaction ................... 72

II.  THE ART OF THE DEAL ..................... 77
The Chase ................................... 78
The Approach ............................... 81
The Six Steps ............................... 86
The Key Considerations for Purchase ........... 94
Why Companies Become Available .............100
Off and Running .............................102
Always Prospecting...........................106
Ones That Got Away..........................108
The Joy of Being Number One.................111

III.  THE KINNEY WORK ETHIC...................115
Learning the Work Ethic .....................116

In the Footsteps of a Self-Made Man . . . . . . . . . . . . .120
The Chickens Came First. . . . . . . . . . . . . . . . . . . . . .124
School Days . . . . . . . . . . . . . . . . . . . . . . . . . . . . . . . .131
College Years. . . . . . . . . . . . . . . . . . . . . . . . . . . . . . .133
The Navy . . . . . . . . . . . . . . . . . . . . . . . . . . . . . . . . . .137
Setting a Good Example. . . . . . . . . . . . . . . . . . . . . .140
Portioning Out the Day . . . . . . . . . . . . . . . . . . . . . .143

IV.  THE ALL-PHASE TEAM . . . . . . . . . . . . . . . . . . . .149
A Winning Attitude . . . . . . . . . . . . . . . . . . . . . . . . . .150
The Best and Leanest Staff in the Business . . . . . . .156
Hiring Smart. . . . . . . . . . . . . . . . . . . . . . . . . . . . . . . .160
Performance Reviews . . . . . . . . . . . . . . . . . . . . . . . .169
When Employees Don't Measure Up . . . . . . . . . . . . .172
Everyone Loves Recognition. . . . . . . . . . . . . . . . . . .176
Pulling Out All the Stops on Training . . . . . . . . . . .181
The Advanced Management Program . . . . . . . . . . . .183
The Personal Touch. . . . . . . . . . . . . . . . . . . . . . . . . .185
The Profit-Sharing Plan . . . . . . . . . . . . . . . . . . . . . .192
Managers as Entrepreneurs. . . . . . . . . . . . . . . . . . .195
The Role of Outside Sales. . . . . . . . . . . . . . . . . . . . .199
Keeping Employee Costs in Line . . . . . . . . . . . . . . .204
The Matter of Confidentiality . . . . . . . . . . . . . . . . .208

V.  OUR CUSTOMERS, OUR SUPPLIERS
     AND OUR COMPETITION . . . . . . . . . . . . . . . . . .211
Getting and Keeping Quality Customers . . . . . . . . .212
Promotions That Work . . . . . . . . . . . . . . . . . . . . . . .222
Pricing It Right. . . . . . . . . . . . . . . . . . . . . . . . . . . . . .228
At Least I Tried like Hell . . . . . . . . . . . . . . . . . . . . .230
Spreading the Word on All-Phase . . . . . . . . . . . . . .233
Working the Conventions . . . . . . . . . . . . . . . . . . . . .237
Tough but Fair Negotiator . . . . . . . . . . . . . . . . . . . .241
Deals with Manufacturers . . . . . . . . . . . . . . . . . . . .247
The High Value of Vendor Relationships . . . . . . . . .250

One Step Ahead of the Competition . . . . . . . . . . . . .255
Staying on Guard . . . . . . . . . . . . . . . . . . . . . . . . . .260

VI. ALL PHASES OF OUR BUSINESS . . . . . . . . . . . . .263
How a Branch Makes Money . . . . . . . . . . . . . . . . . .264
The All-Important Profit Margin . . . . . . . . . . . . . . .271
Inventory Transfers . . . . . . . . . . . . . . . . . . . . . . . . .275
Regional Distribution: A Giant Step . . . . . . . . . . . .279
The Physical Plant . . . . . . . . . . . . . . . . . . . . . . . . . .281
Wheels and Wings . . . . . . . . . . . . . . . . . . . . . . . . . .285
Living Through the Computerization Nightmare . .287
How Banks Have Helped Us Grow . . . . . . . . . . . . . .293
The Value of Planning . . . . . . . . . . . . . . . . . . . . . . .298

VII. MUSINGS . . . . . . . . . . . . . . . . . . . . . . . . . . . . . . . .305
What Would I Do Without My Tape Recorder? . . . . .306
My Love Affair with the Telephone . . . . . . . . . . . . .310
Pet Peeves . . . . . . . . . . . . . . . . . . . . . . . . . . . . . . . . .312
Governmental Nonsense . . . . . . . . . . . . . . . . . . . . .317
The Greatest Threats to Business . . . . . . . . . . . . . .321
Problems Mean Opportunities . . . . . . . . . . . . . . . . .329
Ingredients for Success . . . . . . . . . . . . . . . . . . . . . . .332
The Blessings of Good Health and Energy . . . . . . . .335
An Unexpected Ordeal . . . . . . . . . . . . . . . . . . . . . . .339
Four Men in One? . . . . . . . . . . . . . . . . . . . . . . . . . . .346
An Entrepreneur's Personality . . . . . . . . . . . . . . . .349
The GEM Award . . . . . . . . . . . . . . . . . . . . . . . . . . . .351
A Sporting Chance . . . . . . . . . . . . . . . . . . . . . . . . . .353

VIII. BUILDING FOR THE FUTURE . . . . . . . . . . . . . . .357
Our Silver Anniversary . . . . . . . . . . . . . . . . . . . . . .358
Our Thirtieth Anniversary . . . . . . . . . . . . . . . . . . . .359
The Woman Beside Me . . . . . . . . . . . . . . . . . . . . . . .362
Our Children: Our Proudest Achievement . . . . . . . .365
Passing the Torch . . . . . . . . . . . . . . . . . . . . . . . . . . .368
The Second Thirty Years . . . . . . . . . . . . . . . . . . . . .370
The Ultimate Satisfaction . . . . . . . . . . . . . . . . . . . .376

# Acknowledgments

*The seed for this book was planted one day in June 1983 when my son Stephen asked me to recount the history of All-Phase Electric Supply Company. We turned on the tape recorder, and it wasn't turned off until 500 typed pages later. My thanks go to my daughter Marla and Sylvia Paine, who organized my dictated manuscript and made it readable. I also want to thank my loyal employees, who really define the character of All-Phase and make it successful. And finally, I want to acknowledge my friends inside and outside this electrical industry who have helped make it all worthwhile.*

# Foreword

*Thirtieth-Anniversary Luncheon Address, May 2, 1989*
*Ritz Carlton Hotel, Chicago*
*National Association of Electrical Distributors*
  *Annual Convention*

Thank you all for joining me to celebrate the thirtieth anniversary of All-Phase Electric. Thirty years ago I started All-Phase in
an old A&P store building in my hometown of Benton Harbor,
Michigan. Today we have ninety-seven locations stretching from
Pennsylvania to California and are ranked as the fifth-largest electrical distributor in the country. If our rate of growth continues,
as we surely expect it to, we will double the size of the company
every four or five years. (In the past ten years we quadrupled our
size.) Since you arrived in this room one hour ago, All-Phase has
conducted more business than we did in our entire first year of
operation.

Thirty years seems like a long time when you consider that I'm
the only "original" employee who doesn't need the corporate archives to look up a detail. I am the only remaining eyewitness to
a great deal of corporate history. But history is of interest only to
historians. We have learned from where we have come, but the big
news is in where we are going.

One shining example of our future direction is our Regional
Distribution Center that opened in St. Joseph, Michigan, in
December 1988. It adds another 100,000 square feet of warehouse
space to a system that already encompasses more than fifteen
acres across the country. I'm pleased to say that the RDC concept
is working so well that we now have a 40,000-square-foot addition

*vii*

under construction, taking the building to a total of 140,000 square feet.

The Regional Distribution Center is one way All-Phase works to keep our system energized every day of the week. We want to keep our employees motivated, we want to keep our programs innovative, and we want to maintain a competitive spirit in all of our operations.

The world is moving from a transaction environment to an alliance environment. We as a company are changing along with the total industry. We are managing our own changes, and we are not allowing external factors to influence the manner in which we do business. Like most of our key vendors who are sitting in this room today, we want to lead change, not follow it. We recognize the importance of alliances and true partnerships. We are not interested in simply doing business with our vendors—we want to have them as full partners. That takes it out of the transaction environment and into true strategic alliances.

I'm reminded of a couple of Boy Scouts who took a hike through the woods with their troop. They found an old railroad bridge and wanted to try walking the rails. Scout after scout lost his balance and fell off the track—except for two, who were hanging back, whispering. These boys bet the rest that they could walk the entire length of the trestle without stumbling. The troop took the bait. So Scout One jumped on the first rail, Scout Two on the opposite rail. Their arms reached across—shoulder to shoulder, to balance each other—and off they walked! They won the bet.

It is precisely through that kind of cooperation that we have come this far—balancing each other, shoulder to shoulder in mutual respect.

Prognosticators suggest that as much as one quarter of the distributors doing business as recently as two years ago will be gone by 1995. And during this same short period, the number of branches owned by the remaining top 100 distributors will increase almost sixfold. The locations won't necessarily disappear, but you can bet they will be operated differently and by different people than we know today. Today, just nine of the largest full-line electrical distributors have more branches—1,093—than did all of the top 100 distributors in 1971. And, interestingly, three of those nine have offshore ownership.

All-Phase doesn't have to be number one. Rather, our goal is to be the best in the markets we serve. Our goal is to be perceived as the premier electrical distributor in each of the communities where we have a branch.

Our mission statement today can be summed up in five key words: Quality, Leadership, Consistency, Commitment and Empowerment.

Quality—in the vendors we represent, the people we employ and the customers we sell to.

Leadership—in this wonderful electrical-distribution industry, setting trends and always being on the cutting edge.

Consistency—in how we deal with our partners and our customers.

Commitment—in how we go to market, and leveraging our size to benefit both our vendors and All-Phase Electric. This will be important in the months and years ahead. And we will be asking for innovative market support in taking your products to the customer.

Empowerment—of our employees so that they will have the confidence and the skills to do the right thing at the right time.

The All-Phase we all know is a sound and stable industry citizen, the result of thirty years of labor and loyalties.

Every company has its own culture—its own values, rites, rituals, heroes, everything from leadership style and decision making to the way we dress and the sports we pursue.

One hallmark of the All-Phase culture is stick-to-itiveness. Another is single-mindedness. We have always devoted our ambitions and energies toward a single industry, while maintaining a small-town spirit.

We also are growing with American-made products. The Industrial Distribution Association handles 5 to 10 percent of its products from offshore. Catalog houses have over 50 percent imports. All-Phase sells less than 1 percent in imports.

This demonstrates another All-Phase characteristic: pride!

All-Phase people have lots of it. Pride in an industry that is clean, essential, more stable than most and highly visible. Pride in the company beyond a place to work—a corporate-wide pride beyond individual recognition.

All of these factors make up the All-Phase difference. A difference that makes work worth doing. A difference that gives dignity to the individual, character to the business and satisfaction to the customer.

Now comes the big question: How can we top our recent accomplishments? One thing is certain: Complacency is not in the All-Phase vocabulary. We don't even think about slowing down; we're too busy thinking about how we can improve.

New markets, new customers, new products, new marketing approaches—all of these are moves All-Phase is targeting in the immediate future. It all stems from good strategic planning.

Strategic planning is building a bridge of reality between the present and the future. Further, it requires us to start building with vision, mission and scope. We decide how far we expect to go and how to get there. Then we find out what it takes.

Let's get specific. Let me give you three numbers. We are looking for 20 percent growth in sales per year—10 percent growth in market share and new openings, and 10 percent through acquisitions. Over the past few years we've added an average of one new location per month.

In conclusion, let me say that strategic planning—which translates into strategic management—will power our future. We need to accelerate the decision-making process if we are to gain the flexibility required to react to rapidly changing market conditions. I challenge all of you to remember that the greatest risk is uncertainty, the most costly decision is no decision, the most shameful waste is an idea cut off before it finds a voice.

All-Phase is an idea I had thirty years ago, and with your continued support, it will become that much greater in the next thirty years. Thank you.

# *CHAPTER I.*

## BRANCHING OUT: HISTORY AND GROWTH

# New Life for the Old A&P

I RETURNED TO MY HOMETOWN of Benton Harbor, Michigan, in January 1956, after a six-year absence—four years at John Carroll University in Cleveland, Ohio, earning a bachelor's degree in business administration, and two years as a commissioned officer in the United States Navy. My first job when I arrived back home was that of salesman for one of my father's businesses, a rather small company doing perhaps a quarter-million dollars a year in retail heating, air conditioning and appliances. Within about a year I went from salesman to service manager to general manager and majority stockholder. After two and a half years with my father, in the fall of 1958, I decided that the company would never be large enough nor lucrative enough to support what eventually would be a family of six children. At best, I thought, I might realize $25,000 net profit after tax for a full year's work.

Just as important, I felt that the retail business was not the one for me. I did not like the idea of dealing with a new customer for each sale. I preferred serving the same customers day in and day out, building rapport with my clientele.

To be sure, we had a fair number of repeat customers who were satisfied with our sales and service, and I had had a few opportunities to succeed at repetitive sales. I might, for example, sell a family the furnace for their home, then an add-on air-conditioning unit, then some appliances. But after all, how many times do you buy a kitchen full of appliances or a furnace? I wanted to establish relationships with people based on more than a fleeting, one-time sale.

That fall and early winter I conducted a small survey among local building contractors—and more specifically electricians—to see whether our community needed a business that offered such repetitive contact. Six or seven people suggested I consider the wholesale electric-supply business. There was only one distributor in the Twin Cities of St. Joseph and Benton Harbor. The electrical contractors bemoaned the fact that if the existing distributor was out of an item, they had to depend on service from some outlying community up to thirty-five miles away.

Once I settled on the electrical-supply industry, I had to find a place of business. Right across the alley from our heating and appliance store was the back entrance to an A&P store. I used to have morning coffee with the A&P manager, and he told me he was relocating from downtown. I obtained the name of his landlord and negotiated a three-year lease for the 10,000-square-foot supermarket building.

I hired a staff of seven. The first was Erv Bradford, who was a purchasing agent from South Haven, Michigan; then we added Danny Wegenka, a counterman from South Bend, Indiana, along with three salesmen, an accountant and a combination warehouseman/truck driver.

The driver, Al Ray, had been influential in my decision to enter the business. He had worked for me as an electrician at the heating and appliance store. One day, when we were delivering a refrigerator, too much weight pressed against his chest and he had a heart attack. After that, he could no longer do heavy work. I told him I would somehow find a new job for him that would require less physical exertion.

Most of us were new in this business, so we had to set up our own shelving, build a Cardex file for inventory control, structure a set of books and, most important, negotiate with manufacturers for lines. This was particularly difficult because my competitor in town had been in business so long that he had a strangle hold on the good lines. But I managed to put together a fairly representatative list with manufacturers who had been alienated over the years by my competitor. With these lined up, we opened on April 1, 1959.

The old A&P sign that hung outside my new building accommodated the name I chose for our company—All-Phase Electric. I repainted the metal sign myself, using the existing letters. I considered hundreds of names before deciding on All-Phase, and I've been very, very pleased with its national acceptance and recognition. I'm happy we did not go with Lake Michigan Electric or Great Lakes Electric—which would have been too regional. Also, I detest companies being called, say, "Wholesale Electric" or "Electric Wholesale" or "Electric Supply." Such names have absolutely no character or meaning whatsoever, but it's amazing how many firms in our industry use them. It's even difficult to remember the names of some companies we subsequently purchased, because many were so similar and nondescript.

Another plus with the name All-Phase is the double connotation of the word "phase." It is an electrical term, and also it implies more than one phase of the business or more than one phase of customer. I've been complimented many times on our company name. It's so popular that I continually battle with new companies trying to use it.

FINANCIAL FOOTINGS

Naturally, capital is a basic requirement of a new company. I was fortunate to have the Kinney name, because in our community it was synonymous with business acumen and success. My father, John J. Kinney, was a very successful coal merchant who had left Olivet College in Olivet, Michigan, after his sophomore year to start his company from scratch. Over thirty years he built his business to one of the largest coal dealers in Michigan. Eventually his company evolved into a heating and air-conditioning business, along with several other ventures.

With my new stockholders, namely my father and my two

brothers, Pat and Jack, each of whom had invested $17,500 in the company, All-Phase was able to start with a fairly nominal investment of $70,000, with a similar line of credit from the local bank. We came up a little short on working capital, and my mother bought the remaining $5,000 worth of stock. At the time she simply wanted to loan me the money, but I told her that she was entitled to more than just interest and that by purchasing stock she would get the appreciation on the growth in value. I'm proud to say that within ten years I was able to buy back her stock at the fair market value of $100,000, indicating a growth of some twentyfold. She felt that this was too much money, but I told her it was only fair. Eventually I reached an agreement to buy out both my brothers also.

Pat and Jack went on to become very successful in their own fields. Pat has a highly respected law firm in St. Joseph and is one of the top tax lawyers in the county. He has been of great help over the years in advising us on legal matters and, of course, preparing our purchase agreements and contractual arrangements. He also has taken the lead in our All-Phase real-estate partnership. Jack became a very successful asphalt contractor, operating out of Benton Harbor. He has passed this business on to his sons.

From the start I disagreed with the banking policies we met with, to an extent that shaped my later dealings with bankers. The local bank loaned money based on inventory and receivables. When we grew big enough, we needed to bring in a correspondent bank, the National Bank of Detroit. Then the policy became more complicated. If anything in our accounts receivable aged out beyond 120 days, the bank would not lend money on it. I remember a large industrial account disputing a $5 bill and, because the account remained unsettled, NBD would not loan money on some $5,000 in receivables we had with that company. I resolved that as soon as I was in a position to do so, I would never again depend on a correspondent bank but would move up to a larger bank every time I felt the need or had the opportunity.

Over the years we have moved from the Farmers and Merchants National Bank of Benton Harbor (now a branch of NBD) to the American National Bank in Kalamazoo (which introduced the Prudential Life Insurance Company for a long-term loan) to the Michigan National Bank in Grand Rapids. Eventually we turned to Continental Illinois National Bank and shared a line of credit with the National Bank of Detroit. All of these banks have been helpful in the growth of All-Phase, but they have certainly received their payment in full for any exposure or leveraging in which they were involved. Although it was unfashionable to negotiate interest rates in that day, I still managed to secure a favorable rate.

DESTINED TO GROW

I'll never forget my first customer, Baroda Hardware. The owner was one of the people who had encouraged me to get into the business, and I had expected to go back, open up my order book and write some sales. But the first thing I heard was a question about my price for building wire. I said I didn't know for sure, but I had plenty to sell. "Well," the owner replied, "of course, your price has to be competitive with West Michigan Electric or we won't be able to buy from you." I thought I would get orders in appreciation of my having created a new supplier for these contractors. I hadn't realized it would be a matter of price. What a rude awakening to the facts of life!

In the beginning almost every dollar I could accumulate went right back into All-Phase. I always kept my salary relatively low. I paid my purchasing agent $250 a week; I received $200 a week. I continued to be the second-highest-paid employee at All-Phase for several years.

All-Phase was destined to grow. In our first month of business we did $5,000 in volume. Of course, that was not nearly enough to support eight people and 10,000 square feet of space, but I did my part to cut overhead. I did all of the collecting, served as sales manager and ran the showroom until we could afford to hire someone to run it as well as do secretarial work. Needless to say, I spent every day of every week at the office, including Saturdays and Sundays.

After eighteen months we were in the hole $18,000. (I told my wife, Eva, that I was no longer making $80 a week; I was losing $1,000 a month.) That seemed astronomical to me at the time. My starting capital was proving inadequate. The bank line was still good, thanks to the family reputation, but we were strained. I even went so far as to send inquiries to plumbing manufacturers to see if that might be a better field for me.

Fortunately, just at that time, my competitor, West Michigan Electric, was having a little difficulty with personnel. The general manager, Ray Hafer, had left the company and had moved to Grand Rapids, Michigan, as a manufacturer's agent for the DayBrite Lighting Fixture Company. This gave me the opportunity to go after some of the accounts Hafer had serviced over the past twenty years. Our successes were immediate. When we turned the corner, we were able to make back all of our losses and reach the break-even point within the next twelve months.

OUR FIRST ACQUISITION

On Memorial Day weekend in 1964, Ray Jeffirs, the owner of West Michigan Electric, called to ask if I might be interested in talking about buying his company. He said he had been negotiating with Westinghouse Electric Supply Company out of Pittsburgh and was getting short-tempered with the red tape. He was determined to sell—and soon. I met with him on Memorial Day with my brothers and my father. Jeffirs laid out the requirements for an asset purchase of his main house in Benton Harbor as well as a branch in Kalamazoo. We met in his lawyer's office on the following Monday morning, and it took us a full week to structure a contract agreeable to both parties. We then discussed the Kalamazoo branch and completed that transaction the

7

following week. By July 1, 1964, All-Phase had gone from $1 million in volume to $3 million.

My father had been a silent partner in West Michigan Electric in the late 1930s and early 1940s, but he and Jeffirs had had a falling out. They eventually mended their differences, for they had too many common friends and acquaintances to remain enemies. They declared a truce while leaning on a heating pipe in the boiler-room basement of St. John's Catholic Church one Sunday after Mass. Eventually they became such good friends that they traveled together on many trips and frequently entertained each other in their homes.

Our first acquisition was not without its difficulties. Here, as with succeeding transactions, the conflicts had to do with personalities. When we took inventory to determine the value of the assets, we came up with a discrepancy of some $10,000 between inventory value and our actual physical count. In looking over the physical inventory taken prior to our count, we found that ten chandelier shades had been counted as complete chandeliers valued at $1,000 each rather than $1 each. When we pointed it out, Jeffirs said the error wasn't important and that we had agreed to buy his assets as listed on his books. We could either take it and pay him the $10,000 premium, he said, or walk away from the deal. We came awfully close to going our separate ways, but this was the opportunity of a lifetime and I convinced my stockholders that we simply had to go forward with the purchase.

When we approached inventory day, Hafer called me and said Jeffirs was about to sell all of his wire inventory at 5 percent over cost to someone else, hoping to make a profit of 5 percent more than he would get from me the following day. He also would receive cash rather than the deferred payment to which we had agreed. So I had to jump in and pay his 5 percent premium to purchase the largest single commodity—copper—which amounted to some 20 percent of the total inventory.

Obviously, there were many complications in putting together two companies that had been at each other's throats for five years. We had to decide whether to stick with our purchasing agent, who was our first employee, or accept theirs, who had been in the community some twenty years. Our person won out. Then there was the question of combining sales forces. I'm happy to say that the original All-Phase group was retained, as were just about all of the West Michigan Electric people, although some were eventually deployed to Kalamazoo and other new branches. I delayed for six months hiring one of our former salesmen who had defected to them a year before the purchase.

Inventory was a severe problem. First, we had to combine both inventories into one building that was somewhat smaller than theirs—Jeffirs had retained the major-appliances and television-franchise portion of his business in half of his three-story building, leasing us the other half. More important, we had to satisfy perhaps half a dozen manufacturers in a particular commodity classification where we needed only three; in this regard the stronger of the lines always survived.

Despite all of this, our expanded company prospered from the outset. We had a deferred-payment program directly with the seller that was satisfactorily retired on time.

# "Seven by Seventy" and Beyond

IN FEBRUARY 1966, ABOUT A YEAR AND a half after the West Michigan acquisition, we acquired an old-line company in Holland, Michigan, that had fallen on difficult times. It took us two or three years to make it profitable. We were so confident, though, that we built a new building after about eighteen months in the city.

Then came the Michigan City, Indiana, branch in the fall of 1967. This was our first move into a new state. We tried to buy our competitor in that city, but he was difficult to deal with and became rather emotional over the issue, so we ended up opening a new branch. And we did it within twenty-one days after deciding to do so. This was quite a record, considering that again we took an old supermarket building, cleaned it out, remodeled it, bought shelving, installed the counter, built offices, stocked the inventory and were ready for business—all within three weeks.

Early in 1968 we bought a company in Battle Creek, Michigan. It was our fifth branch and one of our most unusual acquisitions. The company, B.C. Supply, dealt in all types of products—lawn mowers, pizza trays, beach umbrellas, mailboxes, garden implements, you name it. We sold off these extraneous lines largely because of a philosophy All-Phase adopted early on: Do one thing and do it well.

We have had opportunities to sell many things—plumbing, heating, electronics, mill supply, hardware supply—but we have always resisted. In Muskegon, Michigan, for example, we almost got into wholesale sporting goods. I love sports and really would have enjoyed selling uniforms and equipment to high schools and colleges. But it was just too far afield for us. I firmly believe that one of the keys to our success is that we put our blinders on and decided to concentrate on electrical products and market those as well as we could.

Up to this point all of our purchases had been of an asset nature. That is, we would buy the assets—typically the inventory, accounts receivable and fixed assets of equipment and rolling stock. Asset purchases involve simply the net asset value with no premium paid for blue sky, good will, a noncompete clause or the going aspect of the business. All-Phase Electric stayed away from the building and land assets. Instead, I formed a partnership called All-Phase Real Estate Company with my brother Pat to make investments in real estate.

We departed from our usual asset-purchase practice on the next acquisition when we bought the parent company of our Holland branch, Independent Electric Supply of Muskegon, Michigan. When we appraised the assets, we found that the company had a deficit net worth. We were very concerned about proceeding with the purchase. But we managed to negotiate a fair price on the purchase slightly below book value. For the first time we had a tax loss carry forward on the books, so we kept Independent Electric as a separate corporation until it could make back the money shown as a deficit net worth.

Because we did not want a reputation for dealing in companies that were in financial difficulty, we made it a policy not to repeat this type of purchase unless all parties involved thoroughly understood we were making the deal as a last-ditch effort to help the owner and creditors. (We did, incidentally, satisfy all Muskegon creditors 100 cents on the dollar on all claims.) Even today, the first thing a potential seller often says is, "I don't have to sell" and "You're not buying a company in trouble." I'm always happy to hear that, because no one wants to take on a turnaround situation that requires an infusion of people and time—sometimes years—to straighten out.

## CONTIGUOUS EXPANSION

As we expanded we set a policy that every city we entered be contiguous to another All-Phase city. We didn't want to have a city in between branches that we couldn't service with our shuttle-truck inventory exchange or with our salespeople. We would develop new branch cities by sending an existing salesperson in to cultivate business. After that person had garnered some $5,000 gross profit in volume per month, we would consider opening a branch.

This was the case in Sturgis, Michigan, in the fall of 1969. We had been servicing this little community out of Kalamazoo for about five years and had developed it to where we felt it could sustain branch number seven. It was profitable from the first month. That proved that our success in Michigan City, where we'd built our first branch from scratch, hadn't been a fluke. The Sturgis opening allowed us to reach our goal of "Seven by Seventy," a motto that kept us going in those early years.

We perhaps became a little too bold over our success in Sturgis, because within a couple of months we entered the very competitive market of Grand Rapids, Michigan, where there were seven electrical distributors. It took more than five years to turn the corner and become profitable there. That slowed us down a step or two. Our next branch came almost two years later, in the summer of 1971. The location was Cadillac, Michigan. We opened there from scratch too, with one of our countermen from the Kalamazoo branch as our manager. It was very successful from the outset. Then we reached over into Lansing, Michigan, where we acquired the common stock in Capital Electric, which had been founded in 1893 as a manufacturer of bicycles. Through this acquisition we became, for a time, one of Oldsmobile's largest suppliers.

In some cases, as in Lansing, which was key to our contiguous spread through Michigan, we had to apply pressure on the stockholders to sell. We went so far as to imply that if they were not amicable to a sale to All-Phase, we would open our own branch. We simply could not have a void in this city blocking our progress in Michigan.

That same month, November 1971, we bought a company in Valparaiso, Indiana, taking us farther south in that state. We bought just the electrical apparatus and supply divisions of a company that also was involved in carpeting, fireplaces, plumbing and heating, bathroom fixtures and the like. This was quite a move, because not only did we take inventory over a weekend, but we also moved everything out and carried it half a block to another end of the building.

Staying in that building turned out to be a mistake, because a few years later there was a fire that spread into our area. We had a fire wall between the two parts and would have been safe had it not been for a small opening the size of a concrete block where employees of the former company used to pass invoices back and forth. Smoke poured into our building through that little hole before we realized what was happening. It totally consumed both the building and the inventory. Unbelievably, this fire occurred on the Saturday morning of the last day of our fiscal year and we had just completed our physical count, so every single item could be accounted for on our fire-insurance claim.

When they called me to tell me the building was on fire, I ordered every file cabinet moved to the front lawn. We saved every piece of paperwork. You can imagine my amazement when I pulled off the turnpike to drive that last five miles to Valparaiso and saw a plume of smoke a mile high.

If there is such a thing as having a fire at an opportune time, this was it. Of course, we still lost money. We had to buy land, build a new building, replenish the stock and get established again. We had no business-interruption insurance to help in the interim, but because we had no local competitor and were able to stock inventory in temporary quarters, our customers never really suffered.

## A MASS EXODUS

About a year later, in the fall of 1972, we opened a new branch in Owosso, Michigan, complementing the Lansing facility. We opened with all new people from the community. We had some difficulty acclimating them to our business philosophy, and one day the manager just decided he'd had it with us. He laid the keys on the desk and walked out the door, and everybody walked out with him. He left the building unlocked and vacant. We rushed a man there to take it over, but I learned then not to trust a new branch to an unknown, outside person. I don't believe there has ever been an acquisition or a new opening that we haven't sent in at least one All-Phase person for the initial indoctrination and branch opening.

A couple of months after the Owosso opening, we bought the electrical apparatus and supply division of Commercial Electric in Toledo, Ohio, which also had a major-appliance and television division. Here again we inventoried and moved on the same weekend, but this time the move was across town into a large, 21,000-square-foot facility. I remember this acquisition vividly, because the owner had one of his staff members standing at each exit with a walkie-talkie, reporting on every activity. I guess he was afraid we were going to walk out with some TVs.

Later in 1972, after several thwarted attempts to buy an electrical distributor in our neighboring city of South Bend, Indiana, we finally decided we had to start from scratch. We obtained the key supplier lines we needed and staffed the branch with local people and existing employees. A key employee was our resident salesman, who had been in South Bend for about ten years.

In the summer of 1973, we acquired the company in South Haven, Michigan, from which we had hired our first employee, Erv Bradford.

At about this time we entered Fort Wayne, Indiana, the first city in which we operated two branches at once. First we acquired the Anthony Wayne Electric Supply Company there, and a year after we opened another branch on the north side. The two coexisted for five years until we decided we could serve the entire community out of the larger Fort Wayne North building. Halfway through the remodeling of that facility our contractor went bankrupt, and for the first time I learned what it was like to receive, or in this case fail to receive, a waiver of lien. I was faced with the harsh reality of having to pay for concrete work on the truck dock twice, the first time to the contractor and the second time to the supplier who had not been paid by the contractor.

Next we concentrated our expansion efforts on Ohio and the northern peninsula of Michigan.

The Lima, Ohio, acquisition was somewhat of a quirk. My oldest daughter had completed her first year of college at St. Mary's of Notre Dame and was taking a semester abroad when she asked us to look into Dennison University in central Ohio. I've always hated to make any trip without tying it in with business, so I looked at the map and saw that Lima was on the way to the college. Eva and I stopped there and had lunch with the owner of State Electric and his wife at the country club. We got along so well we ended up buying their company.

Then we were contacted by the owner of a company in Cheboygan, Michigan, who had a branch in Sault Ste. Marie. He couldn't figure out why he couldn't make any money, but I could see that the generous salary he was paying himself was a big part of the problem. This branch too was an asset purchase. It pretty much completed our sweep of western Michigan, all the way from the Straits to the Indiana line.

Our single largest acquisition to date followed: the purchase of W.W. Electric in Springfield, Ohio. It was a real jewel—52,000 square feet. We had an excellent core of forty-five or fifty people, most of whom were still with us ten years after we bought the company. Again, this was a pure asset purchase, with very fair rental on the building, which we eventually bought.

Springfield has been a true storybook branch in terms of personnel promotions. We have been able to bring our warehousemen up to the counter, countermen up to inside sales, and inside sales to outside sales. At least half of Springfield's outside salespeople today had some inside position at the time of the acquisition. Many of these employees moved on to branch management in other locations.

# Heading East and South

$B$Y 1975 I CONCLUDED THAT IF WE were really going to expand, we needed to abandon the idea of contiguous growth and spread beyond Michigan, Indiana and Ohio. As it happened, a supplier who attended one of our sales-blitz banquets in Lima heard my speech, which closed with my asking everyone to keep his or her eyes open for prospects anywhere in the United States. The supplier told me of a company headquartered in Atlanta that was available. I contacted the owner, who also had branches in Athens, Carrollton and College Park, Georgia. It didn't take long to determine that the company was virtually bankrupt.

After spending a day there, we told the principal we could see no opportunity for All-Phase. He responded that he was desperate to do something with the company. He had been turned down by one other regional electrical distributor and saw no alternative but to allow the financing company with which he was factoring his inventory and accounts receivable to put a lock on the door and auction off the inventory. We said perhaps there was some way, short of bankruptcy, that we could help him. If he could persuade at least 80 percent of his suppliers to accept a cash payment for a discounted portion of the amounts due them, we would pay off the amounts agreed upon and make the acquisition.

He succeeded in getting more than 80 percent cooperation. We paid off the creditors as agreed and also paid off in full those who would not agree to a reduction. We were quite careful to stay out of the mainstream of this settlement, for we did not want the reputation of having bought a company and then offering the creditors less than full payment. Even as it was, I had to contact a couple of manufacturers to push it over the top. I would hesitate to become directly involved in such a transaction again.

In terms of the number of locations tied to a single purchase, this venture into the Southeast was our largest acquisition up to that date. (The Springfield acquisition of W.W. Electric was about the same size in terms of sales volume.) The Georgia acquisition went rather smoothly until we began to negotiate sales commissions. As a result we lost two key salesmen at the outset. That was a bit of a blow, but most of the people stayed.

I often ask myself: Is it better to go into a branch that isn't making money and completely clean house, sending in all new people, or try to maintain what is there and start good hiring practices by replacing the lesser performers? As I look back on this Georgia acquisition, I still think it was best to keep existing people in key positions, because ten or twelve years later the branch manager in every one of those locations, as well as most of the outside salespeople and some of the operations people, remained from that original acquisition.

One mistake was keeping the principal of the Georgia company as a salesman. Although he professed support for our company, I think he was jealous of our success.

While it took an immense amount of time and money, Georgia did end up being one of our better acquisitions. We subsequently backed a minority-business enterprise in which our former warehouse manager held 51 percent and we owned the rest. He is president of this prosperous little company in downtown Atlanta and does very well with government and state contracts.

Later in 1976 we acquired one of the oldest electrical-distribution firms in the United States—the Doubleday-Hill Electrical Supply Company of Pittsburgh. The company dated back to 1884, when its founder actually worked with Thomas Alva Edison on developing the incandescent light bulb.

The company had fallen on hard times, not really of its own making. The previous owner was president of the National

Association of Electrical Distributors (NAED) back in the 1960s and, as such, was a focal point of the industry. The unions decided to organize his company, and he absolutely refused to succumb. They even put signs on his front lawn at home and, I'm told, built fires on the grass. They also boycotted him and caused him to lose the base of his business in Pittsburgh. He fought it, and although he almost lost his company he never did let the unions in. He sold the company to a buyer who couldn't bring it around, and we ended up with it.

It was a loser with a fairly substantial tax-loss carry forward, which we received for $5,000. Today it is a fine moneymaker and very efficiently run, but for a number of years it was in the gray area. We have in our archives one of the invoices written by this company in longhand in 1903, which came out of its active file cabinet when we made the acquisition in 1976. You can imagine what kind of shape the company was in if it still had records dating back seventy-three years.

Before we agreed to complete the purchase of Doubleday-Hill, the valuation of the assets had to come up to a certain dollar level. We were taking inventory and still didn't know whether we had a deal when the owner approached our controller and asked, "What do you think the chances are that this is going to go through?" Whereupon our construction manager came through the wall with a sledge hammer as he was remodeling the entire office and warehouse area. The owner said, "I guess it really doesn't matter; it looks as though you've already taken over." We learned our lesson from this—not to push too hard and to be gentle and considerate, particularly in new regions of the country.

ALABAMA BOUND

Our first entry into Alabama came in January 1977 with Tri-State Electric in Dothan. This acquisition was somewhat unusual in that we had the express approval and agreement of the company's principal, but we discovered that he did not have the approval of the stockholders.

When we arrived for the transition week and signing of the actual agreement, we found not only that the stockholders disagreed over the sale but also that they had not even been informed that such a move was planned. We had to spend many hours convincing them to sell. We left the city without a contract, but it finally worked out. The principal of that company continues as one of our fine supporters in the community.

We came back into Michigan in early 1977 with the purchase of Park Electric Supply Company of Petoskey, a branch of a bankrupt company out of Pontiac. We merely purchased the branch and complied with the bulk sales act, whereby we notified all supplier creditors of the intended sale so that they could stake their claim. We paid everyone in full.

The next spring we returned to Alabama with acquisitions in Huntsville and Albertville. While interviewing employees during transition week, some of them accused the Huntsville branch manager of stealing from the company. When confronted with this on inventory day, he implicated other employees. And then things went from bad to worse.

Over the weekend this manager held a meeting at his home with the employees and convinced them that these people from the North were not good for them or for the company. They quit and joined other companies in the area. Thank God two of the key individuals subsequently returned and helped restore stability to the branch, but for a while they caused us great concern. In the meantime, we had to jump in and transfer one of our people from the Central District down as branch manager and scramble around sending temporary people in from Georgia. These were anxious moments as we wondered whether we'd be able to keep the doors open.

On the shirttails of this came acquisitions in Selma and Monroeville, Alabama, making Alabama one of our largest states, with six locations.

Then a manufacturer friend told me of a small company in Lake Charles, Louisiana, that might be for sale, so in October 1977 I visited the owner at his dilapidated former grain-elevator warehouse. I remember knocking on the framework of the doorway to his office (there was no door) only to find him asleep behind his desk. I couldn't blame him at the time, because the temperature must have been 95 degrees and the humidity about the same. He and his wife joined me for lunch, and we put together a nice asset purchase.

The only mistake I made there was perhaps bringing in too many people for the transition week, thus making this elderly gentleman very excited. He was quick to get over it, and we ended up with a fine relationship, but it taught me another lesson: Never overwhelm someone with too many people. If someone feels he or she has lost control of the situation, it takes a long time to regain equilibrium.

A KEY SPOT

I met the owner of Gulfport Electric Supply at the annual NAED convention in Chicago in 1978. In the course of an evening of visiting manufacturers' hospitality suites, we became well acquainted. On a follow-up telephone call I proposed an asset purchase for his company in Gulfport, Mississippi. He said there was no way he would sell his company for bare assets, but he did have an idea as to the value of the company. So we wrote a purchase agreement based on the figure he had in mind, but with the condition that the assets had to be such that we were satisfied with the purchase price.

When we arrived in Gulfport after attending the National Football League Super Bowl game in New Orleans, we expected to have a signed agreement within an hour or two. But his attorney was so difficult about the contract language that we stayed on into the late hours of the night. Fortunately, the assets did come up to our anticipated level and we were able to complete the purchase.

This owner was very people-oriented. As I sat in his office one day, he received a phone call from a customer asking for a quotation, and he assured the customer that he would have the quotation there on time, that it would be complete, that it would be competitive, that he would get the very, very best price and not just the street price. As he was about to hang up he said, by the way, "Who am I speaking to, ole buddy?" He was everybody's friend, sometimes to the extent of overlooking the day-to-day operation.

Fortunately, he had an excellent partner who continued to work for us for many years in this fine city. We built a new building in Gulfport—some 20,000 square feet on the main artery into the city. We literally bought the front lawn from Sterling Drug. Never have I had an opportunity to locate in such a key spot as this one in Gulfport.

In 1978 we bought a small company in Crawfordsville, Indiana. The owner was amenable when it came to agreeing on an asset purchase, but he became more difficult once we arrived on the site to appraise the fixed assets. We finally concluded the deal, but not without excessive and difficult arbitration.

# *Lessons Learned*

WE BECAME VERY BOLD IN THE FALL of 1978 when we jumped all the way to the Northwest with the purchase of Palmer Electric in Seattle and Port Angeles, Washington. Upon hearing of the company's availability at a western regional NAED convention in Phoenix, I sent my wife home and jumped on the first plane for Seattle. Arriving late in the evening, I was led into a darkened hallway, where I met the principal of the company, who was wearing a trenchcoat and hat. He whisked me off to the manager's home to discuss the deal. I've never seen anything so cloaked in secrecy. I felt as though I were dealing with Howard Hughes.

The thing that really concerned me about the move was not only the distance from our Benton Harbor headquarters but the presence of not one but two different locals of the Teamsters Union. Still, I decided that if ever there was a time for us to test the waters on a union, this was it. Whatever the outcome, the branches were too far away to affect the rest of the company.

One Teamsters local represented the seven people working in the warehouse and counter area, and another local represented the two truck drivers. The wisest thing I did was to contact a professional labor lawyer in Chicago, who guided me through a decertification process. We planned this from the outset, even to the point that as I was showing the indoctrination films and began discussing the profit-sharing plan, I stopped the projector and asked the union members to leave the room because this benefit was not available to them as long as they belonged to a collective-bargaining unit. That created anxiety and interest on their part, and the next morning they couldn't wait to ask those who had stayed just what this profit-sharing plan was all about.

I held individual interviews with each union member, asking them please to place union membership on the shelf and deal with me directly. If they felt that I wasn't treating them fairly and found it necessary to bring the union into play, they could do so. Finally we arrived at that window, the ninety days to sixty days before union contract negotiations, when I was able to get them to request a vote. Fortunately, one leader was not afraid to take the bull by the horns and initiate the paperwork. He petitioned for a vote. It was close, but we won four to three.

I'm pleased to say that those former union members who remained with the company attained extremely fine positions. One of the countermen became a purchasing agent, one of the warehousemen became our inside salesman, and the person who took the lead in decertification became our star outside salesman. The others now have retired or left the company. We promoted one truck driver to salesman and eventually the other decertified, so we were rid of both unions. I guess it goes to show that if people remain within a union they just move like cattle from one grazing pasture to another in response to prescribed increases in wages and benefits, but in our case every employee who forsook the union but remained with the company took quantum leaps to better-paying and more prestigious positions. I can honestly say that every one of those nine union members is better off today because he rid himself of the shackles of the union.

I would not hesitate to take the same steps again—except that if I were considering a branch in a unionized city contiguous to another All-Phase operation, I would have to be very, very careful about work restrictions. I would not want that cancer to spread throughout our company, and there are certain cities where I doubt we would ever be able to rid ourselves of the union. Unions are the main reason All-Phase has stayed out of such larger cities as New York, Chicago, Detroit, Philadelphia, Boston and San Francisco. Things may change, but for the present, at least, this is our posture.

The Northwest also represented a couple of new industries for us in lumbering and aerospace. Aerospace has been very difficult to crack because of competitive bidding, but the timber industry is exciting and volatile. The only problem is that it is feast or famine. When the housing industry is going great, the Northwest goes great, but when it's down, it's really tough.

## INCIDENT IN NATCHEZ

In the fall of 1978 I received a phone call from a real-estate agent in Natchez, Mississippi, about the availability of an electrical distributor in that city. It was the first time I had received an overture from a Realtor. As it turned out, we did buy this small company from a group of local stockholders. The principal of the business stayed on with us for a short period, but we transferred a young man from our training program in Atlanta to this branch as his first branch-management position. Incidentally, the principal did eventually return to our employment and had a brilliant career in sales.

Our Friday-night cocktail party and banquet culminating the transition week took place at one of the antebellum homes for which Natchez is noted. But the affair is memorable for other reasons as well. During dinner, after a rather long cocktail party on the porch, I suggested that we all stand up, introduce ourselves and say something about our roles in the company.

As we got to the last table, the counterman stood and said he was giving his two weeks' notice. That was the first time anything like that had happened. The former owner, who was sitting next to me, told me not to pay any attention to the man; he'd just had a little too much to drink. After a fine southern dinner I made the mistake of going around the room again and asking people what they thought of this new opportunity. Of course, I heard a lot of good things about All-Phase opening in Natchez, but finally this man's turn came again. By this time, he had had another couple

**25**

of drinks. He stood and said he was withdrawing his two weeks' notice and was quitting immediately.

With that I jumped from the head table, scurried around to his table, grabbed him by the scruff of the neck, and told him to get out of the room and out of our company and to turn in his keys. He threw them on the table and rushed out, leaving his wife behind. She was badly shaken and in tears. It was one of those isolated instances where things kind of backfire, but the evening did end up well. By the time the rest of the employees left in the wee hours, we were all friendly and everyone agreed that this fellow was a rotten apple. He came back the following Monday morning looking for his job, but naturally we did not accept him back. He subsequently rammed our metal building with his car, but it did little damage. To say the least, he was a hothead.

## ONE THAT TURNED THE CORNER

In March 1979 we were back in our home state with a new location in Marquette, on the shores of Lake Superior.

This acquisition showed us the importance of researching the marketplace before plunging ahead. All we knew was that Marquette catered to the mining industry, that taconite mining was surging, and that we wanted a piece of the action. We didn't bother to find out that all of the electrical components for this large mining expansion had been purchased before our arrival. Two years after starting up, the branch was still losing considerable money. We decided the answer lay in concentrated sales and service. With the help of sales blitzes, an open house, telemarketing and identifying "target accounts," we turned the branch around. We also changed managers several times along the way.

Eventually we became so successful in Marquette that Westinghouse Electric Supply Company closed its branch there, and the other local competitor moved from his large facility into a much smaller one. We literally control the market. In fact, this branch has done so well that it now has a sub-branch in Escanaba, Michigan—a small, 3,500-square-foot facility some fifty miles away servicing the paper and taconite industries.

## HARD KNOCKS IN MOBILE

In the spring of 1979 we also acquired the most prestigious electrical distributor in Mobile, Alabama. Our sales-development manager, Jim Cleworth Sr., and I had made an overture to the owner a couple of years earlier, and now he was ready to sell. He had gone through a divorce, and his wife ended up with the building. That caused quite a problem in our negotiations, but the man appeared to be a real southern gentleman. He mentioned that the only problem still facing him was an obligation on a computer that was running several thousand dollars per month. Though he was selling us his electrical apparatus and supply business, he was retaining a residential-fixture showroom across town (managed by his new wife), so the computer was far more powerful than he needed. I felt compassion for the man, and in an effort to make the deal easier on him I offered to pay a couple of thousand dollars per month for two years until he completed his contractual obligation on the computer. This was done after the deal was completed and was simply a gesture out of the goodness of my heart.

I didn't realize it, but he was something less than ethical with me and ended up causing us severe problems. My first mistake was not requiring a noncompete clause. But, as he had put it, it would have been almost impossible to define clearly what he could and couldn't handle in the residential showroom (for example, we'd both carry light bulbs, some recessed lighting fixtures, fans and hoods, and so on). So I agreed to forgo any noncompete agreement.

However, this man did several things that led him right back into the business. He kept his old telephone number, so people who were accustomed to calling his former electrical distributor-

ship called his lighting center rather than our company. He also
kept his old post-office box, which meant our mail went to him. For
months, purchase orders and even customers' checks went into his
lock box, and he took his time delivering them to us. The mail
always arrived opened. We got some vendor invoices so late that
we missed cash discounts. He also took with him a major manufacturer's line, Crouse-Hinds (a line that at the time we were having
difficulty keeping as we bought its distributorships), which meant
he was no longer just a lighting center but really was back in the
business. I had real difficulty accepting that.

The last straw came when we mistakenly paid an additional
two months on the computer beyond the two-year agreement. He
refused to send our check back. He told me he thought that it was
our way of continuing the agreement—and all of this on a piece of
equipment we never once used. I felt I knew his attorney well
enough to call him directly and ask him to reason with his client,
and he said he would try. When he called me back, however, he
said there was no way to recover the money and that he was sorry
to put me in that position, but I would have to find some other
means of getting it.

I sued for the money—I think it was about $4,000—and took
the matter to court, but the southern judge completely misunderstood the case. At one point during the trial he thought I was the
defendant when, of course, I was the plaintiff. After we had been
in the chambers perhaps an hour and a half, he said, "Look, I just
can't spend any more time on this." He said, "As I understand it,
Mr. Kinney, you're a large corporation from the state of
Michigan," and I said, "Now just a minute, your honor, I can see
in what direction this is going, but I'm just the owner of a series
of small branches and one of them is here in Mobile." "Well," he
replied, "whatever the case might be, I have to dispense with the
case, as I have a backlog of cases waiting in this courtroom, and
I'm going to find the defendant not guilty. He does not have to
return the money to you, but I don't want you to be discouraged,

and please don't take this as a setback in your business career."

Outside the courtroom I ran into the defendant and his attorney, and I told him he was the most immoral businessman I had ever met. But that only served to fuel the fire, and he got me again when he put the building up for sale. We offered $350,000. He responded through his real-estate agent that while he felt it was a fair offer, his ex-wife turned it down. We found out subsequently that the building was sold to another party for $360,000. We were never given the opportunity to negotiate. He simply found someone to top our price by $10,000.

We suffered another setback in Mobile when, after having been in business for about a month, we were hit by a hurricane. The winds literally came in one end of the building, blew down a wall and went out the other end. The storm left everything in a shambles, but the real damage came when neighborhood children came in and stole our tools and office equipment. Our branch manager brought a mattress down to the branch and literally slept on the counter for six straight nights.

We announced to the trade that we were open twenty-four hours a day and sold a tremendous number of generators, flashlights and batteries and other emergency electrical equipment. (Today we have a disaster-relief division whose sole purpose is to have ready for delivery at all times a sufficient quantity of all merchandise needed in the case of a hurricane or other disaster.) This tragedy also showed the loyalty and camaraderie that can develop among branches. The employees from the Dothan branch rebuilt the wall themselves and helped get the Mobile branch back in business. All of the neighboring Alabama branches fed materials into Mobile until it could get back on its feet.

Soon we also moved into Virginia with the purchase of a company in Martinsville. The owner there, too, was a problem, in that as we started to take the inventory count on the usual Thursday evening, I noticed some large quantities of slow-moving merchandise that I hadn't seen when I'd walked the inventory on a prior visit. I confronted the owner, saying he must have transferred in some merchandise from his other location in Charlotte, North Carolina. He denied it but finally admitted it. We ended up loading that stock back onto his trucks. I guess we should have walked away from the deal as a matter of principle, but we went ahead with it.

A couple of years later we opened in Danville, Virginia, where the local distributorship had burned down and supposedly was not reopening. In the end, however, it did. With four distributors, this small city of perhaps 30,000 people is simply overpopulated with electrical distributors. Thank God we are the major force there. Danville has been so successful that we subsequently built a new building.

We learn something from every acquisition. Taking a lesson from Mobile, today our contracts stipulate that the telephone number stays with the new All-Phase branch, as does the address and post-office box. We also state that no merchandise can be transferred to the acquisition location from some other branch before the purchase, nor will we buy any merchandise that has been returned from a job site. Almost every time we complete an acquisition we come up with additional stipulations.

# Four in One

IN MAY 1979—THE MONTH THE Martinsville and Mobile branches became part of the All-Phase network—we also made two more acquisitions.

Our third that month was in Port Arthur, Texas—our first venture into that state. Now we had branches in eleven states.

The company, J&M, handled not only electrical supplies but also mill supplies, hardware and such miscellaneous items as rags, optical equipment, rain gear, tarpaulins, chain, rope, garden utensils (wheelbarrows, hoes, rakes, post-hole diggers)—just about as great a variety of merchandise as you could imagine. Because of this hodgepodge, we went into negotiations with a rather negative attitude. At the first meeting I told the owners we weren't interested in the major portion of their business, and they agreed to price the inventory so that I would pay the current acquisition cost on the electrical merchandise but would buy all other items at a discount—from 75 percent of the original cost down to 25 percent, depending on the age of the item on the shelf. We were able to sell that merchandise rather quickly at a fairly good profit.

We also bought the building, which was in a very poor neighborhood. As it turned out, there was so much inventory that we also bought a two-story, 20,000-square-foot building (a union hall built in 1927) across the street for the nominal fee of $20,000. We have moved out of both buildings and into a beautiful new 15,000-square-foot warehouse on one of the main highways bypassing the city. Port Arthur eventually carved its niche in the history of All-Phase by setting new sales records in 1988 in eight of nine consecutive months—a record that probably will never be equaled.

In the last week of May 1979 we moved into Lexington, Kentucky. As in Mobile, we actually bought half of a company, because we did not purchase the residential-fixture showroom.

As I look back, it seems impossible that we could have had four acquisitions in four states in one month. At the time we didn't even have our own airplane, so all travel was via commercial airline. I think I spent one day in my office that month.

To commemorate the feat, we formed the "Four in One Club" consisting of the eight or ten people who had been involved in every acquisition. I gave each person a silver platter with the inscription "Four in One Club." After the Lexington cocktail party and celebration, I took the group to the races and gave each of them $2 to bet on one race. They made their selections and I took their money, but I decided to book the bet myself without turning it in at the window. There wasn't a single winner in our group, so I came out even. I continued to book the bets throughout the evening and, in the end, paid out some money, but not nearly as much as the group bet. I had provided a great evening of entertainment for only a handful of $2 bills.

TRAVELING ON

July 1979 saw us enter our thirteenth state, Tennessee. The branch there in Kingsport services the Tri-Cities of Kingsport, Johnson City and Bristol, with a combined population of about a quarter of a million. The three owners of Kingsport Electric were excellent individuals, and I recall traveling to Allen-Bradley with one of them to convince the manufacturer to stay with us, which it did.

Then it was on to Syracuse, New York, for a similar meeting with Crouse-Hinds. Although the executives there acknowledged that they had never seen a more professional approach and presentation than ours, their minds were made up: They weren't going to get along with All-Phase. It's unusual that we were able to convince Allen-Bradley, with whom we were just starting to establish a relationship, but not Crouse-Hinds. Thankfully this relationship took a turn for the better a few years later with a change in Crouse-Hinds management.

Nineteen-seventy-nine continued to be a big year for us. In October we acquired two branches in Washington state—Bellingham and Burlington—owned by a good Irishman. In fact, the symbol for his company was a little leprechaun. Bellingham, the northernmost metropolitan area in the continental United States, is known for paper milling, mining, oil refineries and fishing. The only problem is that its economy swings with the building industry. Also, the former owner forgot to tell me that his key man was retiring and his top salesman had just left, so we had some personnel problems when we arrived. We sent in a manager from one of our smaller branches, but unfortunately he did not get the job done. We ended up replacing him with another All-Phase manager, but we had lost market position and momentum and eventually closed this branch.

## A DISMAYING SETBACK

This aside, we ended a very successful 1979 with a new branch opening in Monroe, Louisiana. This was probably the strangest and most devastating experience of my business life.

We had signed a purchase agreement to acquire the company BECO. When we arrived for the usual appraisal of assets, we found that the inventory on the books far exceeded our actual count. After a meeting on Saturday morning with the owner and his accountant and attorney, we called the deal off. We left the city that afternoon, discouraged and disappointed that for the first time in the history of All-Phase we weren't able to buy a targeted company. The worst of it, however, was yet to come.

That evening I received a phone call from one of the BECO employees, who implored me to return to the city, open a new branch and hire BECO personnel. I refused to listen to this for a week or ten days, but after repeated calls from several of the employees, I agreed to return to Monroe and take a look. If they could assure me they were leaving voluntarily and that I would not be walking into trouble, I would consider opening a branch.

After chartering a plane to Monroe and interviewing people, we decided to find a building, line up some lines and open there with a small crew of former BECO employees—all of whom had left voluntarily.

Approximately a year later we were notified that BECO's owner was suing us for breach of contract, unfair business practices and defamation of character. We hired local counsel from Shreveport and, with an attorney from our insurance company, proceeded to build what we felt was a strong defense.

We were successful in getting the trial moved to Federal District Court. However, that court happened to be located in Monroe, and the jury consisted of people living within a 100-mile radius. Without going into all of the details, as unbelievable as it might seem, we lost not only the $175,000 suit for personal slander (incidentally, the owner had asked for only $150,000) but we also lost a $900,000 suit by the then-bankrupt BECO Electric. We appealed, of course, and were able to get the $175,000 slander suit thrown out, but the $900,000 suit stood firm. After our insurance settlement it still cost us $300,000, plus a great deal of time and harassment. This was one of the severest setbacks All-Phase Electric—and I—have ever suffered. To add insult to injury, poor local management eventually forced us to close this branch.

Had I any less resolve, I could have become paranoid over this outrageous injustice to the point that I might have become fearful of ever again entering a courtroom to defend ourselves, but the exact opposite happened. I am more determined than ever to hire the very best counsel available, prepare our team to the ultimate, and be willing to go to any extent to protect what is legally and rightfully ours. I would rather fight my battles in the marketplace, but if one chooses the courtroom, then I'm just as ready to do battle there.

I do feel that jury trials have the potential of rendering biased verdicts. During the first hour or so of jury selection, so much happens so fast that if you're not right on top of the situation you could find yourself with a group of inadequate people with whom you will spend the balance of the trial trying to reason. In the Louisiana case we had a difficult time literally keeping the jurors awake long enough to make our points.

# *I Was Nearly Mortally Wounded. . .*

IN MAY 1980 WE MADE OUR LARGEST acquisition to date—a five-branch operation in South Carolina. I felt proud that we had swept the state in one large purchase, all the way from Greenville to Anderson, Spartanburg, Columbia and Charleston. Little did I realize that I was on the beaches of Dunkirk. Or was it the edge of hell?

Whatever the analogy, it was our poorest acquisition. You might ask how this could happen after such a track record, but I guess it boils down to the business ethics of the three partners with whom we were dealing.

One of the three owners had been caught, tried and sentenced for tax evasion for collaborating with their largest customer in failing to show the proper paperwork for materials supplied. That largest contractor, who provided them with over half of their $20 million volume, had no loyalties to All-Phase, and we lost his business. Of course, we didn't realize going in that we would have such a problem. It seems this partner took the rap for both parties and served a jail sentence on a work-release program.

I remember the late-evening meeting Monday when I arrived for the formalities of signing the contract, intending to start the transition Tuesday. But the second owner, the president of the company, decided he didn't like the noncompete wording in the contract—he felt he might want to work for the contractor who was his largest customer. Rewriting the contract to accommodate him, however, upset the third owner, who felt that the other was receiving preferential treatment. We had a series of private meetings and negotiations past midnight to try to resolve the surprises that kept cropping up. I wasn't prepared for this; having thought it was just a formality meeting to sign the papers, I didn't even have our lawyer with me.

We finally worked out the details and agreed to purchase all five of the locations rather than the three that were in our original plan. We should have stuck with three. Eventually we closed the utility operation in Columbia (we sold the building and took a tremendous loss) as well as the branches in Charleston and Greenville.

The next morning, after signing the contract, we assembled the employees for the announcement. The president came into the room, looked at the floor, looked at the ceiling and, without looking anyone directly in the eye, said, "I've sold my company to All-Phase Electric; this is Ron Kinney, their president." I was left standing alone awkwardly to explain just what had happened and who we were.

I did my best to convince them that this represented an opportunity for them. But I was simply shorthanded—I had only one other person with me. We had to try to speak to these people as a group, then meet with them in smaller groups, then one-on-one. I probably didn't get the job done as quickly and smoothly as I should have, but there was no way that two of us could have begun to cover five branches. We immediately had an exodus of people.

The first person to leave was the branch manager in Anderson, who went into business for himself, taking some of our people with him. We lost several key people at the main house in Greenville; the sales manager, an additional salesman and an inside man went to work for a new company. Then our purchasing agent, operating manager and an additional salesman left and started their own business in Greenville. Our branch manager in Spartanburg left and went into the agency business. Our branch manager of the utility company in Columbia left and started his own utility business. We made an attempt to switch that company from utility to apparatus and supply but, after considerable investment in time, money and people, we closed it instead.

Finally, in Charleston our former manager started his own business as well, hiring two of our salesmen and our operating manager. Within two or three months, we had no more than a skeleton of the original company. We had lost our two major customers, all of our branch managers and all but two of our outside salesmen. Of course, we had tried to hire the best people we could get, and as a result paid a premium, but received poor quality in return.

The turnover was immense. People were coming and going faster than we could put the paperwork together for the payroll records. We ourselves were going through managers rapidly. The only person from the former company who stuck it out was the one of the three owners who had a one-year employment agreement with us. We should have let him go with everyone else, because when he completed his year with us he went to work for a competitor in a southern city. Meanwhile, he hung around and played golf with his cronies, giving us nothing to show for an expensive salary.

Today we have only Anderson and Spartanburg to show for all of our hard work and frustration. I will never make back in South Carolina the money I lost in Greenville, Charleston and Columbia, although the two remaining branches are now successful.

## BAPTISM BY FIRE

We learned so many lessons in South Carolina that it's hard to enumerate them. The venture gave me an education I could never have gotten at home, in school or in the navy. I really got my baptism by fire.

One mistake was to alienate the manufacturers' agents and representatives. In an attempt to stem the exodus of people and lines, I invited the agents to the local country club for cocktails and dinner, followed by our audiovisual presentation. I then fielded questions from the floor. Unfortunately, I was too direct and outspoken for these Greenville people.

I criticized the people who had left our company and told everyone in the room to choose sides—to go with our ex-employees or stay with us. It turned out that we had about seventy-five friends in the audience, but about a half-dozen people decided to leave All-Phase and support the competition. Ex-employees held personal vendettas against us, and though we fought with a vengeance, we just couldn't overcome the influence of this southern state.

I think South Carolina is unique among states below the Mason-Dixon line. I've never felt such bias in my life as I did there against northerners. Perhaps we brought on part of it with our independence and honesty. One rep commented to our manager that he couldn't do business with All-Phase because we were just too honest. We refused to succumb to demands for kickbacks. We wouldn't allow them to drag us into that whirlpool. Unfortunately, competition and the new companies formed by our former employees went along with the game and captured the bulk of the business.

Another problem is that we changed managers several times. No one seemed to have the kind of business ethics and principles we demand: If it can't be done right, don't do it at all. Even the people we sent down there seemed to fall into the local bad habits. As much as five years later we released one of our transplanted branch managers as a hopeless drug addict. We also had our share of bad debts.

Late one afternoon I flew into Charleston on our company plane and met with all of the employees in a cocktail lounge at the local hotel. I cautioned our company representatives who had flown in with me not to be too rough on the employees, because we needed to settle things down and get some harmony out of at least one city in South Carolina. During the cocktail hour I went around the table and asked people how they were doing with their accounts. I didn't like the answers I was getting, so I started to bear down on a couple of people, and I guess I put them on the spot in front of their peers.

They kept telling me about the great orders they had booked, but when I asked about profit margins I found they were between 2 and 3 percent. Since the cost of doing business in this industry runs around 17 percent, we were losing tremendous numbers of dollars with each sale.

We went into the dining room and ordered one more cocktail before dinner. I turned to the manager next to me and said, "Well, certainly I've heard just about everything that's wrong with Charleston. I do hope that your collections are coming along well." Whereupon he told me about a bad debt that was imminent in the amount of about $30,000. I stood up to go to the restroom, turned back to my seat, picked up my glass and shattered it against the wall to show how disgusted I was. I walked out to the parking lot. Our district manager followed me, and we talked it over and returned to the table for a reasonably quiet dinner. I was trying to make the point that I couldn't continue to put up with this poor performance. The next morning two or three of our people didn't show up for work. I then had to go around and reassure the rest of the employees that their jobs were secure.

The branch manager subsequently left the company, and we finally got out.

The day after the incident I flew to Columbia to meet with our manager. When he picked me up at the airport I asked if he was free for lunch and he said, "Only if you promise to have your drink in a paper cup." I had a good laugh at how quickly word travels.

Before we closed the doors in Greenville, only one employee remained out of the original twenty-four. The thing that really hurt is that the situation eroded over a period of time. We would have been much better off had everyone walked out the first day.

We didn't make another acquisition in 1980. I was nearly mortally wounded by South Carolina.

# One New Branch per Month

E ARLY IN 1981, WE STARTED AN aggressive expansion campaign in Pennsylvania with the acquisition of Power Electric in Scranton and Hazleton. The owner had four locations, but we purchased only two because he had buy/sell agreements with his branch managers in the other two. Scranton nearly didn't make it either, because the owner's local branch manager was a partner and had a buy/sell agreement, and he almost decided to buy the company himself. In the end he threw in with All-Phase, at least temporarily.

This man subsequently left the company and started a new business in competition with us. That wouldn't have been so bad, even though he was a hometown boy and had a following, except that he ended up taking twelve of our twenty-four employees with him.

The Scranton acquisition was unique for its tremendous degree of nepotism. Of the twenty-four employees, at least fifteen were related to some other person in the branch. The epitome was the showroom manager, who had two sons working for him in the showroom and a third in inside sales. Two of the sons eventually left our company but the father stayed on. It is a true testament to the surviving local branch manager and his loyal employees that we have continued to prosper and grow to a point where we built a new 25,000-square-foot warehouse in 1989.

This experience reinforced our commitment to our policy against nepotism, whereby we never allow relatives to work in the same branch together.

The Hazleton branch ranks as one of our largest operations.

It occupies a well-planned 52,000-square-foot warehouse and has very capable management personnel and a seasoned sales staff. It's amazing that a company in a city of 26,000 people can do more than $1.5 million a month in business, until you consider that the sales territory extends a hundred miles east and west and approximately thirty miles north and south, dominating this portion of northeastern Pennsylvania.

Something unusual happened at the time of the Power Electric acquisition. The owner, an explosive individual, had arguments with our transition team and even fought with our purchasing agent to the point that they weren't speaking. Even though we had agreed to the pricing levels, he tried to change them once we got into pricing, extending and totaling. When we had pulled off all the obsolete lighting fixtures from the shelf, per the terms of the agreement, and we had more fixtures in the aisles than were left on the shelves, I tried to meet with him to negotiate a price. He didn't like the way the conversation went and told me to forget it—he would keep the obsolete ones. He proceeded to fill an entire semitruck with them.

When we were about to finalize the deal, he became somewhat easier to negotiate with. I think we had a difference of some $100,000, and he told me he wanted to split it with me. I said his middle name should be "Split-the-Difference," and I refused— because it was still much, much more than would have been fair. He then wanted to flip a coin, "all or nothing," but I felt that it was too much money to be dealt with so playfully. He finally was realistic in his appraisal of his fixtures, and we bought them for a reasonable and equitable price. It was tough for me to go to the warehouse manager and tell him to unload that entire truckload of obsolete fixtures and put them back on the shelf. I think I almost lost the man over this.

I must admit that the owner was fair, but he always had to make one last attempt to get the best of the deal. During the closing he said, "Look, you have to recognize that I'm an actor, and

I'm always on stage. Don't always take me so seriously." This was after we had completed a multimillion-dollar deal—the largest we'd ever been involved in.

He was a self-made man, a hard fighter who never would have sold his business were it not for failing health. One of the final items of negotiation was my agreement to take him to the Super Bowl game if the Philadelphia Eagles were playing. The Eagles made it to the final game so I put him on our airplane, flew him to Mobile for a weekend, then to New Orleans for the Philadelphia Eagles/Oakland Raiders Super Bowl game. It wasn't much of a game, and Philadelphia lost. But I kept my end of the bargain.

A couple of months later we purchased this man's archrival, Allen Electric, in Bethlehem and Allentown, Pennsylvania. I had visited the company while in the midst of acquiring Power Electric. When Power Electric's owner asked me where I had been that day, I eluded his question. He said, "Oh, you have something on the side," and I just smiled. Had he known that I was starting negotiations with his bitterest enemy, I'm sure he would have terminated our agreement, were it possible.

He came to the open house following the Allen acquisition. He looked at his former competitor and said, "You know, this is one of the few pleasures of my life, to be sitting here in your office, eating a ham sandwich on you." They never spoke to each other again, and unfortunately both died of physical ailments relatively soon after.

The Bethlehem branch consistently vies with Hazleton as one of the two or three top branches in the network. Again it brought to us an excellent, well-trained team of veteran salespeople and inside sales support. Bethlehem has our largest showroom in terms of square footage.

Both Pennsylvania transactions were asset purchases, and in the case of Hazleton we got quite a bonus because we were able to buy the building for book value, which was considerably less than market value.

## GETTING STRONGER IN PENNSYLVANIA

Later in 1981 we opened a new branch in Beaver Falls, Pennsylvania, as a sub-branch of Pittsburgh. This community was severely depressed because the steel industry was in decline. With our low overhead and favorable rent in a old A&P store building, we thought we could buck the tide and be profitable. But we hadn't done our homework and ended up with a bad deal that we closed as soon as our lease ran out.

Finally, in August 1981, we opened in Williamsport, Pennsylvania. We call it a new opening, but actually the branch grew out of negotiations with Lowry Electric. Lowry's owner had contacted me to look at his operation, but after seeing the condition of his inventory and his severe labor problem, we decided not to make an offer. When we went to his office to tell him so, he said, "Look, how about discounting this inventory deeply, then you tell me what you might pay me for it at your very, very rock-bottom price." I gave him a figure that I thought was a fair proposal, and he told us to write the agreement.

We conditioned the purchase on the acquisition of this single asset item of inventory. We did not want to buy the corporate stock or appear as though we were even buying the company. This was for one reason and one reason only: labor-union problems. I believe that Lowry had about thirty-five employees, about twenty-five of whom belonged to the union, including his office staff, counter and warehouse people, truck drivers and even some upper-level managers.

They had absolutely grabbed control of the man and his company. It had gotten so bad that at 10 a.m. a whistle would sound at the counter and all of the employees would head into a little coffee room for their ten- or fifteen-minute break, leaving customers standing around at the sales counter until they finished. I just couldn't believe this was happening. Lowry knew it, and he knew that this had caused his once-proud company, one of the finest in northeast Pennsylvania, to sink to the low ebb that it had. So we bought only his apparatus and supply inventory and hired only his two outside salesmen and purchasing agent. Lowry kept his major appliances and he kept his union. We built our own fairly formidable group and formed a new company that has been profitable from the outset.

We had by now accomplished quite a feat. We had gone from a single branch in Pittsburgh to seven Pennsylvania locations by year's end doing more than $35 million in volume. We had come from nowhere to become the third-largest electrical distributor in that state. Obviously, our image in the eastern United States soared. I have never had so many overtures from companies in my entire life as those that came from the rest of Pennsylvania, as well as New Jersey.

I sincerely like the work ethic of the Pennsylvanians. I don't think there are any harder workers than the families of people who have worked in the coal mines and steel mills. That certainly is what Pennsylvania is all about. As one of the countermen in Scranton once said to me, "You'll never find anybody with a better work ethic than we have right here in Scranton.$CQ He was right."

## ENTERING FLORIDA

We were so busy in 1981 that by September we had added one new branch per month. One of those new openings was in Florida. For a number of years we had felt that we needed to be in the growth-minded Sunshine State, and the area of Port Charlotte, halfway between Sarasota and Fort Myers on the west coast, appeared to offer a unique opportunity.

General Development Corporation was developing a tremendous amount of land, and tens of thousands of homes were scheduled to be built in the 1980s and 1990s. We wanted to be part of the boom. Also, the Square D line was available. Although we would have preferred to purchase an existing company, the only one readily available was in Tampa and on the verge of bankruptcy.

So a combination of factors led us to go it alone. One was Jim Cleworth Sr., who had been a very dependable and valued employee since our acquisition in Kalamazoo, Michigan, where he was branch manager. He eventually moved to Benton Harbor as manager of sales development, then on to Atlanta as southern regional manager. In the late 1970s, however, he developed a heart problem and had to retire. A year or two later he returned as our company pilot. In fact, he was a big factor in our purchasing an airplane. But when I took several staff members to the Mayo Clinic in Rochester, Minnesota, Jim was told that, because of his heart problem, he was never to get behind the controls of an airplane again.

I thought so much of Jim that I asked if there was some way he would stay with the company. He said only if he were able to go to his beloved Florida, where he had a winter home and could work in a warmer climate. I told him I would arrange it. Once again it was because of good, loyal people within the company that we expanded into new territory. Eventually we built an 18,000-square-foot building, one of the showplaces on the west coast of Florida.

Port Charlotte wasn't a strong force in our company until we bought additional locations in the state. When you consider that the present population of approximately 50,000 will be part of a completely planned community accommodating a quarter of a million people, it's not hard to get excited about the prospects.

*More New Territory*

IN THE SPRING OF 1982, AFTER attending the southern regional NAED convention in San Antonio, our southwestern and southeastern district managers and I planned what was probably our twelfth visit to Houston to scout opportunities. We were resigned to the fact that there probably wouldn't be anything for sale and that we would have to build. As it was, we were having problems arranging for the desirable manufacturers' lines and coming up with the kind of staff we might want. Fortunately, because of inclement weather, we were unable to fly our plane into Houston and became sidetracked to Orange, Texas—fortunate because at about that time falling oil prices were sending Houston's economy on a long downward slide.

Orange, on the other hand, had some 25,000 people, six major industries and no electrical distributor. We arrived early in the morning and by noon had found a building, gone to the bank that was foreclosing on it, negotiated a very favorable price and terms, and interviewed the prospective branch manager. I never accomplished so much in a half day. One week later, on April 1— which happened to be our twenty-third anniversary—we opened our sixty-second branch.

A month later we negotiated to buy a company in Shreveport, Louisiana. The parent company had twenty-one branches, and this was the only one outside Texas. It looked like a fine opportunity, and the negotiations went very smoothly. It was a pure asset purchase, with the condition that we would purchase nothing that was obsolete. Thus we started off with a clean, yet heavy inventory.

What we didn't realize was that this operation had just completed a million-dollar order for an oil-rig project and that the branch manager had sacrificed almost all of his regular daily business to service this project. He had so alienated the rest of the trade that they were fed up with the branch.

The company had further offended one of its largest customers, the local utility, by letting union members camp in its parking lot during a strike. And the utility wasn't willing to change its ways just because All-Phase purchased the branch. Also, one of the salesmen and the operating manager liked their former owner so much that they moved back to Texas with the company. When we discovered that 60 percent of the remaining volume was being conducted with only three accounts, all of them credit risks, we realized we had opened a Pandora's box.

We responded by reducing overhead, cutting the dozen employees to six. Of these, we insisted that two be full-time outside salespeople, with the branch manager supplementing the sales force at least 50 percent of his time.

But there were too many problems to overcome. We stayed with the branch far too long—six years—before closing it. We finally reasoned that both Monroe and Shreveport would lose so much money before the oil economy would turn around that we would never be able to make up our losses.

## KOKOMO AND KIRKLAND

About mid-1982 we heard of a company in Kokomo, Indiana, that was having difficulties. The owner decided to close and consolidate his operation in a neighboring city, leaving as the only remaining competition an Allen-Bradley distributor and a branch of Westinghouse Electric Supply Company. There was no one to handle the Square D line. So we opened in a 5,000-square-foot building (priced right at $500 per month, with an option that we later exercised to buy at a competitive price). We had three employees—a branch manager, an outside salesman and someone to service the counter, warehouse and delivery. The branch was slow getting off the ground and never reached the maturity we had hoped for. We eventually closed it but came out all right, as we sold the building for twice what we had paid.

One problem in Kokomo was that our largest single customer, an electrical contractor doing project work, ran into credit problems. I now interject a new question whenever we're looking at a possible acquisition or opening: Do you have any single customer who generates more than 5 percent of your volume? If so, who is it? I then ask for a full description of that company. The district manager or I may even make a sales call to determine whether we can transfer the loyalty of this account to our company. This is one of the key steps in analyzing the market.

Ever since we started to prosper in Washington in 1982, we've been interested in additional locations there. This state, however, seems like Florida in that everybody does fairly well and a company seldom comes on the market. At our biennial Advanced Management Program, we discussed expansion in the Northwest. With the district manager and his supporting branch managers and staff, we decided to seek a community in greater Seattle for a sub-branch. Someday we will have to vacate our expensive, highly commercial location in Seattle, so we figured an additional branch could forestall future problems.

That spring we found a 5,000-square-foot building in Kirkland with great exposure just off the main artery. (We subsequently doubled the size of the warehouse.) It was within fifteen or twenty minutes' drive of the Seattle branch in the direction of our Burlington location. We negotiated a lease, remodeled the building, erected shelving, stocked the branch and hung our sign—all within forty-five days. If nothing else, this kind of quick start-up is excellent experience for a district manager.

## A POWERHOUSE IN HUNTSVILLE

Perhaps one of our most successful acquisitions was Wholesale

Electric in Huntsville, Alabama, in 1983. The initial contact came about in a most unusual way.

We had been in Huntsville since acquiring Lewis Electric in 1977. We had never really done well and certainly had had our share of problems. This was the branch where almost everybody had walked out by the time we opened our doors Monday morning. Later we discovered a theft ring and obtained signed confessions and eventually restitution from three of our eight employees. Thus we were struggling along with five people. Also, our building in Huntsville was the worst in the entire network.

One rainy day an employee named Dean Green needed to put up an order in the warehouse, and with our dilapidated building, it was raining as hard inside as it was outside. She called me, very irate, and said dripping water in the warehouse not only ruined her new hairdo but soaked her new dress. She said something had to be done. I sympathized and asked, "What would you have me do?" We'd looked for another location but hadn't found anything better, and we weren't doing well enough to invest in a new building.

"Why don't you buy my old boss's company?" she asked. "He has an excellent building." That boss had started Wholesale Electric Supply Company approximately twenty years earlier after having spent about twenty years with Graybar. He had a magnificent new building at the crossroads of Huntsville's main artery and a highway, right in the center of the city. A $750,000 building appeared difficult to justify for the size of the city, but I contacted the owner and we had a pleasant discussion. He told me another party was ahead of me and that I would have to wait until he completed those negotiations. Depending on the outcome, he would call and we could take it from there.

I decided to pay him a visit anyway. We spent half a day together and got along extremely well. I could see that he liked me, that he liked the image of All-Phase and that he genuinely wanted to be on our team. But he had this other obligation.

About a month or two later he called to tell me that while the other national company had met all his conditions, they did not want to buy his building. If I could meet the conditions *and* purchase the building, we could make a deal.

I returned to Huntsville and negotiated an agreement whereby we would purchase his inventory at a very fair price. The building's price was confirmed by an independent appraiser, and the fixed assets were to be negotiated at closing. We paid a premium in the form of a salary continuance for the owner for two years, whether he stayed with the company or not. This cost about $100,000.

This man was highly influential in the community, having worked diligently for the chamber of commerce to bring new industry to town. He knew who was going to build and had an inside track on new business. He had served on an advisory council for President Lyndon Johnson and was a personal friend of Governor George Wallace. He even had brought Ronald Reagan to Huntsville before Reagan was elected president of the United States. He also was a friend of Wernher von Braun, the famous German scientist who developed rocketry for Hitler's Nazi government during the war and, of course, was the influencing factor in the space age, which started in Huntsville (NASA had its origins there before Lyndon Johnson was influential in moving it to Houston). Many scientists who worked with von Braun in developing the space center stayed in Huntsville and developed high-technology offshoots, a very progressive form of business for the community.

I was amazed at the amount of business available in Huntsville—something we hadn't realized when we were operating out of our small location. We just hadn't done our marketing work— perhaps because I was trying to do it all myself. I'm happy to say that our third Advanced Management Program was devoted to training our district and branch managers in how to rate a market and do a market survey of their communities. As a matter of fact, we made this an absolute requirement for their reporting for fiscal year 1984.

The Huntsville owner ran his company autocratically. He was a man whom employees, customers and vendors either loved or hated. Many of our customers said that as long as he sat in that office, which they could observe from the counter, they would never darken our doorstep. That was one reason we asked him to move back into his private office, out of sight from the counter.

On the other hand, he brought an image to our company second to none. Because he had built such a prosperous company so quickly, he had earned the respect of the industry. We definitely had purchased number one in the city of Huntsville, and for that matter in probably all of northern Alabama. It positioned us to change a small, mediocre branch into a powerhouse—all with a minimum of people. We had six employees at the time of the acquisition, and Wholesale Electric had thirteen. We combined staffs, hired a couple of new people and still had just over twenty people developing an annual sales volume of more than $6 million.

As a rule of thumb, at that time we looked for gross profit in the neighborhood of $5,000 to $5,500 per month per employee. This means that if we had twenty employees, ideally we should develop $100,000 to $110,000 per month in gross profit. In Huntsville, the second month we were in business we went well over $100,000 in gross profit. The branch leaped into the elite ranking of number four within the network—from the worst facility to one of the best. It was a magnificent success story.

SMOOTHING THE TRANSITION

Here, once again, we held to our belief that if employees would just give us thirty days to prove ourselves and not be enticed to leave the company or join some other firm because of a sweeter offer, they would probably want to stay with All-Phase for the rest of their careers. We were so careful to give Huntsville the attention it required that the district manager spent perhaps 20 percent of his time there for the first forty days.

In the case of the salespeople, we continued their existing agreements. Deciding which salesperson from the two companies was most influential in developing sales and gross profit with a certain account was one of the most difficult points of negotiation. It worked out that all six individuals were happy and prosperous.

There was a greater problem with inside sales, because people who had been competing with each other for years now had to get along amicably and put aside any competitive, bitter feelings. This took a great deal of counseling. There was a tendency to refer to the Wholesale Group and the All-Phase Group, and we had to continually work on the theory of unification. The former owner himself helped by addressing the employees at the unification cocktail hour and banquet the Friday evening after the inventory. He said the only thing we had to fear was self-defeat, and if we started bickering and fighting we would be self-defeating. On the other hand, we could be the strongest distributor in northern Alabama if we set aside personal feelings and aggressively attacked our competition, not each other.

The entire transition went extremely well for several reasons. There was good awareness of what had to be done, and many people participated in the transition week. Also, we didn't rush out of town Friday night or Saturday morning but instead left three people behind to help with opening week. Finally, it helped that a third of the staff already knew the All-Phase regimen, its philosophy and paperwork. Huntsville went so well that I now look at cities with less-than-prosperous branches and consider purchasing the largest competitor distributor there.

# Westward Ho!

Our WESTERN DISTRICT BEGAN taking shape in March 1984 when we purchased Coast Wholesale Electric in Burbank and Oxnard, California. When the owner of that company was ready to sell, he consulted his business confidant, who in turn called Hubbell Wiring Device, the company to which the confidant had sold his business. The principals at Hubbell told him Ron Kinney could be trusted, was rapidly expanding and was very honest. This kind of recommendation went a long way with him and seemed to open all doors.

The evening of the open house in Burbank, the seller toasted me in front of some of our most valuable suppliers, among them Allen-Bradley, Crouse-Hinds, Hoffman, Hubbell and G.E. He said he wouldn't have sold his company to anyone other than Ron Kinney. Somebody from our staff jokingly said, "Jack, why don't you go out and buy more companies so that we can buy them from you?" I in turn toasted him, saying I have never had a better relationship with anybody we purchased a company from, and I felt completely comfortable in placing absolute confidence and trust in him. It was a very auspicious beginning for our Western District.

Still, we had to negotiate a pretty tough arrangement. The seller admitted as much when he said he didn't necessarily need every last dime, but only wanted to feel that he was being treated fairly and was getting as much as he could for the company. I told him that he was really tough in his negotiations when he asked for an additional year at $75,000 for the noncompete clause. Ironically, he ended up apologizing to me for being so tough.

As I look back on this transaction, I consider it one of the best investments All-Phase has ever made, even though we did pay a nice premium in the form of a noncompete clause as well as a very high rent obligation for five years. But I guess the rent can be chalked up to the area. As a matter of fact, we renewed for an additional five years.

We have continued to grow our business in southern California to the point that we are recognized as the largest Allen-Bradley distributor in the Los Angeles basin. Much of this success results from our professionalism in the industrial-technology side of the business.

## EXPANDING OUR CLAIM

In line with our general practice of staking a claim within a geographical region and expanding from there, we looked around northern California and bought Gilson Electric in Pittsburg in June 1984 and, eight months later, another Gilson outlet in Oakland. The Oakland purchase resulted from a side trip I took while attending the Super Bowl game at Stanford Stadium between the Miami Dolphins and the San Francisco 49ers. That was the second time a Super Bowl trip had led to an acquisition.

Gilson, which dated back to the early 1900s, was the oldest Bay Area distributor in the business. It had very good lines: Allen-Bradley in Pittsburg and Square D in Oakland.

We ended 1988 with twelve branches in California and are recognized as a major factor in the industry there.

# Strange Circumstances Lead to More Florida Acquisitions

In 1986 WE MADE ONE OF OUR BEST acquisitions, in south Florida.

It all started in 1983, when the president of Allied Electric called to say his company was selling certain branches from its north Florida subsidiary. When he named the cities and locations, I realized that I had visited them several years earlier, before Allied bought them. I had been horrified at the condition of the inventory and facilities. I turned him down without further conversation.

A few years later, in 1986 as I left the NAED Central Regional Convention in West Palm Beach, I met a manufacturer friend at the airport. He asked if I was interested in south Florida. Allied, he said, had gone into Chapter 11 bankruptcy, and some of the branch managers, along with the president, were trying to buy the company but couldn't come up with the necessary financial backing. He gave me the name of the chairman of the board of the parent company, Imperial Industries, which also was in receivership.

Back in Benton Harbor I called the chairman. He said he was disappointed that I hadn't accepted their overture a few years earlier, and that they were well into negotiations with the operating principals of Allied. But because they were having difficulty financing the deal, there might be an opportunity. He promised to call me back. A month went by, and then one weekend I heard from him. He told me about the problems they had had in the negotiations and the troubles the company was facing.

It turned out that the electrical-supply subsidiary, Allied Electric of South Florida, was now in the hands of a trustee, the local representative of the National Association of Credit Managers, who was to decide how to dispose of the company. I asked that all financial data be forwarded to me on Monday. This was before the days of fax machines, so I'd have it Tuesday. The plan was that I'd take the plane down and spend the last three days of the week there.

By Wednesday noon I still had not received the information. I telephoned the man, who told me his secretary had misunderstood his instructions but that I would have it by Thursday noon. I told him we would board our plane at 3 p.m. Thursday and arrive by 8 p.m., in time to meet with his lawyers to review the information. This, of course, was on condition that the information we received was adequate for us to start making a decision.

As I thought more about this on Wednesday afternoon, however, I decided I must be dealing with the wrong man—at least, I wasn't satisfied with the answers he was giving me. I decided to forget about Florida. I called a supplier contact and told him I would like to keep an appointment we originally had scheduled for Thursday afternoon. Although he said he had made other plans, I explained that my calendar was open because I had canceled my trip to Florida. As we talked, I found that he was very conversant about this Florida distributor, and he suggested I call the major creditor, a manufacturer's agent in Florida, who had not only gone into debt with Allied at the rate of $80,000 but also guaranteed the payment to this supplier in the amount of $450,000. In other words, this agent had so much confidence in Allied that he was on the hook to the tune of $530,000.

My contact introduced me to him over the phone at 5 p.m., and I received fine cooperation. By 10 p.m. I had arranged to have dinner the following night, Thursday, with the representative from the trustee in bankruptcy for Allied.

On Thursday morning I rushed into the office, picked up our

audiovisual materials on All-Phase as well as details of our benefits program and other corporate brochures, boarded the plane and arrived at Allied's northernmost branch, in West Palm Beach, at 1 p.m. Fortunately, one of our people was vacationing at Boca Raton, and he rented a car and picked us up at the airport for a series of visits to their branches. We arrived at our final destination, Miami, at 5 p.m.

I did not know that our largest competitor in this industry, Graybar Electric Supply Company, was doing exactly the same thing. They started their trip at the southernmost end of the Allied network, Key West, visited other branches and arrived in Miami at precisely the same time I did. Ironically, Graybar happened to be downstairs viewing the inventory while I was upstairs in negotiations.

When I found that we had competition, I canceled the return of our company plane, booked a room, stayed overnight and continued negotiating until the following afternoon, when we signed a contract. I remember sitting in the attorney's office when a phone call came from Graybar asking to be allowed to submit a price. The man said it was too late; the company had just been sold.

ACTING FAST

Thursday evening was my first opportunity to meet the president of Allied as well as the representative from the trustee NACM. We got along very well and ended up going to dinner together along with the representative from the manufacturer's agent (their largest creditor). I am convinced that purely because of a fast friendship struck up at this dinner meeting, we were in a favorable position to make an offer.

In fact, the gentleman taking the bids even told us we didn't have to bother putting any value on the fixed assets, furniture fixtures and so on, because there wasn't much value involved. Furthermore, he would keep the accounts receivable and collect them for the creditors if we wanted it done that way. (Of course, he would pick up more commission by collecting these receivables for the creditors' committee than if we bought them outright, reserved something in escrow and collected them with our people.)

After a late evening of dinner and drinks, we all agreed to meet with Allied's attorney from Detroit at 11 a.m. on Friday at the trustee's office. Little did I realize that he was there to liquidate the company at 5 p.m. that day. I found this out only after we had signed a purchase agreement at 4:30 that afternoon.

Allied's people brought us up to date at an early-morning breakfast meeting. At the 11 a.m. meeting we said we would purchase the inventory at a 35 percent discount, pay nothing for the fixed assets and pay $50,000 over the mortgage balance on the two buildings. They counteroffered with a figure about $330,000 higher than our $1.12 million bid.

Concerned that Graybar might already have a higher bid on the table, I offered an alternative in which we would select certain lines and price them at varying discounts, depending on the quality and condition of the inventory. This was to ensure they would be willing to negotiate if we didn't have the right number going in. As it turned out, that wasn't necessary, for these people were ready to wheel and deal with us.

We left the room for a fifteen-minute consultation and returned with a price $80,000 higher than our original but $250,000 less than theirs. They accepted the offer without further discussion. At 4:30 p.m., less than thirty hours after arriving in Florida, I signed a letter of agreement to purchase the company for $1.2 million. Two working days later, we paid the amount in full at the lawyer's office in Detroit. Only four working days went by from the time of the first contact to the final payment—a record.

"TURNING TO"

I think the only reason we ended up with this company is that I simply stayed with it until the end.

Immediately after signing the contract on Friday afternoon, I rushed to the office where all of the employees from four out of the five branches had been assembled. (Key West was too far for its people to get there.) I gave them an hour-and-a-half presentation on All-Phase. After showing the audiovisuals, I answered questions and tried to pump them up on the company. It wasn't too difficult when I explained that, had our negotiations lasted half an hour longer, the company would have been liquidated and nobody would have had a job.

This acquisition made me extremely proud of the way All-Phase can respond. When I picked up Allied's customer list that Friday evening and flew into Benton Harbor at midnight, I was met by our manager of Management Information Services and our credit manager, who went to work that same night setting up customer masters on our 1,100 new accounts. Believe it or not, by 3 p.m. Saturday we not only had all of the new accounts set up but also had a letter in the mail to them and to our 1,100 vendors nationwide announcing the acquisition. That's what I call "turning to."

At 11 a.m. Saturday we assembled a group of staff and administrative people, giving each assignments to carry out in Florida. They would convert all of the paperwork, interview the people, arrange for bank accounts and so on. After all, we had to open the doors as All-Phase Monday morning. The company plane left early Sunday afternoon, and by 7 a.m. Monday we had an All-Phase person in each of the five locations: Key West, Homestead, Miami, Hollywood and West Palm Beach. It happened to be December 22, so I was asking a great deal of our people to stay there until late Christmas Eve, when they returned to their homes. Our corporate director of personnel even stayed over the Christmas holidays to get the job done. We sent his family down to be with him for the holiday.

I also was fortunate in that veteran All-Phase employee Jim Cleworth Sr., who had retired to Key Largo, was putting in some time with us and was able to go to work full-time to help establish us in this great area.

Another reason I felt such euphoria over this five-branch purchase was that we had made only two in the previous eighteen months—Oakland and Canoga Park, California. It was great to get back on the acquisition trail. Over those eighteen months we had closed or consolidated four locations: Martinsville, Virginia (which we subsequently reopened as a service center); Beaver Falls, Pennsylvania; Kokomo, Indiana; and Bellingham, Washington. By ridding ourselves of real losers, we added significantly to our bottom line, yet we were able to retain most of the business in neighboring branch cities.

One of the nicest bits of negotiation in this deal was yet to come. I notified one of our top vendors of wiring devices of the purchase and said I would give him 100 percent of the competitive line of wiring-device business. I asked him to get there right away to start writing orders. I added, however, that we had many competitors' devices on the shelves and that I expected him to do his part in cleaning up this inventory. He would need to accept items back on a one-for-one basis, meaning that we would place an equal order for new merchandise, not only his own items but also those of his competitors. After much negotiation and deliberation, he agreed.

We used this same method of negotiation with many other suppliers—those on our preferred list who were giving us good reason to do business with them.

Eventually Allied's parent company went bankrupt. We upheld our end of the bargain and saw to it that every manufacturer got as close to 100 cents on the dollar as possible. We paid our purchase price in full. I am very proud of that, because I know of other companies in our industry who buy troubled companies and end up making the supplier suffer a loss.

I was convinced that within six months we could make this new acquisition profitable. We had to work hard to turn the company around, and along the way released every manager except the one in Key West. We replaced at least 50 percent of the personnel, but after eighteen months of losses we finally started making money. Because of these early losses, we didn't realize nearly the income I had hoped for and eventually closed the West Palm Beach branch. But it was still a good investment, as we helped many of our loyal manufacturers out of a jam and received their loyal support as a result.

## Timely Opportunities

WHEN WE PURCHASED CENTRAL Electric in Denver in June 1987, we felt that we had rescued the company from the brink of bankruptcy—some said it was only a week away. Again, we saw to it that suppliers received every penny without exception. Central at one time had been ranked among the top fifty distributors in the country. In fact, I found one ranking in which the company was one spot ahead of All-Phase. At that point it was doing in the neighborhood of $40 million in sales, but its volume had dropped to less than $20 million by the time we stepped in.

Colorado had severe economic difficulties in the mid-1980s, but this company went down faster and farther than others. Central's management told us that every time they came up with a forecast and lowered their expectations and reduced the number of their employees, the results inevitably came in far worse than they had anticipated.

It took a little over two years for us to turn it around, but we did become profitable and grew rapidly. When we took possession, Central had five locations. We promptly closed the one in Grand Junction, leaving Denver, Colorado Springs, Fort Collins and Boulder. We didn't even let Grand Junction see daylight; we took the inventory on a weekend and closed the branch Monday morning, transferring the inventory and fixed assets back to Denver. We later recognized that we may have acted rashly, and we subsequently reopened the branch in the same building, but at a rent less than half the original amount. We eventually purchased the building. We opened additional branches in Steamboat Springs, Glenwood Springs and Aurora. This Rocky Mountain District has been a real success story for All-Phase Electric, one of which we're extremely proud.

Another notable purchase that year was our Merced, California, branch. During negotiations I was appalled to discover that the company had made a tremendous investment in fixed assets, principally as a result of its motor-rewind business. As a matter of fact, negotiations came to a standstill when I closed my book, made a motion to stand and said that I absolutely could not pay the kind of money listed for fixed assets—something in the neighborhood of $250,000 to $300,000. These people appeared to have marked up their items to approximately list price.

"Please get a hold of yourself," the owner said. "Sit down and let's talk about this. What would you actually offer?" I said I didn't want to throw a number at them but would confer privately on the phone with my confidants back at corporate headquarters. I did so and returned to the bargaining table with a figure of something like $125,000. "Let's go with it," the man said. I thought he said, "You may as well go," so I started to get up again. "No," he said, "I mean it's a deal." The purchase turned out to be a fine one for our company. The negotiations were very fair and both parties were happy with the end result.

## A PERFECT FIT

I was particularly proud to add Martin Electric of Dayton and Hamilton, Ohio, to the All-Phase family. I started pursuing the company in 1987 and finally made the deal in November 1988. It was well worth the wait. I dealt with a wonderful seventy-eight-year-old gentleman named John Martin, who was proud that the company had been founded by his father forty-eight years earlier. It was a true quality organization with outstanding industrial lines—every line that one would want to represent in an industrial electrical-supply environment.

One thing I especially appreciated was the excellent training both inside and outside salespeople had received at Martin. One man told me he had been at the Allen-Bradley Hi-Tech School eight times—and I know it ran between $1,000 and $2,000 per session. Knowing that Martin provided similar education to approximately fifteen people, I developed a great deal of respect for the quality of people we were hiring.

Another reason Martin Electric suited us so well is that it was perfectly located to fill in a gap between our successful operations in western Ohio—Toledo, Lima and Springfield—and Lexington, Kentucky. In fact, All-Phase and Martin had overlapped on their respective customer bases by about 30 percent, so we often were competing. Martin, however, was more oriented to industrial supply and we to construction, so the marriage was perfect.

The day we were driving from Dayton to Hamilton to announce the acquisition, I asked Mr. Martin how it happened that he sold his company to All-Phase and not to a large competitor of ours in Detroit. He said he had heard from that competitor in March 1985, but at that time he wasn't interested in selling. A month later, he changed his mind. Then he opened his calendar and showed me that he had placed a call to the principal of that company in April 1985. He even had written down the telephone number. When he called the man, the woman who answered said he was out. Mr. Martin asked if he would be back later in the day, and she said, "I don't know." He then asked if he would be back the following day, and he got a curt "I don't know." Finally, becoming exasperated, he said, "Do you think he'll be back sometime this week?" She almost shouted into the phone, "I don't know!" Whereupon he hung up and decided never to call him again.

There is a moral to this story, in that if he had completed that phone call, I wouldn't have been able to buy this $15 million company. That's the least of the matter, because this other company already had customers in Dayton and would have loved to have serviced them more fully with this new location. Not only that, but I budgeted this $15 million company for a sales volume of $25 million in its very first full year of operation—a 40 percent increase. Couple that with the fact that we now have an entree into the Cincinnati market, and you really have something of value. This reminds me of the story whose moral is: "For want of a horseshoe nail, a war was lost."

I was surprised to learn that in fiscal year 1988 Martin was the fourteenth-largest single-house distributor for Allen-Bradley. And compared to other distributors, Martin had phenomenal growth. The top twenty distributors for Allen-Bradley grew at a rate of 13 percent, all of their distributors at a rate of 20 percent and Martin at a rate slightly higher than 40 percent. Other industrial suppliers had had similar growth experience with Martin.

When we took control of Martin Electric, we accommodated our major supplier, Allen-Bradley, by closing out peripheral competing lines. This kind of commitment from us went a long way toward solidifying our relationship with them.

We also agreed to close our Cincinnati sales office so that we would pull out of an APR (Area of Prime Responsibility) that was not assigned to us. Allen-Bradley had been very upset that Martin Electric was selling its products in Cincinnati and was pleased we could remove the problem. All of this was in keeping with our policy of supporting as few sources of supply as possible and playing the game right with each supplier. We may have lost a little volume in Cincinnati, but we felt that we'd more than make up for it with the commitment we would receive from A-B's Dayton district office.

## ROUNDING OUT THE EIGHTIES

Because most of our success in the late 1980s was occurring in the East, we concentrated more of our efforts in eastern Pennsylvania. We pulled back from parts of the Southwest and closed our branches in Monroe and Shreveport, Louisiana. After a half-dozen years, we finally decided we simply didn't have the right lines or customer base to be profitable. So we picked up everything and sent it to Pennsylvania, opening new in Allentown and Montgomeryville.

We relocated the physical assets into communities that really needed additional electrical distribution. All of this was accomplished in such a manner that we received great plaudits from our suppliers. They understood that we simply repositioned our assets, and they never viewed it as giving up on something or quitting. And every person at the closed branches was offered a job with All-Phase, and both branch managers accepted a transfer.

We completed a very successful expansion year in eastern Pennsylvania with the opening of a new branch in Pottsville.

The 1980s weren't to conclude, however, without one more acquisition—this one in Grand Haven, Michigan, just one-and-a-half hours from headquarters. The purchase was a logical one, positioned in the heart of our Grand Rapids-Holland-Muskegon trading area.

# On the Wild Side

ACQUIRING NEW LOCATIONS IS always great cause for celebration at All-Phase, and I have collected innumerable stories from our openings through the years. Some of the parties we gave to bring new branches aboard really were a little wild—especially in our more youthful days.

When we moved into Port Arthur, Texas, for example, we decided to use the old Union Hall across the street from the branch for our party. It had a stage, and we simply had to supply the sound equipment and musicians to create a real party atmosphere. But we made the mistake of serving what was called "Kickapoo Joy Juice," a very high-proof, clear alcohol that, when mixed with grape juice, tasted harmless but had a tremendous kick. All of the northerners, of course, enjoyed this drink to excess. The next morning when I was rounding up our troops to finish inventory, I found three of them in one bed sound asleep, with one fellow's feet sticking out from the end of the bed. It was our guitarist/branch manager, who had performed marvelously the night before.

The Port Arthur company had been selling cowboy hats and boots, along with an unbelievable array of other merchandise, when we took it over. In appreciation for everyone's working so hard, I gave each person involved in the transfer a cowboy hat and pair of boots. I guess we made quite a spectacle of ourselves the next day as we passed through Chicago's O'Hare Airport in our regalia.

In Lake Charles, Louisiana, we took all of the people involved in the move to dinner at a downtown restaurant. The parking lot was adjacent to the county jail. As we entered the restaurant, the inmates who happened to be looking out their windows shouted some obscenities at us and, of course, we returned the gesture. Upon leaving the restaurant a few hours later, full of food and drink, we were surprised by a tremendous clattering of tin cups against the bars in the jail. Every window in that four-story building seemed to have an inmate standing at it rattling his cup and shouting at us. Since we were even more in the mood to respond than we had been earlier, we shook our fists and hollered right back. It's a wonder the police didn't show up and arrest us for disturbing the peace. The next morning, as we were boarding the plane for home, we noticed a front-page article in the local paper saying there had been a riot at the jail and that the inmates had been subdued with tranquilizer guns. It really had gotten out of hand. Had we any idea that we might have caused such a problem, I would hope we wouldn't have done as we did.

I'm also reminded of our grand opening in Kalamazoo, Michigan, at the time of our first branch acquisition in 1964. We could not get the former owner to leave the building after the event, he was so partied out. He finally fell asleep in his chair. We couldn't get him up so we locked the building and left. He awoke in the middle of the night and took a cab fifty miles home.

When we acquired Coast Wholesale in Burbank and Oxnard, California, we had a marvelous, emotional moment at the unification dinner when I gave an impassioned speech of thanks to the former owner, Jack Smith, and his marvelous wife, Abby Dalton, who is a movie actress. I guess I spoke with such emotion that when I finished, Abby had tears running down her cheeks. Later, she mentioned that she was going to participate in a televised sporting event for celebrities and was planning to wear an All-Phase hat. Unfortunately, the officials wouldn't allow her to do so. Even sadder was the fact that her team won, and there she was on national television, bareheaded, when she could have been sporting our logo.

# Service Centers: A New Concept

ANOTHER FORM OF EXPANSION HAS been our small service-center branches, which we opened throughout existing districts in the late 1980s. Mostly the centers are in remote communities where we have little if any local competition. Located in Michigan, Colorado, California, Indiana, Ohio, Alabama, Tennessee, Virginia, Florida and Pennsylvania, these service centers have a dual benefit in testing markets for us and providing great training for young, ambitious managers, countermen and inside salespeople.

The service centers consist of approximately 2,000 to 3,000 square feet, about $60,000 in inventory and two or three employees. Mainly they service the customer over the counter; they have no delivery other than that made by the larger neighboring branch. Quotations, purchasing and outside sales also are covered by the parent branch.

We saw the service center as an easy way to feel out a market and, if successful, to let it grow into a full-fledged branch. We typically sign leases for one year, with a series of additional one-year renewals. It is an easy-in, easy-out proposition. About 10 percent of these locations don't make it, but we realize going in that there is a sizable risk.

Most have been quite profitable, particularly Stroudsburg, Pennsylvania, under the direction of Hazleton, where we have made money every month since we opened. We knew we had a winner here because it was so hard to find a building—the community is that prosperous. We ended up completely remodeling a dilapidated warehouse—and obtained a good term on our lease, with a renewal.

The service-center concept is working so well that my appearance at the grand opening of one in Ludington, Michigan, in May 1988 was my first time ever in the city. In other words, the employees selected the site, remodeled a building, installed a residential-fixture showroom and got the branch opened before I even became involved. The same thing happened in Panama City, Florida; Steamboat Springs and Glenwood Springs, Colorado; and will continue to happen, I am sure, throughout the country.

Another feature of service-center branches is that we can erect a building and move in within sixty days. This was the case in Angola, Indiana, where the economy is so strong that there were no vacant buildings to rent. We bought a couple of acres from the industrial-development board, contracted to construct a 3,000-square-foot building and, were it not for some delay in receiving approval from the local government, we would have been up and running within two months.

With the help of service centers we were able to add one new branch a month in 1987 and 1988.

# An Instantaneous Reaction

ONE THING THAT SETS OUR COMPANY apart from the competition in making an acquisition is our ability to react instantly. This came to mind on a Friday afternoon in 1989 while I was in Minneapolis doing the final review for this book. My son Richard called at 4:30 p.m. Central Standard Time to tell me of a phone call he had just received from a friendly manufacturer. The manufacturer told us there was a $20 million to $25 million company in the northeastern cities of Providence, Rhode Island, and Worcester, Massachusetts, that might be available.

I immediately placed a call and was able to talk to the president and CEO, although it was now 5:45 p.m. Eastern Time. We spent approximately an hour on the phone while he explained that he thought his company had been sold to a large nationwide distributor, only to have his hopes dashed at the last minute when he couldn't guarantee that the purchaser would be able to represent Allen-Bradley and other important industrial lines that had been a tradition of his company. (Apparently, a competing distributor out of Boston was the strongest contender for these lines, and he intended to open a branch.) It was supposed to be a net asset sale and had all of the ingredients for a quick turnaround by the purchaser, but the deal was on the rocks.

Fortunately, this principal also had his outside accountant and his executive vice-president in the room with him, so I was able to speak with all three individuals, thus getting a good feel for the current condition of the company. I made an immediate decision to fly out early the following Monday and be at his place of business by 9 a.m.

We had to scramble over the weekend to assemble four people for the trip: our vice-president of finance, our vice-president of field operations, our attorney and me; as well as lining up the plane, assembling the necessary brochures and audiovisuals and, of course, that all-important purchase agreement. Just to be safe we packed an overnight bag, optimistic that, if there was a deal to be made, we would do it instantaneously and not let it hang out there for someone else to salvage. (I wasn't quite as thorough as the others and took only my toilet kit and a razor but no change of clothes. I had to wear the same shirt two days.)

Timing is everything in business, and if we leave no time for others to move in, we can lock up the deal.

## THE KEY LINE

Like the other potential purchaser, we had the onus of securing the Allen-Bradley line, not only for its prominence and success in the marketplace but also because the other industrial suppliers were watching what the lead supplier was doing. They were poised and ready to remove their lines from this distributor and give them to other local competitors. One had moved so far as to commit to another distributor already.

Knowing that we had our work cut out for us, we arrived at the distributor's office and set about negotiating the terms and conditions of a purchase. Things moved along rapidly and satisfactorily to both parties, until finally it was time to negotiate with Allen-Bradley.

I went to the phone and called its headquarters in Milwaukee. I caught the principals just minutes before they entered a meeting with their president and CEO to discuss their position on this very distributor. Had I called thirty minutes later, it would have been too late. As it was, although it was going to be difficult, there was still time to save the company.

After making various commitments on the sales and marketing of the product—and a promise that we would add considerable resources, not the least of which would be financial and human resources—as well as telling them that the purchase agreement was contingent upon their accepting All-Phase as their distributor, they went into conference and said they would call back immediately.

Forty-five minutes later I received the good news. They were going ahead with our company, but at the same time they were legally and morally obligated to allow not only the national distributor who had been there before us the opportunity to come back, but also all other properly performing Allen-Bradley distributors. I rushed back into the room to tell the principals of the company the news. They literally jumped with joy—springing from their chairs and shaking hands with me and then proceeding with the negotiation.

By 6 p.m. we had agreed to all terms and conditions. The only thing remaining was for our lawyers to draft the final agreement, which they set about doing at 7 the next morning. At 6 p.m. on the second day we signed the contract, securing the largest single purchase transaction in the history of All-Phase Electric—a deal that brought into the fold a $23 million company that we forecasted to reach $35 million within the first year or two.

After the first day, when it looked as though we would make the deal, I sent the plane back to Michigan to pick up our human resources group, our internal auditing manager, our security officer and our vice-president of materials management. They arrived on the second day and began interviewing the employees and indoctrinating them into the company. I opened the second day by meeting with all employees in both locations and handing them a brochure about All-Phase, shaking hands with them and giving them my calling card. I told them over a thirty-minute visit the history of the company and said we were pleased to have them in the All-Phase family. This met with great reception.

I'd just love to duplicate this feat about once every six months.

## REACHING A MILESTONE

What makes Worcester and Providence special—beyond their quality and size—is that these are branches ninety-nine and 100, so we reached that milestone that we sought for so long. What a great way to celebrate our thirtieth anniversary!

I have always wanted a district in New England. We were patient, and now we have it—the twelfth for the company. The new branches fit us ideally—an industrial base with excellent customers and suppliers, a great group of employees and a tradition dating back to 1946. Also, we sent only one permanent employee to New England, the new district manager, so we were not required to deplete our ranks of experienced people as a result of the purchase.

The acquisition wouldn't have happened were it not for our great supplier relations and the kind of image in this industry that attracts the loyalty and support of the best manufacturers. I am convinced that without my close relationship with the principals of Allen-Bradley, as well as of the other fine lines represented at this company, we never would have been able to buy it.

All of this was accomplished, from first contact to unification dinner, in a scant ten days. We've rarely concluded a deal so quickly.

# CHAPTER II.

## THE ART OF THE DEAL

# The Chase

AS THE FOUNDER OF THE COMPANY and someone who's well known in the industry, I should be the key figure in our acquisition of new locations. From the initial contact to the final negotiations, people like to deal with the person in charge, particularly when he's an entrepreneur who developed and grew his own company. I'm sure my successor will be able to negotiate deals too, but right now I can't imagine anyone else having the advantage I enjoy.

I recall that the owner of Wholesale Electric in Huntsville, Alabama, had great respect for the fact that he was dealing with a nationally known figure and that we could make decisions while sitting across the desk from one another, without having to get on the phone or return to a board of directors for permission. He liked the "shoot-from-the-hip" type of operation All-Phase had and the flexibility of making the deal. He was particularly impressed that I always carry three important items in my briefcase: a purchase agreement, a typical lease agreement and a check... always ready to make a deal. I remember with our first acquisition, the seller had been encountering so many delays and so much red tape in trying to deal with Westinghouse Electric Company headquarters that he finally gave up and called me.

In my office I keep a file on every state, and within each file I have a record of any contact I've made with a company within that state. It might be notes on a brief telephone conversation that I make as soon as I'm off the phone, or maybe a penned note to somebody I ran into at a convention. I think I have something in every state's file, and some files are bulging (I never clean them out or throw any of this material away).

Some of the information goes back ten or fifteen years, and some of the contacts I've established still are viable. Sometimes we make a second contact with a company, and these files provide us with valuable history.

If there's any hope of making a deal with a certain company someday, I generally draw a Dun & Bradstreet report on the company after talking to the owner. In some cases, if we have been progressing well after our first conversation, I ask for other background information—anything I can keep on file for future reference.

An especially valuable tool is McGraw-Hill's biannual *Directory of Electrical Distributors*, listing every electrical distributor in the United States. I refer to it three or four times a week in returning a call, looking up somebody I've talked to or checking out a city I'm about to visit to learn about the competition. The book gives me just enough information to talk intelligently to a prospect.

After a deal is made and we have purchased the company, of course, I open another file containing the purchase agreement and all information since our first conversation. This file continues to grow over the years with correspondence and records of every conversation I have with the former principals of that company or its employees. It is an excellent tool in, say, bringing a new branch manager or district manager up to speed on the history of a branch. There is a separate file for leases on the properties we rent for our branches.

A prime function of mine personally—and ideally of all staff and district managers—is to continually and aggressively track down new acquisitions. I've even written a manual so they can do some of the field work on prospects, at least as far as the initial contact is concerned. We should be visiting prospects, getting to know them, telling them about the history and image of All-Phase, and building a relationship so that when and if they decide to sell, they'll think of All-Phase.

The owner of Wholesale Electric never would have thought of us, nor would we have known he was thinking of selling, had we not made this kind of solicitation. Opportunity abounds. All we have to do is be smart enough and aggressive enough—and use an approach that will keep us in people's minds.

# The Approach

I NEVER HESITATE TO SOLICIT AN acquisition, no matter how large the target might be. I have made innumerable such inquiries, to companies large and small, and only rarely has the telephone conversation ended on a sour note.

I approach it thinking, what have I got to lose? The principal of the company might be a little offended at the outset that I would ask if he might someday consider selling, but generally, by the time I'm finished, he says he's genuinely pleased I would think so much of his company as to call him. So even if I say to myself, "Well, that company would never consider selling because he has second-generation management within his family," I try not to hesitate. Who's to say whether his designated heir has the ability or the inclination to run that company?

I am careful not to make this type of call on a Monday morning, when people are nervous about the week's business ahead. I try to avoid Friday afternoons as well, when people are starting to wind down. Generally I'll make the call late in the day, when the person has settled in and the immediate business of the day is out of the way. I then try to soften the person up and take a long time to get to the point.

I made a very delicate call once to a woman in Baton Rouge, Louisiana, whose husband had cancer and wasn't expected to live out the month. It was touchy, because I wanted to buy their business before it got into his estate. The call went quite well. In fact, she told me I could call back a few days later, after she'd had time to talk it over with her husband and their business advisers. I did so, but they had decided to keep the company. The man passed away a week later. If I hadn't called, I always would have wondered if I had missed an opportunity.

## A LITTLE PSYCHOLOGY

Psychology plays a big part in initial inquiries. After having handled so many acquisitions, I've learned how to read the early signals.

The comment I most detest from an owner is: "Everything I have is for sale at the right price." That's a real put-off. It means absolutely nothing and generally denotes that the person will be happy only if the price is exorbitant. It usually tips me off that I needn't bother going further with the solicitation.

Another negative comment that's almost as bad is: "I'll show you my projections and we'll talk about the marvelous future of this company. Then we'll talk about a multiple of future earnings." This means that the prospective seller expects to base his price on future earnings, not historical data.

I had such a proposition from an $8 million, three-branch electrical distributor based in Houston. After one hour together, he shared with me his financials, which showed his company to be in a deficit condition with a negative net worth of $200,000, a tax-loss carry forward of $1 million and an asking price of an unbelievable $2.1 million. In other words, if the tangible assets were truly as they were presented, and if his deficit was only $200,000, and if the tax loss carried forward were fully valued, he would still be asking $1.8 million in blue sky.

I couldn't believe my ears. And this was all based on the fact that, despite having lost $500,000 in 1983 and another $500,000 in the combined years of 1981-82, he still projected an income of around $300,000 to $400,000 per year and felt perfectly justified in asking for a figure of five times that. In fact, the company was bankrupt.

I am always wary of any indication that an owner or his people are trying to make a company look better than it really is in preparation for selling. One dead giveaway is the manner in which they handle inventory depreciation. If someone never takes into consideration the slow-moving or obsolete inventory they've accumulated but continues to price everything at current replacement price and is on a FIFO (first in, first out) inventory method, then you know that the inventory is bound to be overstated.

Of course, not all owners have such distorted views. In one negotiation a distributor sat down with me and said he was at a disadvantage, as I had bought forty or fifty companies and this was the first time he was attempting to sell one. I would have a much better idea than he what the value of the company was, he said.

I asked him whether he had any children, and he said yes, he had four. Are they all alike? I asked. He said they were so different you wouldn't even know they were brothers and sisters. That was the answer I was looking for, and I told him that's the way companies are. They are so different, one from another, that there is no set pattern for evaluating the worth of a transaction until all aspects are investigated and valued. This tends to make the person feel more at ease.

Another thing I find is that an owner may be reluctant to call me, thinking it might reveal weakness within the company. I try to overcome any doubt from inquiring distributors by assuring them that I would put the same price on an acquisition regardless of whether I made the inquiry or it came to me.

I try not to come across as overly professional or sophisticated. Rarely will I walk into a place of business with a briefcase; I go in empty-handed. I don't want to look overprepared. That only frightens people who may already feel intimidated by my reputation.

When I go after someone, I know that person has something I want. Perhaps he's in a city where I want to be, or handles the right lines, or has a good image and reputation within the industry. If it's a turnaround situation, it must benefit both parties before I proceed. I would rather purchase good companies with great track records and pay a premium than make a net asset purchase where we end up getting poor inventory and inexperienced people. Our best acquisitions still are those we go looking for.

The majority of acquisitions have resulted from recommendations by manufacturers, who are excellent sources of information about companies that may be for sale. The second-best source is my solicitation in a city where I think we should be located. Often I just call all of the desirable distributors in a city. Another important source of leads is electrical distributors themselves. They may have read about our company in a trade magazine, or perhaps know us as a competitor within their community and think of us when it's time to sell. I receive an average of three calls per week on the availability of an electrical distributor somewhere in the United States.

## DEALING OWNER TO OWNER

I've learned always to deal directly with the owner from the very first contact. It is a lesson learned the hard way, after negotiations for the purchase of a company in southern California fell apart. It took me a while to realize this, but other than a single half-day meeting I had at the prospect's place of business over lunch, all of my other dealings were through the company's accountant. He kept encouraging me and telling me we were on the brink of making the deal. He even claimed he was forgoing his commission to put the arrangement together. But as I think back on it, he probably was the single reason we weren't able to go forward.

When negotiations broke off he told me that the owner thought I was "nickel-and-diming him to death over the rental terms, etc." I am sure it was he who put words in the owner's mouth. The owner, a good Catholic family man and easy to get along with from the first, would not have made such an insulting remark, I'm sure.

The moral is to keep every deal from the first contact to the final conclusion on a direct, person-to-person basis and under no circumstances deal with an attorney, accountant, banker, real-estate agent, broker or adviser without the presence of the principal, even if it means traveling across the country to do so.

It is my competitive nature that drives me to explore every expansion opportunity and never to give up until the deal is definitely gone. I have learned to go with my instincts and intuition when it comes to making an acquisition. I believe that you can reason these things to death, especially if you have legal counsel involved. If you tried to satisfy all their questions and suspicions, you'd never close the deal in a timely manner.

I know that the New England acquisitions in Providence and Worcester never would have happened had we slowed down and taken time to turn over every last stone. Instead we forged forward and made our largest single purchase to date. The company turned around and became a jewel for us within nine months.

I shouldn't have any regrets over missing an expansion opportunity. After all, we've certainly had our share of growth and profitable branches. Even though some turned sour, I believe that we're the kind of company that reacts to a situation and either makes it better, so it will be profitable over the long haul, or closes it. We don't sit around hoping things will get better. How can we possibly have regrets when we have moved this fast and have a company as profitable and professional as All-Phase?

# The Six Steps

OUR STANDARD OPERATING procedure in an acquisition follows six steps.

## STEP ONE: THE INTRODUCTION

This is generally accomplished by a personal phone call from me, a face-to-face meeting with the principal of a distributorship at some trade-association meeting, or an unsolicited telephone call from a prospective seller.

If there's interest, I send a confirming letter along with information on our company: a reprint of an *Electrical Wholesaling* article covering the history and operations of All-Phase, three or four issues of the company newsletter, "Employee Current," our corporate brochure and usually a line card. I will ask in turn for some information on the prospect's company—particularly a list of the manufacturers it represents and their respective purchase volume and, if I haven't already obtained it, a list of locations. If the first contact has been especially promising, I might also ask for a balance sheet and the last five years' profit-and-loss statements by branch (although it is pretty difficult to get that far over the phone).

## STEP TWO: THE VISIT

I then travel to the prospect's facility to meet in confidence with the principal. Generally I do this by myself. I sometimes have taken along the district manager whose territory would include this acquisition, but I find that someone else's presence tends to inhibit conversation.

The most important thing to ascertain at this first face-to-face meeting is whether our corporate cultures are the same—whether we have the same operating philosophies. I believe that in the final analysis, this is the single key ingredient for success in an acquisition. With this as a common base, many other barriers are removed. (One time this certainly wasn't the case was our bitter experience in South Carolina. We couldn't have been more different than the company we purchased, and we paid for the discrepancy in ethics and salesmanship.)

If things progress well, the owner might introduce me to his lawyer or accountant or banker or all three. Usually one of these people is on his board of directors, if he has one, or at least serves as his business adviser. I encourage the owner to have this person present so that we can move along. On occasion he'll bring in his number-two man, particularly if that person owns stock in the company.

This meeting is designed to sell myself and our company and to visually appraise the company's assets. I walk through the building, observing the inventory, and then I may look at the aged accounts receivable and the fixed-asset and rolling-stock depreciation lapse schedules; obtain a list of manufacturers (and, if possible, the annual volume done with each), tax returns, lease agreements, building appraisal (if the real estate is owned and available for sale), and a list of employees' salaries and commissions and their history with the company.

If we accomplish this much at the first visit, we both should have enough information to decide whether to proceed. At some of these meetings we even discuss the method of purchase, which generally involves purchasing the assets. In that case the most important step is the method of pricing the inventory.

Today, an owner often is not interested in selling his company merely for asset value, or book value. The trick, then, is to pay a premium and yet not pay more than the company is worth.

A good businessman will have used some method of identifying inventory that hasn't moved. In Huntsville, the procedure was to price at today's current replacement-acquisition cost all of the inventory that had been in place for one year or less. Inventory on the shelf over one year receives a slight depreciation calculation that increases with each year the item remains on the shelf.

Of course, anything on which the warranty has expired would be purchased at a reduced price. Also, anything that is obviously unsalable—because it is marred, chipped, dented or has parts missing—would be pulled off the shelf at the time of counting, placed in the aisle and subjected to price negotiation.

There may well be outdated items whose obsolescence can't be determined at a glance. We count those items and let the pricing clerk check for them in the current manufacturer's catalog. If they can't be found, they're treated like any other obsolete inventory, subject to negotiation by the two principals.

If we agree to these pricing procedures, we talk about the method of appraising the fixed assets, the rolling stock and, if a building is involved, either the terms of a lease agreement or the purchase of the land and building by All-Phase Realty Company.

We peruse the accounts receivable looking for accounts that have been on the books too long. We also escrow some amount of money to assure collection of the accounts receivable. This amount remains in escrow for perhaps six months. If the accounts receivable drop below the amount of the escrow, we reimburse the seller, and whatever remains uncollected at the end of the escrow period is paid to All-Phase, with the balance of the accounts receivable going to the seller. Any interest accrued on the remaining escrow is split between buyer and seller, in accordance with their final payment. The remaining accounts receivable are returned to the seller for final settlement. We exhaust every possible attempt at collecting before this happens.

There has to be some additional payment to the principal beyond the agreed value of the assets. This takes one of several forms: salary continuance or a noncompete clause or some payment for the going aspect of the business.

We never pay good will, because it is not depreciable on the books and will sit on our balance sheet forever. Our most common agreement is a noncompete clause, which might be a fairly sizable employment contract for a period of years to the principal of the company, and maybe other stockholders as well. This contract, of course, remains in effect whether the person works for us or not, and in the event of his death it would be paid to the heirs.

Generally, the total premium paid, while dependent on the size of the deal and the attractiveness of the company, may run from $50,000 to a million dollars. But there must be justification for every premium paid. The profitability of the company is the major determining factor in calculating the premium that we will pay.

STEP THREE: THE CONTRACT

Assuming that our first face-to-face meeting has resulted in a mutual agreement concerning the generalities, we prepare the purchase agreement, then send it to the seller, who makes any modifications required. The seller signs it and returns it to us. We sign it and return it with our down payment. Or we might—and generally do—conduct the signing and payment in person.

A sizable portion of the remaining payment is made on the Monday morning when we take possession of the assets, and final payment ten or fifteen days later, after both parties have had an opportunity to review the asset valuation.

By this time I generally have made a minimum of three or four trips to the new location. I might add that we don't have a standard contract form, though we do start with a typical purchase-agreement form. Each acquisition is individualized, and at least half the wording in every contract is tailored to the specific company.

STEP FOUR: TRANSITION WEEK

This is a very large step. I usually arrive on the scene on Monday. At the beginning or end of the working day, the owner gathers the employees together, announces the transaction and introduces me and my staff. I give a brief overview of All-Phase, stressing the compatibility of our two companies. I introduce myself to staff members and ask them to tell me a little about themselves.

After the ice has been broken, and if things are going well, I introduce our transition team, which is made up of eight to ten people from headquarters who remain on the premises for the rest of the week. It includes our vice-president of materials management, who is in charge of the inventory pricing; vice-president of field operations; someone from accounting; two or three people from human resources; a credit manager; and an inventory-control manager. We also might have our security officer along to investigate the security of the building and, in a mild sort of way, interview employees. The acquisition team should include at least one woman, for those new employees who might be shy or reluctant to discuss certain issues with a male member of the team.

One big responsibility of the transition team is to provide extensive training for the new employees, whose allegiance is crucial to a successful launch of the new branch. We divide them into groups and show the films "My Career at All-Phase," "Come Grow with Us," "Branching Out to Serve America" and "Employee Wages and Benefits," as well as "Team All-Phase." Then we conduct one-on-one interviews to be sure there are no hard feelings or misunderstandings about what we're trying to do. If possible, the district manager is present at these individual interviews, and he certainly becomes involved in any discussion of salaries, wages or commissions. Beyond this, the human-resources team explains all of the benefits as well as our profit-sharing and 401(k) plans.

I am generally available during transition week, but I spend most of my time with the principal, seeing to it that he's satisfied with the way things are going, perhaps calling on a few major accounts and meeting some of the principal suppliers. I try to stay away from appraisal of the fixed assets, turning that over to the materials-management person, but I do become involved when we negotiate the final value of assets. I also try to stay out of inventory pricing once the ground rules are set until the final meeting. However, I am available as a backstop for any transition-team members.

I give the inventory instructions, and we begin taking inventory on Thursday at 5 p.m. We work until 10 p.m., with dinner brought in. Then we commence inventory again Friday at 8 a.m. and generally finish about midafternoon. If we haven't finished, we work until about 6 p.m. We always stop by that hour for a get-acquainted cocktail hour and "unification banquet" Friday evening. This is one of the most important aspects of the entire transition week. It is the ice breaker where the All-Phase people who are to work with the new branch become acquainted with the new people.

We have a head table, where I act as master of ceremonies. The previous owner speaks, other principals from within their company and from our transition team say something positive, and everything is kept very upbeat. I present my traditional pocketknife gift to everyone present. The whole purpose is to build morale and camaraderie.

Saturday morning we start again at 8 to complete whatever pricing, extending and totaling might be required to arrive at our final figure. Typically we're able to leave the city by noon.

Monday morning we open the doors as All-Phase Electric, generally with all of the acquired company's personnel.

It is critical that the manager of any new branch understand the philosophy, procedures and paperwork of our company. For this reason, if we choose an existing employee as manager, the person must receive at least three days of indoctrination and training at our corporate headquarters. Also, when we open those doors Monday morning after the transition, some of the transition team must be available to extend advice, particularly on paperwork and procedures. We find it most effective to have the human-resources people stay for the first two or three days.

Everybody is anxious to return home from an acquisition, but we never cut the time short just for personal reasons.

## STEP FIVE: SALES BLITZ AND OPEN HOUSE

A blitz is a unique feature within our company and a marvelous way to launch a new branch. We match a manufacturer's representative with each of our people, and these two-person teams completely blanket the marketplace. They receive index cards with the name of the account assigned to them for the day, along with addresses, telephone numbers and directions on how to locate the customer. The team often calls ahead to make an appointment or arrange a luncheon.

We generally bring in help from neighboring branch locations as well as pressing our internal staff into service. Generally we send out somewhere between fifteen and twenty-five teams. Preparation is the key to success in a sales blitz, along with a proper kickoff. A morning breakfast is followed by an energetic reporting session in the late afternoon, at which we award prizes and recognize those who did the best job. The success of this program has been phenomenal: We contact between 150 and 300 customers or potential accounts in one day.

We follow the blitz with an open house, generally a barbecue, at the facility. We try to make the open house very special. The important thing here is to sell the company and its image. Rather than have the event catered, which can be expensive, we try to do everything, even cooking, with our own personnel. That seems to make it all the more special. Lately we've added some cute gimmicks, such as a blimp that flies overhead and a robot that performs tasks and speaks with customers as they arrive. We give everybody a name tag and a tour of the facility. We have the usual giveaways and door prizes, as well as a ribbon-cutting ceremony by the mayor. The local media, the chamber of commerce and other public figures are always invited. This is particularly important when we are moving into a new building.

One of the key individuals in the success of the transition, blitz and open house is the former owner. He must be in the forefront and continually speak well of the company. During the open house, he and I stand at the reception desk and shake hands with everyone who walks through the door.

Afterward, I send a letter to the homes of every one of the employees involved in the open house, thanking them for their participation and contribution. Generally this is the second letter they will have received at home from me; the first is a letter of introduction to the company. Everybody likes to feel they're part of a team, and it's important that people be recognized from the outset. A letter of appreciation also goes to all of the manufacturers participating in the blitz and open house.

## STEP SIX: AUTOMATION

Within four months after an acquisition, and sooner if possible, we send our computer-automation team into the new location to bring the branch onto our system. I would like to do this on the very first day, but to pile computerization on top of the trauma of coming on board and learning a new company's way of doing business simply would be too much. We have the procedure down to a science, and I have never seen a department function more smoothly. There is no doubt that tying into our computer is one of the true advantages of joining the All-Phase system. We're on the cutting edge of this major technology.

# The Key Considerations for Purchase

As A PRACTICAL MATTER, WE should never buy a company that has been in business less than five years and preferably not less than ten. Such companies haven't built a solid customer following and usually don't have the best manufacturers' lines. Also, the people haven't been around long enough to have the knowledge and wisdom this industry demands. There are too many great companies available that are twenty-five years and older to be bothering with the problems of an undercapitalized new company. There's something to be said for tradition and corporate culture built over years of operation.

It's essential to thoroughly investigate every aspect of a potential purchase before making a deal. There have been times when we became so excited about the opportunities that we overlooked some of the negatives. Or if we recognized the negatives, we tended to minimize them. Now we do our homework better. We step back for a moment and let the smoke clear. We try to remove the element of emotion.

If our acquisition investigation had been up to par in Dothan, Alabama, for example, we would have learned that it had a dominant distributor that so controlled the market that it determined the success or failure of the competition. If that distributor decided to run someone out of the community, it could do so by competitive pricing practices for an indefinite period. This independent owner held the philosophy that no one else should operate in his city. As a result, it took us years to make good money in Dothan. We also would have been more leary of South Carolina, and of Monroe and Shreveport, Louisiana.

I once developed a checklist to be used by anyone making the first contact with a potential seller, but we abandoned it after I made a terrible error while looking at a company in Columbus, Georgia: I pulled the checklist out of my briefcase and systematically went down the list, item for item, asking questions and noting the answers. The approach may have been professional, but it sure turned off the potential seller.

The point is, you can be too professional and absolutely kill a sale, just as you can be too professional during the transition week of an acquisition. If we appear too systematic during our investigation or transition, it can sour people on us. If we appear to want only the hard, cold facts, we discount the human traits of the prospective company, and that could be catastrophic.

Nevertheless, there are some key ingredients to making a purchase. First, we should always find out who will be our major customers in the new location, then determine whether we will be able to do business with them. For one reason or another, some will go elsewhere, either for credit reasons, or loyalty to the old company, or obligations to others. Some simply resist doing business with a multihouse operation. If any of these conditions exists with a major customer, we should evaluate the viability of the purchase. We have suffered in many locations because we didn't adequately analyze the mix of business.

It's also becoming more and more clear that manufacturers' lines play an increasingly important role in evaluating an acquisition. This really hit home when we purchased Coast Wholesale Electric in Burbank and Oxnard, California, and united ourselves with Allen-Bradley on a very large volume basis. The Programmable Logic Controller (PLC) portion of the business alone in Burbank was more than a million dollars, and subsequently reached $2 million. In addition, a new branch opening in Bakersfield, California, where we had the sanction of Allen-Bradley, would produce $1 million to $2 million in PLCs alone. This is in addition to the standard general-purpose control line of products, which added millions of dollars in volume at each California branch.

Of course, another prerequisite for an acquisition or a new opening is the financing. A good benchmark is that $1 million in invested capital should return $5 million in sales and $100,000 in net profit after tax. This, of course, assumes that the accounts payable are offset by accounts receivable (assuming forty-five to fifty days' sales outstanding in accounts receivable, and payment terms with manufacturers that are at least as good). The $1 million investment therefore represents the requirement for inventory and a slight fixed-asset amount covering furniture, fixtures, transportation equipment, computer and leasehold improvements (the investment in fixed assets should represent only about one-tenth of the amount in inventory).

Then there's the matter of the building's location. This ranks rather low in the list of requirements of an electrical contractor or industrial customer, because generally materials are delivered to the job site or plant. It may be more important to us than to most, however, since we also cater to the smaller contractor who does his own counter pickups. We don't have to be on the main street, but we should be just a block or two off the main artery and easily accessible. We prefer to be located near an interstate-highway interchange for ease of trucking.

(In raising capital for acquisitions, it is still possible to negotiate a deferred payment by the owner of the selling corporation. However, this requires the approval of our lenders. If, however, we buy the building in the name of All-Phase Realty Company, we're able to negotiate directly with the owner, as our realty company is a separate partnership, not related to the corporate loans.)

Every purchase is a cash transaction unless it is in the best interest of the seller to have a deferred-payment arrangement.

## TURNING PROSPECTS INTO PROFITS

My philosophy on acquisitions has changed over the years. I

used to bite at every single phone call from someone wanting to sell a company. Now I ask a series of questions and request financial statements before I even make a visit. This probably narrows the prospects down to one for every ten inquiries.

I guess this change in my thinking reflects changes in the industry. Throughout the late 1960s and early 1970s, it seemed we could acquire any company and make it successful. In fact, I think we acquired every single company I visited over a fifteen-year period. Now we seem to acquire only 20 or 30 percent even of those that reach the visiting stage.

Maybe it's that this industry is overpopulated with distributors. It has become so competitive that profitability has been severely affected. Even though we have only one major competitor on acquisitions today, it is increasingly difficult to have confidence that a new acquisition will be profitable from the start.

Sometimes, of course, it is our own expansion philosophy and the way we change the character of a new company that gets in the way of profitability. In the case of Coast Wholesale in southern California, we decided to expand rapidly and hire as many good people as we could find for one year, then look to profitability later. Although this worked fairly well, we lost more money for a longer time than we had planned, and it took almost two years to make profits consistently in that four-branch district.

It is commonly said that it takes two years to turn a profit from a start-up, but I guess I've always expected immediate profits from an acquisition. With an acquisition you already have a following, established lines and a staff with the proven capability to make money for you. It makes sense, then, that an acquisition would be a quicker path to profits than a new opening.

Today, however, that doesn't seem to be the case. The fact that we change more than just the name is the key. We change the entire method of operation, particularly now that we are automated and must place the new company on the computer for control purposes. This automation, coupled with our strong organizational skills, can be intimidating to the new employees, who fear that the personal aspect may be neglected. I try to compensate for this by staying involved through the acquisition, as well as for several months after.

There is a much greater thrill in making a good acquisition than in opening from scratch. I absolutely love the euphoria of adding $10 million to $20 million in sales to the company with one stroke of the pen. It's rare indeed that we can open a new branch and immediately see this kind of volume. I recall that happening only once, when we opened in Sacramento, California, and had a sales volume of $10 million the first year.

## COMPETITION FOR ACQUISITIONS

Once we started on the acquisition trail, we were able to add about one branch per year from 1965 to 1975. The amazing thing is, not once during this decade did we compete with someone else for the acquisition.

Today we can scarcely turn up a company whose owners either haven't already been approached by someone else or want to talk to another party before making up their minds. I guess, in reality, we have only ourselves to blame, because All-Phase Electric has certainly set the trend for this. I could not count the number of times someone has said to me, "I think I'll open some branches or buy some companies. It seems to work so well for you."

We've probably been our own worst enemy in this regard, as I have always sought publicity for the company to keep it in front of the eye of a possible acquisition. But in doing so, we have inspired others to follow suit. This is not all bad for us, for consolidation certainly is the trend in our industry. And we couldn't possibly have handled any more than we absorbed in putting together our 100-branch network. But from time to time I do wish that our company had originated in an extraordinarily prosperous state such as California, where it would have been so much easier to grow. Then we may not have been inclined to enter some of the states where we have struggled.

Some distributors, it appears, seemingly purchase anyone just as long as the deal is right. One acquisition-minded distributor once told me as much when we were attempting to dispose of two of our South Carolina operations. He said that if we were willing to take a deep discount on the assets, he would buy the companies. He added that he "would buy any distributor if the price was right." Of course, we were much better off doing what we eventually did—closing the two branches, selling the buildings and transferring the inventory to our existing locations.

# Why Companies Become Available

W HAT CAUSES A GOOD, SOLID, profitable electrical distributor to become available on the market? One reason is government interference in the form of taxes. More specifically, the tax on excess profits called the Accumulated Earnings Tax. Plain and simple, this means that the U.S. government, in auditing a company, looks at the assets the company is not using—say, a very large bank balance that is never withdrawn for use in the business, or perhaps a securities portfolio of stocks, bonds and other items that are not producing revenues as a direct result of the operation of the company. These "excess earnings" that aren't being used for normal business operation are assessed at a rate of 28 percent. The money is taxed as income because the government says it should be paid out to the principals of the company, and when there's a dividend paid, it is taxed. The government has this right, although it seems extremely unfair not only to tax the company but also to assess penalties and interest.

This appears to have been the major reason the previous owner of our Huntsville, Alabama, branch sold us his company. He was faced with either expanding into more branches or using the cash he had in the bank for the operation of the business, perhaps buying more inventory. I look at one very desirable acquisition candidate in Houston and wonder why he has such outlandishly huge inventories, and I realize it's probably because if he didn't use his cash to purchase inventory he would accumulate a large bank balance and be taxed for it. At the age of seventy-five, he certainly doesn't want to expand into branches.

I recall another company in Wichita, Kansas, that we passed

up mainly because it had an $8 million inventory with a total sales volume of around $20 million. Obviously the owner was burying his cash in inventory, and it was obvious when you walked into the warehouse: You saw items like fast-moving, regularly used wire stacked way up in the top of the pallet racking some twenty-five feet off the floor, where you would put only your very slow movers. He was stockpiling good, salable inventory.

Then there was a distributor in Roanoke, Virginia, whose sole reason for selling his company was that the government had told him he would be taxed for his idle cash on the next audit. If we could find more companies with this problem and could buy them without paying too big a premium, they would be a marvelous source for expansion. So much for government intervention.

When looking at some family-owned companies as potential acquisitions, we have realized that while they might look good on paper, we need to dig deeply to develop a spread sheet charging them for the use of the money and for the occupancy of the building (rent), as well as administrative overhead. We need to view their operation just as though it were a stand-alone branch. Sometimes the offset is that the owner is very generous in personal compensation and perks (automobiles, country-club memberships, airplane, summer homes). All of these factors need to be considered when judging a company's track record.

# *Off and Running*

Ⅰ OFTEN HAVE BEEN ASKED WHY some acquisitions are so much more successful than others—why in some cases can we assume ownership and start off on a Monday morning writing just as much business as the former company did on the previous Friday afternoon, and continue the operation as though there were no interruptions. I guess the answer lies in preparation during transition week. We supply enough people to do the introductions, the orientation, the training and the melding of the two companies.

Another key is maintaining existing employees at the time of an acquisition. This is absolutely imperative. There is no single item more important than these employees to the stability of a new branch.

I look back proudly on our Springfield, Ohio, branch, where after two decades of success, almost every single employee who was there when we took over is still there today. The absent few have retired at age sixty-five or older. This is a prime example of how it should be done. Similarly, in Hazleton, Pennsylvania, another successful branch, we lost only one outside salesman, to my knowledge, out of a staff of approximately fifty.

By contrast, in Bethlehem, Pennsylvania, as soon as we bought the company we released the purchasing agent as well as the counter and warehouse manager, none of whom measured up to our standards. In addition, we lost the two principals (the owners of the company), one salesman and finally, at my insistence when the economy turned downward, another half-dozen people. Of the fifty in place when we bought the company, only about twenty-five remained two years later. Today the branch is extremely profitable, but it took more time than was necessary because of these personnel problems.

## THE FIRST THIRTY DAYS

We can always tell within the first thirty days whether a new operation will be successful—or if we're in trouble. Here again, it boils down to people. I would do almost anything, anything possible, to keep people on the payroll for that first thirty-day period. Even if we find that they're inadequate, that they're not our type of person, that they're fighting the system, I would accept anything short of dishonesty for the first thirty days. The stability is that important. In addition, no matter who the employees are, no matter what their position, they know somebody in our customer following, and if they leave, they'll try to persuade that customer to stop doing business with us. It's only human. Of course, the degree of damage is commensurate with the position that person occupies.

Because any fallout tends to occur within the first month, it's important to keep our pulse on the people every day of that month. But if people make it beyond that point, we know they'll usually stay with us for the rest of their careers.

In fact, there should be a thirty-day grace period where we take no drastic action whatsoever. The only two things we must do are to change the name and change the paperwork and standard operating procedures. Beyond that, everybody and everything should remain status quo.

Perhaps that should apply to the principal of the company too. We generally have allowed him to retire and not be around when we open that first day of business. Usually he sold because he wanted to start taking it easy. But there also have been instances where the manager was young enough that he wanted to stay on. I think it is a good idea, regardless of what kind of relationship we ultimately end up with, to keep that individual in place for the first month. Assuming that we get along reasonably well, the former principal can be our greatest source of continuity for employees, customers and vendors.

We also try to avoid making product-line decisions early on. The manufacturers, their agents and their representatives do have friends on our customer lists and do influence sales. If we choose one manufacturer over another, we've naturally alienated one of our sources of supply, who certainly will go to our competitors and try to take our customers along. We pay dearly for the continuity of employees, customers and vendors, and we certainly can't afford to throw it away.

As soon as possible, I always send our construction man into a new acquisition and spruce the place up a bit. It could be anything from a little paint to brighten it up all the way to building new offices and training rooms, wire-wheel racks and conduit racks, rebuilding a truck dock or ramp and perhaps installing an overhead door—just something to let the new branch know that we are sensitive to their needs and respond immediately. It makes them feel good to see us spend money on something they may have been trying to get done for years.

We also add new vehicles to the fleet. At Martin Electric, we had to replace every truck immediately, because the one with the lowest mileage on it had 250,000 miles, and the one with the most was at 500,000 miles. The vehicles didn't look bad, as they took very good care of them. But they were starting to wear out. We also moved them outside to make room for more storage racking, which is what the branch really needed rather than a garage. I never believe in parking trucks indoors if it means sacrificing warehousing inventory.

## A COMMON IDENTITY

We have always changed a company's name to All-Phase when making an acquisition. Certainly many companies we purchased had outstanding names, reputations and images within their marketplaces. Early in our career, these often were much stronger than that of All-Phase, which in many cases wasn't even known in the community.

From the time of our first acquisition, West Michigan Electric, every company has been called All-Phase. West Michigan was doing three times the volume that we were; other acquisitions had been in business for almost a hundred years. But to succeed, we must have one system, one flow of paperwork, one universal invoice, one purchase order, one statement and so on. It would be impossible to properly utilize computerization within our industry if we had 100 different names; the printer would have to print 100 different corporate headings. Operating as one large unit gives us purchasing power too—we have greater clout as a $450 million company than a single branch would as a $5 million company.

Also, I like that people need refer only to one company, one name, when addressing us. We are able to utilize such things as mailers out of corporate headquarters and a nationwide WATS line that operates twenty-four hours a day, seven days a week, 365 days a year and is, of course, answered at corporate headquarters by the name All-Phase.

But most important of all today is the excellent image and reputation that All-Phase Electric has nationwide. We are viewed universally as a very aggressive, hard-working, honest and forth-right company. I want all the branches and all of our people to be a part of this image.

# Always Prospecting

I NEVER FEEL QUITE SATISFIED, EVEN on a vacation, unless I have something to show for my time. Sometimes one of my side trips pays off handsomely—as it did when I bought our Gulfport, Mississippi, and Oakland, California, branches as a result of attending Super Bowls. This is the type of entrepreneurship I love—being able to travel about the country and make quick decisions. It's the greatest feeling in the world.

Of course, my efforts don't always pan out. On the way to the NAED National Convention in Philadelphia one year, I stopped off in West Virginia to investigate a potential acquisition, and thank God I spent only three hours there.

The Square D distributor I visited had an outrageous expectation as to the value of his company. He had a net worth of $2.2 million, with an asking price of $2.5 million, which sounded very logical and attractive and probably well worth a $300,000 premium. It was the only real distributor in town, with a 26 percent margin and growing volumes. Although he suffered through some pretty tough times in 1981-83, he was coming back strong and never had anything that resembled a loss year. But then he pulled his cash and marketable securities out of the deal, thus reducing the tangible assets to $850,000. Suddenly, he was asking for a premium of $1.6 million.

I should have suspected this was coming when he took me to his accountant's office and they started laying out their projections for the next ten years. They wanted twenty times future projected net after-tax earnings. This company certainly had value, but nothing that would warrant that kind of a premium.

How could I have determined beforehand that the trip would turn out this way, saving me the inconvenience and the expense of half a day? It would have been awkward to do too much quizzing because, as it was, the owner was surprised that I had heard from a mutual friend that he once discussed selling his company. What I wish I'd known is that he had a very capable son whom he was paying $65,000 to $75,000 a year to practically run the business from the inside. He already had turned over 40 percent of the ownership to his son, and it was logical that he had a successor in line. I guess the only thing I could have asked on the phone was whether he had ever set a price on the business, but I'm sure he would have said that he'd leave that up to me when I arrived and that he'd never given it much thought.

Because I try not to let any opportunity slip by, I can recall one day reading in the business section of the *Chicago Tribune* that Sun Oil Company had fallen upon hard times during an oil glut in the United States and had lost a considerable amount of money in that quarter. I called my friend, the president of American Electric in St. Joseph, Missouri, a subsidiary of Sun Oil, and asked if he thought Sun might be interested in selling off some of its operations. Because he is such a good friend, he welcomed my call and told me to go ahead and call the executive in charge of this division.

I reached the gentleman at his home office in Philadelphia but to no avail. As a matter of fact, before I could get off the phone, he told me they would be very interested in buying *our* company if we ever were for sale. Now, of course, things do change, he said, and he would keep my name on file. You never could tell, he said, when a board of directors sitting around a table some afternoon just might decide to dump several of their operations.

## Ones That Got Away

EVEN THOUGH WE HAVE THE marvelous distinction of being the fastest-growing electrical distributor in this industry over the past thirty years, we still missed a few opportunities for which I could really kick myself.

One was L&H in Kentucky. It had three or four locations doing about $25 million to $35 million, and I had no idea that it ever would be for sale. But our competitor out of California sneaked in and made the deal before anyone knew what had happened.

One that hit closer to home, and that I certainly should have known about, was a company in Columbus, Ohio. I knew the principal very well and even had him as a member of my commodity committee while I served as its chairman for NAED. I had hoped that when he was ready to sell his business he would contact me. Somehow, a company from Dayton, Ohio, slipped in and bought it.

In 1984, despite our nine acquisitions and new openings through September—one per month—we still missed a couple of big ones, that time by choice. One was Nunn-Royal Electric, a $27 million company with four branches in California and two in Colorado. It would have been a great addition to our California group.

I initiated the negotiation by going to William Simon in New York (former secretary of the treasury in Jimmy Carter's cabinet) and he directed me to the company's manager in Houston. I visited with him, but the company didn't disclose enough financial information for us to make an informed decision. It really hurt, but I turned it down. All of this could have been had for less than a $5 million investment and I am sure a simple net asset purchase.

## THE COST OF CONSERVATISM

It makes me angry when I stop to consider what conservatism has cost this company. It immediately brings to mind two other situations out of dozens that have occurred:

Blue Grass Electric of West Virginia: We shied away from this one because of concern over undisclosed tax liabilities generated through the underreporting of inventory. One of our competitors ended up working out a deferred ten-year payment plan with the Internal Revenue Service (an arrangement that was certainly open to us as well, but we weren't creative enough to make the deal).

EESCO (formally Englewood Electric Supply Company): It had a sales volume of approximately $185 million, with one of the largest Allen-Bradley distribution networks in the United States. No doubt this ended up as a net asset purchase running something more than $30 million. We should at least have entered a bid. There was no obligation, and it simply would have given us the right to "throw in a figure," but I let myself be persuaded by the more conservative element of our company and never became a contender.

I have to be careful not to take a lawyer's advice as the last word on an acquisition. A lawyer is, by nature, conservative, negative and pessimistic. Maybe I would be too, if I had to read all of the new laws that are put into effect. But that's not the way this business has to be run.

We may have become too inhibited in the 1980s by the bad company we purchased in 1981 in South Carolina and by the 1983 Monroe, Louisiana, lawsuit. I think of the time in Shreveport when we were floundering and failing. My recommendation was to try to buy the top electrical distributor in the city, or at least the one that had the best lines. I wanted to combine the two companies into one strong branch similar to what we had done in Huntsville. I should have gone myself at the appropriate time, but I left it up to my subordinates, and they never made the contact.

Timeliness means everything. The end result was that our competitor bought the company, making him stronger in the marketplace. Consequently we never made money in that city, and we finally closed the branch.

I once became very interested in a distributor in Grand Rapids, Michigan, which also had a branch in Cadillac. I became involved in the negotiation quite late in the game, as they were already quite far along with a competitor of mine. Still, I got my foot in the door and was able to meet twice with the principal of the company. We were almost ready to make a deal, but I was advised by my legal counsel that we might be asking for a lawsuit from the competing company, which had been on the verge of making its deal when I came into the picture.

Despite setbacks like these, we cannot afford to dwell on the past. We must learn from our mistakes and move forward.

# *The Joy of Being Number One*

Ever since the successful purchase of Wholesale Electric in Huntsville took us from virtual obscurity to the number one slot in that city, I have looked at cities where we have less-than-prosperous branches and considered purchasing the largest competing distributor there. This is in keeping with our philosophy that All-Phase should be number one in every city in which we are located—and continually strive to reach this goal.

One of the best things I could do is to call the principal electrical distributor in every city where we are not number one and see whether there is some opportunity to talk about getting together. Just the fact that we've been competitors for years should not influence whether we solicit a deal. The worst that can happen is that the owner becomes upset with us; but after all, he's already our competitor and really not our friend, so what's there to lose?

Just as we have been only moderately successful in cities over one million in population, so also have we had trouble in branches where we are too small (between $500,000 and $2 million in volume) unless we are the only ones in town. In all of these cases, our goal is to be number one.

## HOLDING THE ADVANTAGE

Of the 100 or so cities in which we're currently located, we probably are considered number one in at least sixty or seventy, and that is a fine, fine feeling. Where you're number one, obviously you have some influence on the market and in some cases even control it. Where you feel you control the market, you have in-

*111*

fluence on pricing, and this goes a long way toward profitability. I'm not saying that we can gouge a customer, nor would we want to, but we should at least get a fair price. And having the kind of relationship with customers where they let you write the order even if you weren't priced competitively at the outset gives you an upper hand that is envied within this industry.

An example is our dominance of our hometown market in Benton Harbor. At least two competitors have started and failed, and the latest competitor is struggling to stay alive. When you are established and doing the job right, and you have been taking care of your customers for the past twenty or twenty-five years, it's almost impossible for someone to crack that market, regardless of their pricing practices or the competitive atmosphere they develop. That is, unless they catch the existing distributor asleep at the switch.

In Spartanburg, South Carolina, Graybar entered the market with a splash, offering extremely competitive pricing and giveaways, even to the point of raffling off shotguns and other such merchandise. But after some sixty to ninety days, they settled down to the regular day-to-day operation, and our customers, some of whom had left us briefly, gradually returned to the fold. This type of thing has been repeated many, many times in almost every city in which we operate. If you're trying to buy the business with price, it's a very short-term, competitive relationship. Of course, the risk of killing profitability for years is also always there. No one wins in that situation.

And there are those cities, perhaps just a handful, where we are the only electrical distributor. While I think competition is a good thing, if we're able to keep our people on their toes and extend good service and competitive prices, there's nothing like being the only game in town.

Of course, we're never entirely without competition; there's always a distributor in a neighboring city trying to grab business out of our community. But a local counter, local people and our true civic-mindedness will always give us an edge over out-of-town distributors.

If we do nothing else in the 1990s, we should try to change to number one all of our branches not currently enjoying this position.

# CHAPTER III.

## THE KINNEY WORK ETHIC

# Learning the Work Ethic

A HIGHLY RESPECTED MANUFACTURER told me that I am recognized as the hardest-working electrical-distributor principal in the industry. He said no one had ever seen me at a convention doing anything but meet with suppliers. That was refreshing, since so many people go to conferences to play golf or tennis or participate in other events.

He paid me an even greater compliment in saying that my sons in this business quickly are gaining a reputation as smart, aggressive and hard-working. If they have learned the work ethic by my example, that makes me extremely proud and happy.

There is no doubt that I learned my work ethic from my father, John Kinney. He always had his company on his mind. He never had an interest in sports, neither active nor passive. I never saw him play a round of golf, pick up a tennis racket or throw a football. Nor do I recall ever seeing him go to a movie or read a book, unless it was related to business. He felt that time spent on anything but business literally was wasted. The only exceptions were the hours he spent with his family, including an annual automobile driving vacation that in some years took us as far as the West Coast or even Mexico. Other than that annual trip, my father was totally immersed in his business.

He did have his Monday-night poker/bridge club. The seven or eight couples would play from 9 p.m. until approximately midnight once a week, taking turns hosting it in each other's living rooms.

Other than that, my dad worked. Our hometown of Benton Harbor was a farming community with the largest outdoor fruit market in the world at that time. Saturday was the busiest day for the farmers bringing their fruit-laden trucks to market, so my father kept his coal-company office doors open until 9 p.m. on Saturdays to receive cash payments on account and, of course, to write orders for coal delivery. That was one night we never had dinner together, and we would not see him until late, if at all.

My dad always left home before breakfast, so we never saw him in the morning either. He never came home for lunch, and during the week he would arrive home at approximately 6:30 or 7 p.m., so our one meal with him during the week was late evening. The only day we saw him for any length of time was on Sunday, when he had all three meals with us. Our favorite pastime was to take a ride in our car through the countryside. (Of course, this was before television and the emphasis on major sporting events.)

## MY FATHER'S EXAMPLE

I first joined my father in business in 1956, when I went to work as a salesman in his heating and appliance business. He expected everyone to work a sixty-hour week. No one went home on Saturday afternoon. You worked until the doors closed at the end of a very long day. As a salesman, I was out chasing down cold calls. Quite frankly, Saturday was a pretty good day, as you generally could find families at home. It was really the only time to make a sale to both heads of household—other than weekday evenings, which also were busy for me.

My father set an example by working harder than anyone else in the company. His credo was to set that example so others would follow. I must admit, a lot of that thinking influenced me. Now I feel the same way.

When I became manager of the heating and appliance business in the late 1950s, our days were so filled with sales and service that there wasn't time to review the accounts payable, so my father would sit with me at the kitchen table in the evening and review every bill—and I mean every single bill. I believe he made a great percentage of his income by disputing bills and making deductions. There always seemed to be a reason, although sometimes he really had to reach. He hated to part with his hard-earned money.

At the end of each month, when the bills were due, it was tough convincing him that we should pay bills in full. He meticulously went through every item to be sure we were being treated fairly. His attention to detail drove me crazy, but I have to admit that it taught me thoroughness in dealing with paperwork.

You also had to remove certain phrases from your vocabulary or you would bring down my father's wrath. He absolutely would not accept "I forgot" or "I can't do it" or "I don't know." He would never take no for an answer, and he certainly couldn't tolerate mistakes. I guess that's where I picked up the practice of telling people never to come to me with a problem without bringing me a solution as well. I have conditioned myself to be a little more tolerant than my father was, or no one working for me would ever have taken any risk for fear of failure. We learn from our mistakes, and it is only those who make no decisions who are error-free.

The years I spent with my father also helped me hone my innate leadership skills. And those skills were put to the test one night early on in my career. In those days, it was popular to convert a coal-burning, warm-air furnace to oil. The oil conversion unit would spray a fine mist of oil into the combustion chamber and an electric igniter would spark the flame. If, however, something happened to the power to the house or if the controls malfunctioned, there would be a delay in ignition, which would cause an explosion within the furnace. The smokestack from the furnace to the chimney would blow apart, soot and smoke would fly everywhere, and the control would fly across the room. Naturally, this created havoc in the homeowner's basement, with the noise, the thick, black smoke and soot, and the terror that ran through the household.

One Saturday evening, I received a call at home that just such a thing had happened in a racially mixed neighborhood on the east end of Benton Harbor. I rushed out there and found people milling about the front yard, people on the porch, in the living room and throughout the house. Everyone was panicked.

I knew exactly what had happened, and I took a quick look into the basement, came back to the dining room, stood up on a chair to get everyone's attention and told them there was no reason to be concerned, that the furnace had simply puffed. Everyone seemed to understand that a puff wasn't all that serious, and I was able to quiet them down and get them to leave the house. I then called in a service man, who put the smokestack back up, inserted a new control, started the furnace and everything was just fine.

Because I was able to get people to perceive that this was simply a "puff" and not an explosion, they bought the idea that there was nothing to get excited about. This all happened when I was twenty-three years old.

## In the Footsteps of a Self-Made Man

MY FATHER WAS A SELF-MADE MAN. He may not have been the greatest student in the world, but he was a genius when it came to running a business. He did everything right and was a fierce competitor.

After completing high school, he managed to spend two years at Olivet College in Michigan. His only steady income was the 50 cents a week he received for ringing the church bell. He took any odd job the college had to offer, but after two years he decided he couldn't wait any longer to start his own business, so he returned to Benton Harbor and set himself up as a coal merchant, eventually calling his company Consumers Coal and Oil.

He had never worked for anyone else, so he was not only young but also inexperienced. All he could afford to buy were a shovel and a wheelbarrow. He leased the truck to make his delivery and at the same time sell the next ton of coal. Eventually he was able to buy a truck and hire more people. His biggest venture came in the early 1930s, when he successfully bid on property in Benton Harbor called the Central Docks, on the St. Joseph River. This property, now populated with buildings, is still owned by our family.

Apparently my father was trying to buy the dock property out of bankruptcy and was to bid for it on the courthouse steps. He was concerned that he might be the only bidder and therefore be rejected, so he persuaded an uncle of his to attend and join the bidding. Unfortunately, the uncle became caught up in the bidding and offered much more than they had agreed. My dad's plan had backfired. He paid a premium for the property.

ONLY HUMAN

While my father was an outstanding businessman, his ambitions sometimes led him into investments that were only marginally successful. He invested in a farming venture that at one point included 1,000 acres of farmland in southwestern Michigan. This obviously was a tremendously labor-intensive business that was most successful when the principal was actively involved in the operation. Hiring a professional manager and running the farm like a private business never resulted in the kind of return on investment it should have. Eventually my father sold out.

He and a group of friends formed the Midwest Finance Credit Corporation. Again, they were outside their normal realm of business and depended upon a professional manager who really didn't get the job done. Ultimately, this venture failed.

My father also entered the warehouse-storage business in Muskegon. Here again he was an absentee owner, and he eventually sold this venture at a loss.

The one venture in which John Kinney was successful was the development and construction of an office complex at 777 Riverview Drive in Benton Harbor. The project was funded from the sale of his coal and oil business. Unlike his previous undertakings, he committed his total time, effort and resources to this real-estate venture. It continues to be a successful investment, with All-Phase Electric the principal lessee, a situation that evolved as we ran out of space to house our computer operations at our corporate headquarters on Riverview Drive.

My father's various failed ventures caused me to become absolutely single-minded in my business. I observed how a man with all the talents and ambition in the world could be successful in only one major project at a time. I decided that any thoughts of entering into plumbing-and-heating wholesaling, industrial supplies or even electronics was not compatible enough with electrical distribution to be attractive to us. Thankfully, I have never ventured into anything outside electrical supplies.

## PARENTAL WISDOM

My father went on to become one of the largest coal retailers in the country and even became president of the National Retail Coal Merchants Association. Eventually he added fuel oil, and in the early 1950s took over his brother's heating and air-conditioning business.

At one time he was bringing as much as seven huge boatloads of coal to our two cities and, true to form, he always drove to Toledo, Ohio, to watch them load his coal in the hold of the boat. His theory was that if you weren't there, they would pick up a railroad car and simply dump it from a high altitude, breaking the coal into finer pieces and making it less salable. He stayed the night, watching every carload be loaded onto the cargo vessel.

I remember those trips fondly, as he would always take one of his three sons with him. We never got a motel room. We slept in the car or, if we were lucky, went onboard the ship and were able to lay our heads down for a few hours while he stood on deck, watching them work. He often tried to educate us on these trips in some form, and I remember his talking about the birds and the bees. Following his example, I took responsibility for the sexual education of all six of our children and generally did my talking when we were traveling together to some branch. I'm kidded to this day by some of our children who remember those times.

My mother, Magdalene Kinney, always worked as the bookkeeper at the company, so clearly I come from a family of hard workers. It certainly wasn't fashionable in those years for the woman to work, but I can't remember when my mother wasn't very much involved in the business. She has a very good business head and is a good, tough negotiator. She always liked bookkeeping and did it very, very well. Even at age eighty-six, she keeps the books for our local Birthright Chapter.

My parents had seventeen grandchildren, and my father used

to say that it would be wonderful if All-Phase ever had seventeen branches, one for each grandchild. My father died of a stroke in 1974, at age seventy-one. Even on the day of his funeral, I remember going to the office for a time, something I think my father would have been happy to know.

# The Chickens Came First

$A$T A DINNER ONE EVENING I ASKED my mother, then eighty-six, "How did I differ from my two brothers in our youth?" She said I was always a consummate salesman. She said I seldom sat still for very long. I also was the peacemaker between my two brothers, breaking up fights and settling disputes.

I economized on my time, even when I was in grade school. Since we lived only three-and-a-half blocks from school, I came home for lunch. On the way home, I would stop by the barber shop and tell Foster Dailey, our neighborhood barber, that I would be back in half an hour. He always made time for me, even though he was not in the practice of accepting appointments. Since we always played football, baseball or basketball at my home after school, I certainly couldn't take time then for a haircut.

I also was a good organizer. I helped my mother form a Cub Scout troop, which originally met in the basement of our home, and I organized the first newspaper at St. John's school. My mother also reminded me that, as an altar boy, I served the first Memorial Mass at Resurrection Cemetery, and in those days a mass held outdoors was very, very rare. Even my nightly rosary was well organized. I had a piece of cardboard above my bedpost on which the things I wanted to pray about were written down one side of the matrix and the dates across the top, so I could keep track of whose turn it was to receive my prayers.

One time, as an altar boy in grade school, I wanted to do something extra for the church. So I went into the sanctuary after hours and rearranged the cassocks worn by the acolytes in order of size, to give order and respectability to the closets. I guess that

124

shows both my desire to do something right and my incessant demand for order.

I took piano lessons, and my mother tells me I was very calm during recitals, although she herself became quite anxious. Although I possessed very little talent, I loved to perform, then as now.

Although I can hardly believe today that I was at all mechanically inclined, Mother saw in me the ability to work with my hands and consequently gave me my grandfather's carpenter tools. I loved to build things.

Once I noticed a penny under the pew at the Catholic church. After I pocketed it, I thought that if there was one here, there certainly ought to be others throughout the church. So I returned on Monday and walked every one of the pews. I came up with only two pennies, so I gave up the cause. But I thought to myself, if you never investigate, how do you know?

## GOING TO WORK

I have had a job as long as I can remember. My first recollection of entrepreneurship is the Kinney Egg Company, which my two brothers and I started when I was about ten years old. We raised chickens in the chicken coop attached to our garage on Pipestone Street in Benton Harbor, then sold them around the neighborhood. We used old egg cartons we had around the house and even had our own little printing press to make the labels we pasted on the cartons.

As I recall, we sold a dozen eggs for 11 or 12 cents. We almost went bankrupt when blood was discovered in our eggs. If we hadn't guaranteed our product with a no-questions-asked replacement policy, we surely wouldn't have sold any more eggs.

During the early 1940s when the country was at war, I saved aluminum foil to make money. I accumulated a large ball, principally by stripping the foil from gum wrappers. It must have taken hours. I then took it to the local scrap dealer, expecting to be paid a great deal, but my total payment for all this work was 9 cents. I was very young and didn't argue the price, but I'm sure that shrewd scrap dealer took advantage of me.

As a child I was very tight-fisted. One time I was painting my bicycle, and because I didn't want to spend money on a new paint-brush, I used the only brush I had—the very small kind used for painting a picture. It probably took me five times as long as it should have to do the job, but look at the money I saved!

Sometimes I'd take my old toys, paint them, replace broken parts and try to sell them on our front lawn. I put a sign on a tree in front of our house to announce it. And of course I had a lemonade stand there too. I don't think I sold many of the toys, but I sure did try.

While I was in grade school I became a magazine salesman, and I developed a pretty substantial route consisting of neighbors and friends of my parents. As a matter of fact, I became the seventh-best salesman in the state of Michigan for Collier's Publishing Company, and I had started from scratch, with no designated route. I subsequently won my share of rings and other awards and merchandise. It was my first taste of real money and recognition. A lot of my summertime sales took place down at the boat docks, where I'd stand selling to the Chicago vacationers who came over on one-day excursions on the S.S. *City of Grand Rapids*, a luxury liner that ran between Chicago and Benton Harbor. I think they bought my magazines more out of pity than out of any real desire for the magazines. I had three magazines in my repertoire—*Colliers* at 5 cents, *Women's Home Companion* at 10 cents and *Good Housekeeping* at 25 cents—so I could cover the full breadth of the marketplace.

In the seventh grade I took over my brother Pat's job as janitor at a transit company. Pat went out for the football team and no longer was available after school. To do the job I had to ride my bicycle some three or four miles, round trip, five days a week. When I asked Pat how much I should be paid, he told me I should ask for $1.75 a week, and the boss would give me $2. Sure enough, that's what happened. I kept the job through the eighth grade, at which time I went out for the football, basketball and track teams myself.

## STARTING AT THE BOTTOM

My father put me to work in his business as soon as I was old enough, but he always respected my private time and allowed me to participate in sports after school. I worked on weekends, during vacations and the three-month summer holiday, performing such duties as laying bricks in the coal-fired boiler at the dock, cleaning and relaying bricks in the street, and serving as a mechanic on the coal trucks at the docks. I even doubled as a longshoreman by receiving the lines from the cruise ship, putting them on the spars and helping bring the ship alongside. My brother Pat was the envy of both my brother Jack and me because he was able to work in the garage with a mechanic, lubricating trucks and working with the other grease monkeys, while Jack and I had to toil among the coal piles.

One time Jack and I were assigned the difficult task of chipping the asphalt and tar from the ends of bricks, then resetting the bricks on a sand base in the driveway at the Central Docks in Benton Harbor. Neither of us was happy doing this in the hot sun, and we decided that our wage rate of 29 cents an hour wasn't worth it. I can recall vividly walking into the scale house at the coal yards and demanding from my Uncle Bob that he raise our pay to 32 cents. He said, "If you don't like it, I'll find somebody else to do it, but that is as much as you're going to get paid." Jack and I learned early that collective bargaining wasn't in our blood.

By far the most difficult job I ever had was delivering coal. I was fifteen years old at the time. At first I was sent into the coal bin of commercial establishments, where I was to maul the coal back from the base of the conveyor with my shovel fast enough that the operator could continue to pour stoker coal into the bin.

**127**

One time they buried me to the top of my neck in coal because I couldn't stay ahead of the pace. I had quite a time that evening trying to get clean with Lava soap in the lake at our summer cottage at Sister Lakes. In those days, because we had limited hot water and my mother wouldn't let us into the house dripping with coal dust and dirt, we were relegated to the cold lake for our baths.

I remember shoveling coal into the hold on the S.S. *City of Grand Rapids*. We had only three hours to fully stock the holds with coal that would last the round trip to and from Chicago. I'll never forget the time one of the crewmen came out of the hot furnace boilers and, having consumed more than his share of milk and whiskey, vomited on my pile of coal. The only real break we ever got was when the first mate invited us into the crew's quarters for cherry pie à la mode.

You can't imagine how pleased I was to graduate to shoveling coal off the end of my own pickup truck and into the customer's bin. At least I was working in the open air and not confined to some dirty, cobweb-ridden, sooty coal bin.

STEPPING UP

I really thought I had it made when I was assigned a Plymouth coupe, given an order pad and sent into the rural community selling coal door-to-door to farmers for $2 an hour. But it was a very tough job. Here were these people trying to scrape up a living from the earth under the hot sun in the middle of the summer, and I was trying to sell them coal. The only incentive I could offer was a $1 discount per ton if they'd fill their bins early. I also had the latitude to allow them to pay for the coal in the fall. (I guess that's where I picked up my knack for always asking for rebates and dating.)

I was expected to hit every farmhouse in Berrien County, Michigan. I had some prospects—I worked off the previous year's customer list—but I was also expected to make cold calls.

The experience really taught me some things. I called on one farmer when he was sitting down to dinner with his family. The only thing on their table were the vegetables they had harvested that day—tomatoes, corn and potatoes. Before this, I'd thought everybody had meat with their evening meal. I hadn't realized how good I'd had it in life.

I never made much money working for my father, and I guess that's good. He taught me the true value of a dollar.

When I returned home with my wife, Eva, from two years as an officer in the U.S. Navy at the age of twenty-three, with two young children, I was happy to have a job with my father selling oil and gas furnaces as well as major appliances for a salary of $40 a week—combined with a $40-a-week draw against commission, for a total weekly paycheck of $80. The commission settlement was made once a month, and at the rate of commission I was working under—I think it was 10 percent of the sale price—the payment overdraw seldom was reached.

This was hard selling. I had to go out in the evenings and call on rural prospects we had picked up at places like the county fair, where we had a display. I had to work that area all day, every day during shows, and in those days I can't remember taking a Saturday off. You were expected to be in the office or out selling. The customer's time was my time. It would have been unthinkable to tell a prospect that the time he or she suggested for a sales call would be inconvenient. I accepted every appointment I could make. I had no choice in the matter—this is what my father expected of me.

The hard work gained me recognition from my father, and he subsequently made me manager. That meant a great deal more responsibility—managing not only the other two commissioned salesmen but also the installation crew, which numbered some six or eight tradesmen working as equipment installers, electricians, sheet-metal workers and appliance repairmen.

I learned then to organize my day very well and those of the people who worked for me. I had to lay out in advance their entire day's work—quite a task, since it hadn't been done before. I remained in the office late into the evenings figuring it out. It was great discipline for me.

*School Days*

$\mathbf{M}$Y CHILDREN STILL FIND IT HARD TO believe that I spent my first twelve years of school in one brick schoolhouse with only eight classrooms—two of those rooms in the basement.

The Catholic nuns were great teachers and excellent disciplinarians. I remember more than once being lined up against the blackboard and the nun walking down the row, slapping each boy on the face. It wasn't just a light tap; we all had big welts on our cheeks the rest of the day. But no one complained, and certainly no one informed his parents. For that, we would have run the risk of being slapped again at home for the misbehavior. Things are different today.

When I came home from school, my mother was never there until 5 or 5:30 p.m., so we were pretty much on our own and didn't have a lot of discipline. My father, however, could get very, very tough over our marks in school, our homework, and family rules and regulations. If we came in late, we heard from him the next day.

THE 110-POUND TACKLE

The only thing that kept me out of the work place during my high school years was that I played sports, and both my mother and my father respected that. Because I went to a very small school, St. John's Catholic High, everyone who went out for the team made it. (My graduating class had twenty-eight students, and it was the largest in the history of the school.) Even when I was a little freshman weighing about 110 pounds, the coach put me into a game—just because he wanted everybody to have a chance to play. I almost got murdered!

By the time I was a senior, I stood 5 feet, 8 inches and weighed 128 pounds, which wasn't too bad for that day and age, but still on the light side. I played right halfback. My favorite play was called T-2. The quarterback nicknamed me T-2, because that was the play they most often called for me. It was simply a quarterback hand-off to me between guard and tackle, and when I got into the secondary, I would cut right and pick up blockers down the right sideline. This worked for a touchdown only once, against Lansing St. Mary's. I scored the lone touchdown in a 35-7 defeat. I also recall one game where I gained more than 100 yards against New Buffalo, Michigan.

As a junior I once tried for a tackle and missed, and another member of our defensive team came down on top of me and broke my shoulder. I was out for the balance of the season, which was only two games. I excelled best as a defensive player in the secondary in football, and in those years everybody played both offense and defense, so we got no break in the action. I loved every minute of it and never missed a practice session. I think learning how to get along on a team and how to survive in sports was the best experience I had in team participation.

I was co-captain of the basketball team and ran a relay race on the track team, so I participated in every sport the school had to offer. My mother and father attended as many of my games as they could. It was such a happy experience that for a while I thought I wanted to be a coach. At another point I was sure I wanted to be a priest. In any case, I was destined even then to be a leader: Although several girls in my class had higher academic marks than I, the nuns chose me as salutatorian and commencement speaker at our high-school graduation. I was president of my high-school class three of the four years, and vice-president of my freshman and sophomore classes in college.

# College Years

IN MY YOUTH I WAS ALWAYS THE meek and humble one, the middle child who never made waves. I never caused my parents any problem and really was something of a nonentity. I finally came out of this little shell when I was in high school. And when that happened, I positively roared.

I discovered girls and started dating as many as I could. As a senior in high school I once had three dates on the same night. I dated a nurse from the nursing home next door early in the evening, because she had a curfew, then another girl for the middle part of the evening and finally ended up with a late, late date. Though I did get around, it was never anything but good, wholesome fun.

Many people assume I went to Notre Dame University, because I am such a fan of their Fighting Irish football team. I have been a fan of theirs since I was seven years old, when my father took me there for a game. I did intend to go to Notre Dame and was accepted, but instead I entered a Jesuit school, John Carroll University in Cleveland. It was the best thing I did, for two reasons: I got a very good Jesuit education, and I met my wife-to-be, Eva, who also was in college in Cleveland.

The first couple of years at John Carroll University I didn't take things too seriously. As a matter of fact, I remember approaching my professor in freshman accounting to ask how I was doing. He said, "You're just about at the freezing point." Startled, I said, "Do you mean an F?" "That's right," he responded. I had to scramble like hell to get that mark up to a C. Not an auspicious beginning for someone who wanted a business degree.

Then I met Eva, in the latter part of my junior year, and I became a little more serious about grades, averaging A's and B's the last year and a half. Still, I was far from a star student. I guess the moral of that story is that you don't have to be the brightest in class to succeed. It's what you do with what you have that counts. If you apply every ounce of energy in accomplishing a task and do the very best you can, you can achieve anything.

## ROMANTIC INTERLUDE

I met Eva in the St. Patrick's Day parade on Euclid Avenue in Cleveland in 1952. She was a freshman at Ursuline College.

She was sitting in the back seat of a car that was pulling a float. Since we both attended Catholic schools in Cleveland, we had the afternoon off to participate in the parade. When I saw this cute girl in the back seat, I asked her to roll down her window and offered her a drink from my half-pint of bourbon. She took the bottle from me and promptly passed it over the shoulder of the driver in front. I asked him to roll down his window and grabbed my bottle back. It wasn't exactly a "love at first sight" experience, but it was the first time we saw each other.

Our next encounter came when Eva was chairing a tea party at her college. When deciding whom to invite, she and her roommate, Dorothy (who went on to marry Don Shula, a classmate who later became a very successful coach in the National Football League) spotted me in a yearbook, and she said, "Oh, we'll invite this man for someone else." When I arrived, however, I was attracted to Eva and no one else. Actually, I was quite obnoxious at the party. It was very boring. I kept asking if this was all there was to it, and Eva became so upset with me that she returned to her room and told her roommate she wasn't coming back. After being reminded that she was chairman of the party, she returned, whereupon I asked her to dance. During one song I kissed her on the forehead, and that was the start of our romance. We married on June 20, 1953, and have had a long, happy life together.

## CLASS REUNION

I have always considered myself something of a cheerleader when it comes to inspiring people. When I enrolled at John Carroll University, I wasn't big enough for team sports, so, to stay close to football, I tried out for the cheerleading squad. Believe it or not, I made it. The first game was against Youngstown University in Youngstown, Ohio. There I was on the field with my white turtleneck sweater, white slacks and white tennis shoes helping lead the crowd in cheers. Late that night on a long bus ride with the team back to Cleveland, I questioned whether I wanted to spend four years seeing games in this fashion rather than enjoying them from the stands with the guys and girls. I resigned the next day.

When I returned from my thirty-fifth class reunion at John Carroll University in 1988, I realized for the first time how much I enjoyed going to a small Catholic Jesuit college in a large city like Cleveland. I was greatly impressed by the way Cleveland is rebounding from its economic slump. It was also pleasant to renew old acquaintances and relive old war stories. While our school enrollment was about 2,100 students, fewer than 500 of them lived on campus as I did, so I had gotten to know my classmates in my dorm extremely well.

During the reunion, one friend reminded me that we used to sell a pint of blood to the Cleveland Clinic for $25. Today that might not seem like much money, but in those days it meant 250 draft beers at the Crossroads Tavern, one of our favorite hangouts.

I don't want to sound vain, but it was pretty obvious at the reunion that the prosperity of All-Phase was far and away the most successful story that could be told among my fellow alumni. There were dentists, oral surgeons and attorneys, as well as prosperous business people; but not one could point to the kind of growth and prosperity All-Phase has enjoyed over the past thirty years. Of course, this made me extremely proud.

It wasn't difficult to read the surprise on the faces of my fellow graduates when they found out I had a plane with our pilot and copilot waiting for me to depart that evening, and further that we had ninety branch locations in seventeen states.

I rather enjoyed one exchange with a person who said he was from Canoga Park, California. When I told him I had a branch there, he could hardly believe it, and he asked the name of my company. When I said All-Phase, another fellow in the group said, "Hey, we have one of those in my town of Toledo." I said yes, that was mine too. That started me on a roll, and I could not refrain from boasting about the success of the company. I tried to do so as casually as possible. My former roommate then said, "You must be a multimillionaire." I replied, "I am multi, all right, but it's multi-debt."

# The Navy

I HAVE ALWAYS BEEN VERY GRATEFUL that not a single member of our family ever has gone to war. We have been members of those rare generations—my father was too young for World War I and too old for World War II. I in turn was too young for World War II, in school with a deferment during the Korean Conflict, and out of the service by the time of the Vietnam incident. My uncles, brothers, cousins and all other relatives fell into similar circumstances, so we have never lost a life in the family through war. There has been no international conflict during the young lives of my children, so they too avoided military service. God obviously has smiled on our generations.

I look back on my two years—1954 and 1955—as a commissioned officer in the U.S. Navy with fond memories. Those were carefree days with a mild amount of responsibility and almost no pressure. We simply fell into the routine of military life. We didn't have to think and plan. As long as we didn't step out of line, our military career was a breeze.

I spent six months in the Naval Supply Corps School in Athens, Georgia. At the time I entered school, Eva was seven months pregnant with our first child, Lisa. Because we were the first class to attend the school following its transfer from Newport, Rhode Island, she was the first child born to a class member in the Georgia Naval Supply Corps School.

## LIFE ABOARD SHIP

After completing the curriculum, I was assigned to a destroyer tender in Norfolk, Virginia. I was the ship's service officer, running the dry-cleaning plant, laundry, barbershop, watch repair, shoe repair, clothing store and ship's store, where we sold everything from clocks to perfume. At age twenty-two I had more than 100 people reporting to me. Needless to say, I matured quickly, although my senior officer must have had doubts sometimes. I once caught the swabbies shooting dice on a blanket in the barber shop, and I simply told them to break up the game and go to their bunks. The official procedure would have been to scoop up the money, keep it as evidence and report it to the captain.

I also remember when two of my senior people arrived at the quarter-deck after hours. I told them to hurry to their bunks rather than be checked in by the officer of the deck, who would have reported them late and AWOL, which also would have meant an appearance before the captain. My commanding officer reprimanded me for not taking proper action. I was learning that had I stayed in the navy, I would have had a real problem accepting such military discipline.

I was on shore leave once in Palma de Mallorca, floating around on a rubber raft in the middle of a large pool, regretting that I couldn't be with my brother Pat, who was being married that day. On this same visit to this Spanish island I was assigned shore patrol as the officer of the day, and I delighted in storming through the city in a Jeep, raiding the houses of ill repute and the low-life bars. I did this for ten days, and you can't imagine the headiness and feeling of authority it gives you. I was becoming concerned that I might really enjoy this carefree life.

In March 1955 I was asleep in my bunk in midafternoon while steaming across the Mediterranean Sea when the radioman knocked on my door and told me he had an important message. It was a radiogram from Eva telling me that our second daughter had been born. I didn't see Marla until she was three months old, on my return to the States.

I made the mistake of calling Eva as soon as we made our next port, in Cannes, France, on Easter Sunday, to tell her how beautiful the beaches were and how much I missed her. She managed to say she was pleased for me despite the obvious hardship of caring for a newborn and a one-year-old alone. I thought twice before calling home during my naval stint simply to tell her how great it was.

A captain on my destroyer tender tried his best to talk me into staying with him in the navy and promised me an easy life. I must admit that it sounded appealing compared to sitting behind a desk in some office. Thankfully, I chose to return to civilian life. Starting All-Phase has been the most exciting and challenging thing I ever could have done. Not even shore patrol could compare to it. To guide a company's growth from its birth through its infancy and on to maturity is the thrill of a lifetime.

## Setting a Good Example

I HAVE A SENSE OF OBLIGATION THAT is both a blessing and a curse. I feel that I have to be in my office working when everybody arrives and be the very last to leave in the evening. That goes for Saturdays too. I believe that you can lead only through good example.

This feeling of obligation—to family, company, employees, customers, vendors and even the electrical-distribution industry—has been with me as long as I can remember. I hadn't been away from the company for even a single day until the spring of 1961, when I took a two-week cruise with the United States Naval Reserve. I remember saying to myself, "Thank God, I've made it this far and I can finally get away for two weeks." By then I had been in business a full two years.

At one point when we were having extreme difficulty hiring a knowledgeable warehouse manager in our Kalamazoo, Michigan, branch back in the late 1960s, I was so determined to get the job done without compromising our standards of quality that I personally drove to Kalamazoo every morning, spent a full day and returned to Benton Harbor at closing time, catching up on my own work in the evening. I did this for one week. I did all the receiving and shipping myself and not only supervised the warehouse but did the labor as well. It was a terribly frustrating period, as I felt that I could spend my time better elsewhere. On the other hand, I simply knew there was a job to do, and I also wanted to set a good example for the other employees.

The obvious curse in this feeling of obligation and example-setting is the toll it takes on me. I probably work longer hours and harder than I should. I attend meetings only because I told somebody I would be there and I can't stand not showing up. I even take relatively insignificant trips with employees or vendors only because I've committed to them, and I pride myself on rarely breaking a travel engagement or appointment.

The blessing, of course, is that my sense of obligation has played a big part in my success, in that my loyalty and dedication are returned to me by the employee and vendor.

## WATCHING THE DETAILS

Everyone keys off the lead man, and if I don't do it right, and do it the way I'd like to have it done, I certainly can't expect the employees to.

For example, I arrive at the office by 8 a.m. and generally stay until 7 p.m., a couple of hours past our official closing time. Of course, I always put in time on Saturday and take work home with me for Sunday. These are things I expect of myself, and I don't feel that I have earned my way unless I do them.

Another way I set an example is by controlling costs. I make it a point never to take the plane if I am deadheading back—that is, if the plane drops me off and has to come back empty or wait for me for too long. I also generally try to fill the plane so we economize on the expense. It must be cost effective or it won't fly.

I recently checked into a hotel in Mobile, Alabama, with three other executives from our company and, when I found the nightly rate was $80, I asked for the corporate rate. They said they do have a $70 corporate rate, but it applied only when the hotel was at least 50 percent vacant. I said I had never heard of such a ridiculous rule, and that if they didn't give me the $70 rate, I would not stay. They still resisted, so I turned around, picked up my bag, left the hotel and checked into a Ramada Inn for $59 a night.

Now, that $21 savings times four people adds up to $84. But it isn't so much the money that was saved as the example I set for the three other people who will, in turn, set an example for dozens. It wasn't convenient—all of this transpired at 11:30 p.m., and the Ramada Inn was at least five miles away. But I certainly would do it again.

I have never flown first-class at company expense. Even though I can afford to do so today, I would feel too guilty spending All-Phase money in that fashion. I know it's foolish, and I am often told that I have earned the right to some of life's comforts, but I can't bring myself to do it. I will never use the company's money for my own aggrandizement. Nor can I force myself to do anything halfway and not give it every ounce of energy I have.

That total commitment to the company sometimes has meant personal sacrifice and overlooking some of the details to which I should have attended in my personal life. When I built my new home on Lake Michigan, I was so busy that I had no time to supervise the general contractor on the job. Thank God my wife was there almost every day. When it came to settling the account, the only time I could find to check the bill was the middle of the night one Saturday. I literally stayed up all night to finish it, but I would never pay a bill without checking it first.

# Portioning Out the Day

FOR MANY YEARS I'VE PSYCHED MYSELF up for every work day by clenching my fist in front of the mirror, or as I emerge from the swimming pool, and shouting in rapid staccato style, "Get 'em! Get 'em! Get 'em!" This probably originated from the company logo I chose back in 1959: a fist with a bolt of lightning. It's my symbol of attack and aggressiveness to let the world know what All-Phase is about.

I'm convinced that one way I've kept stress in check is my daily exercise routine. When I'm in town, I arise at 6 a.m., ride for twelve minutes on my stationary bike, do four or five minutes of exercise on a Nautilus machine, ten or twelve minutes in the Jacuzzi and a quarter-mile swim. The whole routine runs forty-five to fifty minutes. Then I take my time getting ready for work, have a light breakfast and reach the office by 8 a.m.

Wherever possible I also swim when I travel. The only problem is that I'm in the habit of swimming in the nude at home, so I feel encumbered wearing a swimsuit at a hotel. One time at 6 a.m. in Stockton, California, I was the only person in the pool, and I thought it was dark enough that I could slip off my swimsuit. As I was doing my thirty lengths I heard this steel gate banging repeatedly. I assumed it was caused by the wind. But when I put my suit back on before climbing out of the water, I looked up and realized that the gate was being slammed by people passing through the pool area on their way to breakfast. You can imagine my embarrassment. I fully expected the people in the restaurant to applaud me when I entered twenty minutes later.

The only thing I'd like to change about my routine later in life would be to sleep longer. It would be heavenly to sleep until 8 a.m. and arrive at work at around 10 a.m. I never mind working late in the evening and feel unfulfilled if I leave the office before 7 p.m. On the other hand, if it's 9 p.m. I feel exhausted.

Now I try never to take work home with me in the evening. Weekends are an exception when I return from a trip, but even then I try to spend only four or five hours maximum on the materials in my briefcase. This is quite different from my first twenty-eight years in business, when I worked all day Saturday and half of Sunday.

A great release for me after the day's work is to relax at home with a vodka martini. In the summer I like to sit outdoors and watch the sunset across Lake Michigan; in the winter I sit in front of the fireplace with a roaring fire, perhaps discussing the highlights of the day with my wife. On the weekend my idea of relaxing is either to watch sports on TV or to participate in sports with my children, if they happen to be available, or, in the summer, to sit in the sun getting a tan and catching up on reading. Since I built the 101 steps from the top of our bluff to the shore of Lake Michigan, I have delighted in putting on a pair of earphones to listen to some great classical music and, with martini in hand, watching the raging surf pound against my rock revetment while experiencing some of the greatest sunsets imaginable. I am particularly pleased when one of my grandchildren joins me. I number these moments among my most peaceful in life, when I can let the pressures of the day melt away.

Given time on a weeknight or over a weekend, I like to outline my day and my week ahead, listing the most crucial items at the top of the page. Again, it's my desire for organization and tidiness.

## A GOOD DAY'S WORK

There is nothing like the feeling of exhilaration over doing a good job. The success of a good day's work is one of the greatest lifts one could ask for. What you accomplish might be as simple as writing a new guide for branch acquisitions, or as major as opening a branch or receiving the financing to expand the company. I am never happy with a day's work until I feel I have paid my salary several times over. It's as though I owe the company a debt every morning when I get up.

By the same token, I often find little satisfaction in a trip that is purely for pleasure. I enjoy myself most when a trip combines business and vacation or when a few days of vacation is tacked onto the end of a business trip. I owe the company more than to take a complete vacation from it.

About the only time I really feel at ease is on a cruise ship or in Europe, when distance and geography put work out of reach. And even then I try to cut the trip short, or I keep calling in.

I have never gone to Europe for more than two and a half weeks. We sometimes have planned a three-week trip, but about the middle of the third week I would decide to catch a plane from the nearest airport. Upon returning home I am fired up with ambition and generally work that very evening, jet lag and all. Most often this means a twenty-four-hour day, but at least I feel satisfied that I have made a dent in the work that piled up.

This may not be good for one's health, but it helps make the company successful.

Outside of brief vacations, I never take time away from business for personal matters. A couple of years ago I allowed a $25,000 life-insurance policy to lapse due to neglect. I'm certainly not proud of that, as I pride myself on being detail-oriented, but I was so terribly busy that I didn't take the time to take care of this personal matter. After having lived in my home for eight years, I have never mowed the lawn—and believe it or not, I like lawn work.

## STRIVING FOR BALANCE

The growth of my company is probably the single aspect that makes this industry so enjoyable for me. Yet while I love to expand through acquisitions and feel a great sense of accomplishment in doing so, I also have grave concerns when I am not in my office managing every aspect of the business. Then after spending a number of days at the office, I become edgy, nervous and anxious to get scouting once again.

There were times, such as 1985, when I overcompensated for the extensive travel of 1984 (our twenty-fifth anniversary year) and got into too many details of management. I caught myself pulling back some of the responsibility I had delegated to others. This simply compounded my problem, in that I continued to take on more work: I was spending every Saturday in the office and several hours on Sunday at home with a briefcase full of work and still not getting everything done. The harder I worked, the more I seemed to have in front of me yet to do. I was uncomfortable with the knowledge that something, even the smallest detail, was left undone. I felt that everything had to be done just so, and if it was any other way, I became unnecessarily upset.

I learned then that you must achieve that fine balance that allows you to spend a week on the road and the next week in the office, or three days out and two days in, without letting business concerns pervade all personal time.

Having the company airplane at my disposal is a real convenience, but it actually gives me the inclination to work even longer and harder. When I travel out of town on the plane, I generally arise at 4 a.m. to get in my swim and workout. Then I fly out at 6 and arrive at the branch at approximately 8 a.m. If it's an overnight, I never finish my day until after dinner that evening. If it's a one-day trip, I never return before 10 p.m.—a sixteen-hour day. One recent day stretched on even longer. After a 6 a.m. departure, I entertained customers and employees until 3 a.m. (130 of them for golf in the afternoon, 230 for dinner), then arose again at 5 for a 6 a.m. breakfast with my best customer. I got on the plane, flew 300 miles to the next city and had an 8:30 a.m. sales meeting with twenty-five of our salesmen. Later that day I closed the largest sale we'd ever had in the history of the company, followed by more meetings, and returned home at 11 p.m. That was pushing it a little hard, and I sure slept well that night.

My wife often asks me why I torture myself this way. I tell her that I want to prove to myself and to others that I can still do it, at age fifty-eight, just as I did thirty years ago.

It is a problem that I can't enjoy the euphoria of accomplishment for long. We could have a great month or an outstanding year, or even just a good day—and I could be ecstatic, but the feeling just doesn't stay with me. The next day I am right back at work grinding it out, demanding even more of myself.

But perhaps I shouldn't think of this as a problem, because I react the same way to setbacks. I have the resiliency to spring back from a bad year, month or day, or even just a bad experience during the day. I can bury my head in work and snap right out of it. I don't let that negative feeling linger.

I hope the day will come, however, when I can spend a little more time enjoying the fruits of my labors. I want to take enough time to thank God for all that He has bestowed on me.

# CHAPTER IV.

## THE ALL-PHASE TEAM

# A Winning Attitude

I LIKE TO THINK THAT EVERY ALL-PHASE employee, from top management down to truck driver, sincerely wants to share, cooperate and help one another unselfishly to attain the corporate goals. I hope this sense of altruism is a characteristic of our company. I don't believe that one branch or division should prosper at the expense of another. We must approach this industry hand-in-hand, united in a common front.

Everyone must realize that to grow and prosper and to make our programs more meaningful—including profit-sharing—we are, and must be, judged as a total company, not individually by branch, district or headquarters. People interested in the growth of our company, such as those financial sources upon which we rely, ask for the consolidated profit-and-loss statement and balance sheet. They look at the company as one unit.

I know that all of this seems a little idealistic, and I'm sure it doesn't totally pervade the company, but we must strive for this optimum goal and guard against excessive competitiveness and jealousy between people and divisions.

I once visited one of the largest manufacturers in our industry and was aghast at the "every man for himself" attitude I observed. It extended to the very top echelon in the company. Immediately below the chairman and his three top executive officers was a group of six sector vice-chairmen who reported directly to the chairman of the board. When I met with one of these division vice-chairmen, who incidentally controlled more than $1 billion dollars in sales, he asked for sales support only for those divisions that reported directly to him. While casually commenting that it would be nice if we supported other divisions of his company, he had only one immediate interest: to gain sales and market share within his own realm and, more specifically, to gain personal recognition for himself in the eyes of the chairman.

I hate to think what would happen if this type of self-dealing ever found its way into All-Phase. I guess this is what's meant by "playing politics," and we'll have none of that. If it's not good for the company as a whole, then it can't be good for any division or individual within the group.

I was very pleased in 1989 when three University of Notre Dame M.B.A. candidates, who surveyed our employees about our corporate culture, reported that our staff is united in its commitment to the All-Phase philosophy. Among their findings were these: "Employees have a strong and common sense of community and ethics"; "Whether they had been with the company twenty-three years or less than a year, they all took pride in the company as an employer and as a member of the community"; "The employees interviewed shared a pride in their product and in their business practices"; and "The employees believed in Ron Kinney's sincerity in his concern for the customer, the employee and the community."

## THE VALUE OF CAREER EMPLOYEES

I am continually amazed that a company really does reflect 100 percent and absolutely the personality and philosophy of the owner and principals. And their corporate attitude is reflected in the people they hire.

One of the major things we look for when interviewing at the management level are personality traits, business ethics and corporate philosophy and culture. If they don't match ours, we will not hire the individual. We never hire people thinking we can change them. It's akin to your daughter's bringing home the town bum and telling you she loves him and is going to change him. You know it just won't happen.

When we hire people, we ask ourselves and the employees whether they intend to make All-Phase their life's career. Often they qualify their answers by saying that if they are treated right they would like to do so. That's good enough for us. But if we find that they want only to get together enough money to go back to school or seek a better job, they will not be on our payroll.

There must be a career path in mind for every person who comes on board, and it should be discussed. Where do these employees want to end up in their business career? Everybody should strive to improve themselves and attain some goal, I hope lofty, within the company before hanging it up. (However, we must guard against any implied contract agreement.)

The backbone of the company is the employee who has been around for five, ten, fifteen, twenty years. That, I guess, is why I personally place as much emphasis on loyalty as I do on ability. I'm not saying that's always right, but it's the way I am. It's difficult to instill loyalty in some people, and some individuals' make-up is such that they would never have loyalty to any company. But I appreciate so much a loyal person that I recognize it and respect it, and I admire it more than any other single trait in an individual. Sometimes that can lead to overpromoting individuals just because they've been around for a long time and speak well of the company. But tempered somewhat, reward for loyalty is a good thing. It's the whole impetus behind our profit-sharing program and the 401(k) program. Each program becomes 100 percent vested after seven years of service.

Along those same lines, we have a golden rule that employees are never to criticize the company openly. If they leave the company, they can damn to their heart's content, but not while they're on the All-Phase payroll.

## INSTILLING THE ALL-PHASE SPIRIT

I once read an article that compared the so-called heroes within a corporation to managers. Every corporation needs a hero from whom others can take leadership. Of course, they also need managers. The one quality that marks a manager is decisiveness. Heroes, rather, are intuitive: They have a vision. They don't necessarily make decisions; they accept things that fit the vision. Managers are routinizers; heroes are experimenters. Managers instill discipline; heroes are playful and appreciate the value of "hoopla"—ceremonies and rewards to honor top performance. That makes me a hero.

My wife always has said that I spend an inordinate amount of time coming up with gimmicks, ideas, promotions, birthday gifts, service awards, audiovisual programs, pamphlets, leaflets, brochures—anything to promote the company and honor the employees. It all boils down to being a people person. I really can relate to my people, and I know that they sense this. I've always said, if you want people to care for the company, you'd better care for them. It's a two-way street, and you'd better show interest in each other or you'll both end up losers.

Over the course of my business career at All-Phase, I have cared for my employees almost as much as I care for my own wife and six children. I am always interested in an employee's well-being and get particular enjoyment in watching someone develop and grow to maturity.

For many years, when Eva and I took a two-week break and went to Europe on vacation, I always returned with a gift for every employee. I continued this until we grew to the point where it became impossible. That saddened me.

I recall the time I purchased a salt-and-pepper set for each employee—some sixty or seventy sets, I think. When I passed through customs, the inspector opened every one of my bags and found salt and pepper shakers everywhere. One time, when I was returning from Barcelona, Spain, I wasn't able to get through security. I had purchased more than 100 letter openers shaped like daggers. Security considered them weapons and would not let me on the plane. I had to pack them hurriedly in a separate box. I'll never forget receiving those daggers at my home with many of them jutting out of the box.

We're continually doing everything possible to make our employees proud of and loyal to their company so that they'll support it in almost any situation with a customer or a vendor.

Merchandise with our name and logo on it helps. Every employee should have—and wear often—one of our popular caps. Countermen should always wear our shirts. We also have jackets and coffee mugs displaying our name and logo. They help build pride and let others know that this is an elite corps—that not just anybody can be a member of the All-Phase family.

One way to let employees know they are truly an integral and key element is to show them that their job and everything they do is essential for the success of All-Phase. I want everyone to align the success of the corporation with his or her personal achievements and accomplishments. I speak of this often, particularly at Break Plus employee meetings and at the time of the annual distribution of profit-sharing certificates. There couldn't be a better opportunity than this to let every employee know how much I appreciate them and how they are interlocked with their fellow employees to form a rock-solid team.

## WINNING WITH HONORS

Awards and recognition always contribute to morale, and we have had many of them. I am extremely proud that we are the only company ever to be honored with three cover articles in the McGraw-Hill publication *Electrical Wholesaling*. I'm told that no other individual in this industry has appeared more than once, and there we were in mid-1989 with the third cover devoted to our company. This gives each employee an added boost as well.

In late 1989 *Electrical Wholesaling* recognized me and the company in another cover article, this one featuring twenty "leaders in ideas and action" who "will set the pace as the industry enters the 1990s." It was called "The Influentials: The Electrical

Wholesaling Community Salutes the Best and Brightest in Our Ranks," and it cited us for proving "that a person can make a difference—not only to a company, but to an entire industry." All-Phase won this recognition for pioneering the regional-distribution-center concept.

Yet another proud moment for employees came when our company received a first-place award for corporate truck logo, design and color. This competition involved all industries nationwide, not just the wholesale electrical-distribution business. And pride in our company comes easily when we review some of our unique accomplishments, such as the Regional Distribution Center, our state-of-the-art Information Systems Division, the premier lines we represent and the fact that the $10 million profit-sharing plan accrues solely to our employees.

In 1989 we were selected as the first recipient of the Spirit! Award from the Northern Michigan chapter of the American Cancer Society. The award honors Northern Michigan companies who support a cancer patient's continued employment during recovery from cancer. We were nominated by the wife of a man whom we kept on our payroll while he awaited a bone-marrow transplant. Unfortunately, this fine young man passed away. It is my policy that we will do absolutely anything to help a loyal employee who is in need. We will support that employee to the very end.

Finally, if we really want a lift, we need only remind ourselves that we're the fifth-largest and fastest-growing electrical distributor in the nation, and that we have become so over a scant twenty-five years. One of the statistics I like to quote is that All-Phase conducts more business today in any given hour of the workweek than it did in its entire first year of operation. That seems to put everything into perspective. It goes without saying that none of this would have been possible were it not for the total commitment and dedication of our employees.

# The Best and Leanest Staff in the Business

I T'S BEEN SAID MANY TIMES THAT ANY company in the electrical-distribution industry is only as good as its people. The industry is very labor intensive—we spend something in the neighborhood of 40 percent of our gross profit on salaries, wages and benefits alone. Because margins are so small—about 20 percent gross profit—it is absolutely necessary to get the best return on investment possible from your staff.

All-Phase in the past has operated with a very lean staff. As a matter of fact, I was told by manufacturers that we appeared to function with the smallest staff of executives they ever had seen for a company our size. I was convinced that they were right, and I was equally sure that it was the right way to go.

It gave me a great deal of comfort during difficult economic times to know that we didn't have any unproductive, excessive overhead at the main office. At the same time, it placed a great deal of pressure on me and the staff. Because I depended on so few people, I demanded absolute perfection and performance above reproach. Everyone had to know his or her job well, be responsible, be a team player and not be prone to error.

For almost thirty years we did not have a sales manager nor a marketing manager but relied instead on district managers to perform any such functions. I think we did miss something here, because those district managers were very, very busy visiting branches, maintaining inventory levels, watching accounts receivable, securing personnel for the operation and so on; and sometimes they just didn't have time to be creative in sales and marketing. But I felt much more comfortable with people who were overloaded and rushed than with staff members sitting around with any spare minutes.

I remember when one of the largest chains in our business, General Electric Supply Company, released $7 million worth of overhead—I guess that amounted to something like 150 people. I would never want to get into a position where we had to make wholesale cuts like that.

## POSITIONING THE COMPANY FOR GROWTH

In 1988 we moved away from our philosophy of "lean" and expanded the corporate staff. Until that time I, as president and CEO, had been the only officer active in the company. I had people in charge of finance, personnel, purchasing and computer, but none had the title of officer. That changed when we created seven new vice-presidents. Although I had resisted this type of structure for almost the first thirty years of All-Phase's corporate life, I came to believe that it was now time to add professionals who would position the company for greater growth and prosperity in the coming decades.

My son Richard became vice-president of administration, with the other six vice-presidents reporting to him. He officially oversees day-to-day operations, although I remain very involved in any area that needs my help. I availed myself of the opportunity to delegate to Richard a great deal of the detail, administration, and strategy and planning for the company so I would have more time to pursue those things I love best—expanding through acquisitions and new branch openings, negotiating with vendors and making calls on end-users with our branch and district personnel. I also took this opportunity to spend more time in the field at the branch level.

The positions elevated to vice-president were: materials management (formerly purchasing and inventory control), human resources and public affairs (formerly personnel manager), finance (formerly corporate controller), and information systems (formerly management information services). We also added vice-presidents for marketing and field operations—two voids in the company that truly needed to be filled. They will make a tremendous difference in the way the company operates and prospers in the future.

The vice-president for field operations deals constantly and directly with district managers and branch managers on day-to-day operations. He spends a tremendous amount of time traveling or dealing with the field by phone and memo. The most significant feature of this new position is that we are closing the gap between corporate and field. There is a much better understanding between them and certainly a much better sense of team building and cooperation. We now operate as one unit rather than as a divided one—head office versus branches. I am no longer the only one who returns to corporate from branch visits stating that we must be more sensitive to what goes on in the field. It is comforting to have someone spending full-time keeping everything in balance and installing a level of consistency at the branches.

The marketing vice-president oversees the district sales managers. He is responsible for all sales and marketing within the company. I had felt in the past that our branch managers were sufficiently sales and marketing motivated, since they had come up through the ranks and, with little exception, had spent time as salespeople sometime in their careers. But I had lost sight of the fact that their days were now being filled increasingly with administrative details involving such things as computer, systems and procedures, human resources and asset management, rather than sales. Consequently we absolutely had to fill this ever-important marketing position, and I am pleased that it is having such a positive effect on the company. We now talk in terms of market share and market penetration rather than simply booking all of the orders we can but with no view to internal growth and getting our share of what's out there.

These two new positions and the elevation of the other four

have, of course, cost the company a great deal of money. But the dividends are awesome. We are growing at a rate of 20 percent per year, and we had to install this infrastructure if we wanted to continue to grow at a profitable level. We had doubled our business over the past five years and quadrupled it over the past ten years, but we were faced with a different ball game. If we wanted to continue our rate of growth into the 1990s, these positions were essential.

By my very nature I am concerned about profitability and control of overhead, so it was difficult for me to accept this higher level of expense with any degree of comfort, but I have grown to realize that it is the only way we can grow this company. I still caution every department that it must have a thirty-day plan whereby it could reduce expenses were our economy to suffer a reversal or our industry to falter. I always want to be prepared for the worst.

We also have to guard against becoming overburdened with bureaucracy and time-consuming reports and meetings. I believe in doing everything in the simplest form possible, and I still think staff meetings should take no longer than two to three hours, no more than once a week. Individual meetings are inevitable, but they should be kept to a minimum.

# Hiring Smart

$A$ CARELESS EMPLOYEE OR AN employee who mistreats a customer can cost our company dearly. The way to prevent this is to recruit only the very best people, pay them well and train them well.

Intelligent, persevering, loyal employees are worth their weight in gold. I think we sometimes failed to recognize this in the past and had a tendency to put everyone in the same category when it came to salary evaluation and promotion. We didn't give enough to those few who accounted for so much of the success in this company. I am not talking just about financial rewards but also about personal recognition. We now have several programs in place, discussed later in this chapter, to address that.

We also stopped bargain hunting on salaries. We started paying well to hire quality people. Only recently have I started to preach that gospel. How much better off a company is when it gets quality work from topnotch people than slipshod work from mediocre to subpar performers.

## UP THROUGH THE RANKS

All-Phase always has preferred to promote from within. There have been some excellent and very well-qualified people who have joined us through acquisitions, and others who have come from another company and have fit very well into our organization, but by and large most All-Phase employees start at a rather low level. Typically they begin in delivery, warehouse or clerical and work their way up through the sales counter, inside sales, quotations, purchasing, credit management, operating management, outside sales and, finally, branch management. While this policy has worked very well for us in the past and is something we are absolutely committed to, the rapid pace of our branch expansion and internal growth has compelled us to seek other sources to fill our needs. To complement our traditional pool of internal promotion candidates we added thirty management trainees within the space of eighteen months in 1988 and 1989. In addition, we embarked on a scholarship program as well as a new sales-trainee program at the twelve schools nationwide where we recruit heavily.

An ideal training ground for branch managers are the several small branches we have doing between half a million and a million dollars annual volume. At two in particular—Sturgis and Owosso, Michigan—the company has trained probably a dozen branch managers. Occasionally an employee realizes all of his or her potential simply managing a small branch. In such a case, the person could remain where he or she is, be moved to a larger branch as operating manager or back to the field as a salesperson. At the 1989 President's Ring Club award trip to Phoenix, I was surprised when I realized that four of these top sales performers were former branch managers. I consider it a real credit to our company to be able to retain someone in this manner and channel their strengths accordingly.

My time with my branch managers is so limited that I've come to rely on some quick indicators to tell me what kind of person is running the branch. I have developed the bad habit of judging managers' aggressiveness by the way they drive. If they slow down as they approach a stoplight fearing the light will change, I feel that they are too tentative and lack decisiveness. As destructive as it may seem, I then often take the wheel on our return to the airport and show them how to drive aggressively. It may be an oversimplification, but my conclusion is that the timid and meek are not my style of manager. If they can't drive aggressively, they can't manage aggressively.

HIRING GUIDELINES

Everything related to human resources—interviewing, hiring, selection—is essential for the success of the company. Members of our personnel and training staff provide guidance and direction for the soliciting of new employees, the selection process, training (which includes manufacturer trade schools, as well as in-house training programs), monitoring and observation, review, promotion and counseling of all employees. In addition, they help determine whether a person fits our company's criteria, not just at the time of hiring but throughout the individual's career.

With guidance from the human resources vice-president and his staff, branch managers are expected to follow specific guidelines in hiring. However, not everybody is a good interviewer; not everybody is a good people person, and often there is a tendency to hire someone the interviewer likes rather than letting the forms and guidelines give the cues. It is for this reason that we spend so much of our branch-manager training time on honing interviewing and selection skills. Of course, we always require background checks, driver's record checks, physical examinations and all of the other necessary required data. (We required polygraph tests when it was legal to give them.)

Because we operate with such a tight quota on people, the one thing we guard against above all else is hiring in a panic. The branch manager must always go through multiple interviews and conduct thorough checking. Just because a branch loses a truck driver, a replacement needn't be hired for the next day's deliveries. The district manager should borrow someone from a neighboring branch until the branch in question can get out of trouble, or pay overtime and have people double up on their jobs. But never should we short-circuit the recruiting process.

I like to think that All-Phase does not raid its competitors for people. My policy has always been that the person must first have left his or her present employer before being hired by us. I know this is somewhat idealistic, and I'm sure that people come to us looking for a job while still employed by a competitor—and we succumb to the weakness of conducting an interview and even, sometimes, making a job offer. But that's not the way it should be done.

It also happens that an individual comes over to All-Phase, then tells his or her buddies about it, and eventually we find a migration, as was the case in Bethlehem, Pennsylvania. We hired one inside salesman from a competitor and ended up with an additional inside salesman and a quotations manager. I would have been furious had I been that competitor.

One thing we do prohibit is a manufacturer's raiding of our company. At one point we lost three salesmen within six months to the very manufacturers we represent. That prompted me to write a statement of policy, which I sent to the principal of every vendor we represent, saying that if they found it necessary to hire the trained and experienced people in which All-Phase has invested so heavily, then I would make sure that it was the last day they ever received a purchase order from my company. It was strongly worded and probably would not have received approval from legal counsel. Nevertheless, I sent it and received many, many phone calls and letters complimenting me on my firm stand. Most important, since that day we have lost very few employees to manufacturers, and that is saying something.

The matter of personnel is so important to our company that at our biennial Advanced Management Program we dedicate 25 percent of our time to it. One of our rules: We should never leave a hiring decision up to a receptionist. In other words, anytime anyone calls or visits us looking for a job, we must always allow the person to fill out an application and, if the branch manager is available, have the manager spend at least a couple of minutes with the candidate. You never know when you might have a fine potential employee on your hands, and I would hate to turn such a person away just because we weren't hiring on that particular day.

LIGHTNING STRIKES ONCE

## A PLACE PEOPLE WANT TO WORK

An essential ingredient in recruiting is to have the kind of image people think well of. The fact that we receive more than our share of résumés and employment inquiries from people within the industry supports my feeling that All-Phase has perhaps the best image of growth, prosperity and opportunity in the entire wholesale electric-supply industry.

We have developed some audiovisual programs that are the best I have seen in any industry. We make particular use of them in on-campus interviews and recruitment. We show "Come Grow with Us," a history of the company; "Branching Out to Serve America," a slide presentation on each branch location and the city in which it is located, plus a summary of the growth of the company; and a program on careers at All-Phase. Each program runs eight to ten minutes, and their combined effect makes a very fine impression on a candidate. They "presell" the candidate on the company much more effectively than our literature can. A recent audiovisual program, "Team All-Phase," has been proclaimed as one of the best in the industry.

These programs also come in handy when we invite a candidate to tour one of our facilities or invite a vendor to visit a branch. They are also presented to civic clubs and shown during open houses, counter days and other customer gatherings.

## A TRAINEE'S PATH

Once a college graduate is hired and placed in the training program, he or she is given a timetable detailing how much time to expect to spend in each of the job classifications within the branch. Normally, that individual is expected to be ready for small-branch management within three years after being hired.

One hazard we guard against is having a branch manager fit a trainee into an available training slot, then leave the individual there, either because that person is doing such a fine job or because the manager is too complacent to further the trainee's career. (Incidentally, the cost of a trainee is charged only 50 percent to the branch, with the other half charged to corporate as an administrative expense.)

Some trainees reach the peak of their abilities before getting into branch management. In such a case, the trainee is counseled about his or her lack of potential for promotion. There also have been individuals who said they really didn't see themselves as outside salespeople and didn't want to go through that phase of the program. However, it is absolutely essential for employees who aspire to become branch managers to spend a portion of their training career in outside sales. They need to realize the difficulties a salesperson faces. If they skip that portion of the program and remain inside in operations, they tend to think that everyone who comes into the building or calls in is going to place an order, and they lose some respect for the value of the customer and the value of an order.

In outside sales, trainees experience major hurdles they wouldn't find any other place in their career. They'll lose sales; they'll be turned away by a receptionist, unable to make contact; they'll have their price quote exposed to competition and will have to know how to cope with a lost order. They'll have personality conflicts and hard knocks that only an outside salesperson can understand. They also will learn how to manage their time and how to change their sales approach from call to call to accommodate the personality of the individual with whom they are dealing.

Most important, they will have to learn to work long, long hours. Many calls on small contractor firms must be made before the contractor leaves for the job site in the morning, which may mean some 6 or 7 a.m. contacts. Or they may have to go to the job site to find the contractor, or to the shop after the workday, or to the individual's home in the evening.

They will learn that they need a mix of customers, because industrial contacts can be made only at certain times of the day and, in some cases, only on particular days of the week. To fill in the rest of the time, the salesperson must have other contractor assignments to keep him or her busy. All salespeople also should make cold calls, often referred to as "smoke-stacking," looking for at least one new contact per week. I'm afraid that this is an area where we have been remiss. And salespeople must develop a marketing plan for their target accounts—those customers with whom we are not realizing our full potential.

There have been instances where a trainee has reached the outside sales position in the training cycle and enjoyed so much success that he or she prefers to remain there. That's fine with me, as long as they are successful and happy.

## THE RIGHT OFFER

As tough a negotiator as I'm reputed to be, I can be faulted for being too hurried in wage negotiations with a high-salaried employee or a prospective employee. I am always anxious to bring the matter to a close so I can get on to the next matter. I never like to take time to sleep on it, so to speak, and as a result I tend to offer perhaps a little more than I would if I devoted more time to it. When I have the time to deliberate I offer a level of salary that I feel is fair, and if I am pressed to go further by the employee or applicant, I tie any additional increase to performance.

I believe in trying to fit the job to the person rather than the person to the job. This means that I analyze people, study their strengths and weaknesses and try to maximize their talents. I know some in management disagree with this, as you end up with a variety of jobs, titles and job descriptions. But I think that with some limitations, it does work.

I also feel that the job offer must be good for both the individual and the company. I try never to talk someone into accepting a position or a job transfer, particularly a person who has to relocate. When I apply pressure rather than simply laying out the facts and letting people make up their own minds, I am constantly indebted to them and have to treat them differently from other employees. In such cases I've had to show some favoritism and avoid coming down hard on them if their performance was lacking. I have learned never to be in an employee's debt.

The fact that we have several female branch managers is evidence that we are a strong proponent of a woman's position in our industry. However, I am quick to point out that any prospect, man or woman, must be exceptional and have the right kind of profile. Our women branch managers are very independent. They feel very strongly about their jobs and their positions in the company.

We have many women on our staff in responsible positions. I think of our computer-training teams, our billing teams, our department heads in payroll, accounts payable, accounts receivable, customer service, traffic and logistics—All-Phase just could not exist without these women. In many cases the traditionally feminine traits of patience and attention to detail are required to run those departments.

## NEPOTISM

I have learned through experience never to hire a friend or a son or daughter of a friend. I have had nothing but bad experiences in the few instances where I have done this. There seems to be an assumption of favoritism, and they expect, and sometimes get, preferential treatment. Certainly anybody who knows me knows that I would not allow any sort of special treatment for them or even for my own children. Nor, with a few notable and quite successful exceptions, do we hire relatives of current employees. (Had we tried to apply our policy against nepotism at the time of our Scranton, Pennsylvania, acquisition, we would have lost over half of our employees there! We should have done it, however, as we had a mass exodus of these people when the manager left and they followed him.)

The problem with having relatives working for you—say, a

husband/wife or brother/sister team—is that if one becomes upset with you, then the other generally does too. It usually doesn't work out in the long run. We have had isolated father/son instances where it has succeeded, however. If the lead person is strong and has a very definite, thorough, open understanding that each individual must stand on his or her own, without any influence from the relative, it might succeed.

## Performance Reviews

IN 1985, I DID WRITTEN EVALUATIONS on all fifteen people who reported directly to me. Although we had a written policy to do so for most of our corporate life, I never had the time, nor perhaps the inclination, to complete the reviews before. But having spent at least two hours in thought and preparation before recording my thoughts on paper for each person, I could see that it was one of the most important and responsible jobs a manager could perform all year.

Two of my district managers had been asking for this evaluation for a couple of years. Once they were completed, my merchandising and showroom manager told me it was the finest moment in his relationship with me. And, mind you, what I said in the reports was very candid, open and honest. I didn't pull any punches, nor was I flowery in my ratings. If anything, I probably gave more subpar than superlative ratings.

After writing my evaluations, I called each individual into my office late in the day, explained the preparation that had gone into the report and spent the next hour discussing it with them. I then handed the report to the employee, asking that they not read it at that moment but rather when they were not bothered with the activities of the day, perhaps even at home. The employee was to make comments on each subject and bring the form back to me. We then covered every one of the topics. We both signed the document, and it became part of the employee's personnel record.

This was the best tool I've ever used to clear the air between me and my subordinates. I allowed them plenty of time to correct anything I said that they felt was in error and to defend anything they felt was unfair.

For the most part, they agreed with my evaluations even on the negative items. Without fail, we both agreed to try our best to be better people for the company and try to make our corporate life a little easier for each other. The results were and continue to be astounding. I don't know why I waited so many years to do this.

## TREATING PEOPLE AS INDIVIDUALS

Everyone has to be treated separately and individually when it comes time to review performance and discuss salary. This is a private matter between manager and employee.

This policy was violated when our former Central Region manager interviewed a man for the job of regional sales and marketing manager, and at the same time talked to another man about the job of regional operations manager. Both people already were on the payroll in different capacities. He sat them across from his desk, gave them a joint review and discussed identical salaries and bonuses with them. I later asked one of the men if he was offended by this, and he said yes, very much so. He did not feel it was the other person's business to know what his arrangement was, and he felt that he should have been treated as an individual, not as part of a unit.

This kind of treatment has the same basic philosophy as a union. I've always said that a union treats every member alike and does not recognize an individual's performance, loyalty and ability. Everybody is given the same increase, right down to the penny.

I believe that an individual should be rewarded for his or her own merits. True, the cost-of-living increase generally is the same for everybody, but that's only a portion of a person's raise. Within our company, we don't even guarantee that much, because I feel that it has to be earned.

That same former staff member gave every one of his new district managers in the Central Region the same agreement, the same guaranteed draw, the same guaranteed commission and the same incentive program. It didn't work. Certainly one of those six people will perform at the top and one at the bottom. Why should they receive the same income?

# When Employees Don't Measure Up

I AM CONVINCED THAT THERE WILL always be that 10 percent of employees who won't be happy regardless of what the company does for them. It's inherent in some people. To my way of thinking, we should constantly be on the search for these people and root them out of our company. As soon as we find someone who feels that All-Phase is not for them, they should be gone. There should never be grounds for a wrongful-discharge suit—if we plan properly and have patience, we can handle things without legal ramifications.

Thankfully, there are some 20 to 30 percent of the employees at the other end of the spectrum who would never leave for any reason and are faithful to the end. Then there is that middle ground of some 50 to 60 percent who can be swayed one way or the other by the actions of the company. We are always aware of the flexibility of these people and give them good reason—such as our fine benefits plan—to be loyal. After all, with the million dollars we plow into profit sharing and the half-million we put into the 401(k) program per year, and with our dynamic growth and our commitment to promote from within, we should always be able to convince an employee that he or she couldn't do better.

Employees are also vulnerable to comments from me, I've found. I have to be careful of what I say about any form of employee behavior, bad or good, because there's a risk that my people will overreact. If I am too harsh, they think I am coming down on them and being unreasonable. If I relax the pressure, they think I'm changing my ways and letting up on them. Strange things happen. Sometimes I need only to mention that I don't think a certain employee is our style of person, and before I can turn around that employee is gone. Or I might pay a compliment to someone, and that person is pegged as an "employee for life."

As for alcoholism and drug addiction, an employee whose work is impaired by it gets one chance for rehabilitation. That might sound a little hard-nosed, but from what I know of the disease, if people don't admit to themselves and their family that they have a problem and if they won't seek a cure, there's no hope of saving them. Our rehabilitation program allows them to go to a clinic at our expense to rid themselves of the problem, after which they return to work and get back on their feet. If the problem persists, I insist upon dismissal.

Sometimes this process takes quite a bit of time, as it's very difficult to prove drug addiction and alcoholism or to release a person for it. Eventually, however, a reason generally presents itself, usually absenteeism or tardiness.

## THE MISBEGOTTEN ONES

When people separate from our company I generally have an adversarial relationship with them. There have been a few exceptions, but as I often have said, once they're off the team they're no longer my friend and generally become my enemy.

I'd like to think that All-Phase reciprocates loyalty; we never have had an actual layoff. We have always needed all of the good, honest, loyal, hard-working employees we could get our hands on. If we have let someone go it has not been for lack of work but only because the individual did not measure up.

This is why I feel perfectly justified in treating former employees as I do. They were given every chance in the world to prosper and succeed, and their failure is a result of their own lack of effort. I am not so vain as to say that there might not have been an isolated case of personality conflict between an employee and a branch manager or department head, but I would venture to say that 80 percent of separations from our company are the employee's doing.

The only exception is when we have closed a branch and it would have been too much to expect an employee to transfer. In those cases we do everything within our power to help the person find a job. Also, when an employee leaves to better his or her station in life in a different field of endeavor and not as a competitor, I do try to support them.

Perhaps from time to time we haven't given the counseling and review that we like to see happen with all employees, and if we fail in bringing an employee along, that's unfortunate. It simply means that somebody in a supervisory capacity is not fulfilling the wishes of management. That being the case, the employee always has the power of appeal—all the way to the president and CEO, so nobody ever should be unfairly treated or discharged. With all of the effort we have put into structuring our human-resources department, there should be no question that an employee was treated fairly. That is why I tend to lose confidence in people when they don't carry their load and eventually seek employment elsewhere.

This brings to mind a book I read, *On Wings of Eagles*, about H. Ross Perot and his rescue of his employees of Electronic Data Systems from Iran during the hostage crisis of 1979-80. The book also talks about how Perot started his multibillion-dollar company. He always honored his employees for good performance. He had in his foyer a plaque on which he engraved the name of an outstanding person every month (very similar to our Employee of the Month award). When someone left his company he became so vindictive—and frankly I don't blame him, because he did everything for his employees—that he wanted to grind the name off the plaque. He never went that far.

I seem to be of the same bent. I view anybody who leaves All-Phase as a traitor who made a terrible mistake in leaving the finest company in the industry and perhaps one of the finest companies in all of the United States. I remove their Employee of the

Month plaque from the wall. (That's the advantage in having a separate plaque for each employee rather than engraving everyone's name on one large plaque.) This serves as an example to others that if you're not on the team, you're nowhere with me.

# Everyone Loves Recognition

Motivation is primary to success. People need a sense of accomplishment. To have that, they must be given attainable goals and, once the goals are reached, they should be rewarded. The reward should take two forms: money and recognition.

We're all salespeople—especially the district managers, district sales managers, branch managers, operating managers and certainly outside and inside sales staff—and all salespeople naturally have an insatiable appetite for recognition. They wouldn't be successful if they didn't have an ego, and one way to respond to that is to let employees bask in the sunlight when they attain their goals. We practice the theory that goals should be attainable, and we like to have at least 80 percent of our people reach the goals they set.

For several years we had a sales contest. The winners were called tigers and the losers were pussycats. The celebration took place on St. Patrick's Day in the men's bar at Berrien Hills Country Club in Benton Harbor. A long table was lavishly laid out with the best steak dinner we could buy, and on that table was a placard reading "Tigers." The winners could order anything they wanted: shrimp cocktail, steak, dessert. Then there was a large round table with a similar placard reading "Pussycats." The people seated there were given a single hamburger without condiments. The hazing that took place was magnificent. Everyone tried to avoid being a pussycat.

After we had more than three or four branches, we could no longer handle this and it fell by the wayside. But employee recognition remains a cornerstone of our corporate philosophy.

Our top performers came in for some hearty recognition during our thirtieth-anniversary celebration. Out of our 225 salespeople, we singled out fifty to receive trips with spouses, plus cash and prizes. But the most valued award was the President's Ring Club ring.

I had worn the ring the entire previous year to show it to all of our employees. They receive the ring with a green lintel stone when they enter the club, and a diamond is added for each of the next nine years that they continue to attain the specific sales levels set for membership. It takes ten years to cop the full prize. The ring is a sign of their All-Phase accomplishments that they can proudly display.

We also issue service pins to everyone who has worked five years or more for the company. I try to pass out these pins when I distribute profit-sharing for the year. Those who receive the award also receive a letter of appreciation from me. Every five years thereafter, they receive a new pin with a tab that shows the number of years of service. I make the twenty-fifth year something special, with a diamond in the pin. Three employees (excluding myself) received such awards in our twenty-fifth year: Erv Bradford, our first employee; Danny Wegenka, our first counterman; and Gino DaDan, our first outside salesman.

## INDIVIDUAL ACHIEVEMENTS

Every month we recognize one employee in each district and at the corporate office as the Employee of the Month. The honorees receive a plaque with his or her picture on it and an engraving recognizing his or her accomplishments. One plaque is hung at corporate headquarters and one at the home branch. Employees of the Month also receive a lapel pin and 100 silver dollars.

I try to present many of these awards personally, but if I am unable to get away, the district manager takes care of it. We try to make it a memorable event. We assemble the employees after work, or at a Break Plus, and try to keep the name under wraps so that the recipient is surprised. It's a terrific morale builder. I remind the crowd that only thirteen people are recognized each month in the entire company.

The plaque has made an impression. After the transition period at our Kingsport, Tennessee, acquisition, one of our bright, up-and-coming residential-fixture showroom managers told me that his ambition in life was to be named Employee of the Month. He received the award within the next year. Now he has advanced beyond the showroom to branch management.

Each district also keeps a monthly listing of the top five or so performers in outside sales. An announcement of the top performers is sent to all branches, and then both the district manager and I send them a personal letter of congratulation.

The corporate purchasing department has come up with a contest of its own to recognize individuals at the branch level for their accomplishments. This covers not only inventory turns but also something noteworthy, such as a return to a manufacturer or a large sale of slow-moving or obsolete merchandise. These awards take the form of cash: $100 to the first-place winner, down to $25. When people receive cash as an incentive, there is no doubt they strive to perform and prove their worth. We also have the 4.8 Club: If you attain inventory turns at the company goal rate of .40 per month for a total of 4.80 for the year, you earn a plaque and your name appears on the companywide plaque at headquarters.

An important thing to remember in pitting people against one another is never to cause anyone embarrassment. We would lose all of the good and then some if we singled out someone as a nonperformer. This is akin to that age-old golden rule that you never criticize an employee in front of others. We always take the person aside and point out his or her shortcomings in private.

## THE MANAGER SETS THE TONE

I am afraid that some of our branch and district managers

become so engrossed in their tasks of the day that they sometimes ignore their people. We all know that whatever the manager's mood, so will be the mood of the branch personnel. So while we must be businesslike in the way we handle ourselves on a daily basis, we do need to add some friendly personality to the job.

I myself practice this philosophy by visiting with the various departments and employees at corporate headquarters on frequent walk-throughs; holding regular staff meetings at the corporate level; occasionally visiting a branch, and, once a year, visiting nearly every branch for profit-sharing distribution. This gives me an opportunity to speak individually with each of the 1,300 members of the profit-sharing program, as well as with the other 400 employees who are too new to be in the plan.

This is a major project, but I intend always to spend the five or six weeks required to visit branches and to let individuals know how very much I appreciate their efforts and contributions to the cause. At the same time, I try to meet with the remaining employees, even though they are not members of the profit-sharing program, mainly to let them know that I am interested in their careers and to tell them what they have to look forward to in the profit-sharing program, as well as the 401(k).

No doubt about it: One reason for high personnel turnover is failure to appreciate people and failure to understand their problems. We let our employees know that we are genuinely interested in them as individuals.

Just to make sure we stay on the mark, approximately every two or three years we run an employee opinion survey. We guarantee that no one will be able to be identified with their comments, in the hope that our employees will tell us candidly absolutely everything that's on their minds.

Not only is this a great deterrent to union organization, it also allows us to judge our managers as to their ability to satisfy employees. It reveals shortcomings within the company, such as dissatisfaction with pay and benefit programs, and it lets us know whether employees are well informed about what we're doing. Our human-resources division prepares a complete analysis of all comments. It presents us with an outstanding report—and goes one step further by recommending courses of action.

## Pulling Out All the Stops on Training

We NEVER HOLD BACK ON training our employees, whether it's a course on distribution equipment, motor control or lighting. Employees who specialize in such areas as programmable controllers, drives and other industrial-technology areas may attend additional classes. But everyone in the company is expected to spend a minimum of 5 percent of their working time in actual formal training.

Why should we pay so much to train our people, since inevitably some will leave us and only be better-qualified people for our competition? That question points to a no-win kind of thinking. We simply have to pull out all the stops on training and hope employees will appreciate what we have done for their careers and repay us with loyalty.

Another form of training is the in-house sales meeting, which every branch manager is expected to schedule regularly. Usually it's conducted every Monday night throughout the year, with some relief during the summer when we're shorthanded because of vacations and when people usually don't feel like sticking around after hours.

When we did some belt-tightening during a downturn in the economy several years ago, one of the first things that went out the window was money budgeted for training. Today we would never react that way, because it means we would come out of a recession with people unqualified to take advantage of good economic opportunities. I might add that training trips are always designed to further education and make the employee more valuable, never as a reward for longevity.

# LIGHTNING STRIKES ONCE

The National Association of Electrical Distributors, through its education foundation, has developed some outstanding training programs. One that is getting a lot of play is the EPEC Program, where an employee signs up for a self-study course on the technical side of product knowledge. We share the cost of tuition in accordance with the employee's performance. NAED also offers management-training schools, which are sometimes conducted right at our offices.

In addition, most of our manufacturers have excellent programs available just for the asking. Our only financial commitment generally is travel to the facility and overnight accommodations. The companies themselves pick up the expense of running the meetings and usually all of the meals at school. This has changed somewhat in the 1980s, as manufacturers of motor-control and high-tech products have begun charging several hundred dollars for one-week training sessions at the factory. However, with the advent of such high-tech items as programmable controllers, the need for such training is paramount.

# The Advanced Management Program

No DOUBT ONE OF THE FINEST THINGS we do at All-Phase Electric is our Advanced Management Program. Between 1979 and 1989 we held six of these biennial affairs, and they have grown better with each passing year.

AMP is the most important single training program at All-Phase. We bring more than 200 employees to corporate head-quarters every other year for more than a week to educate them on new procedures and opportunities at All-Phase as well as to motivate them for success and development. We discuss everything from credit and collection to reading a balance sheet, motivating employees and enhancing interpersonal relations.

Among the many, many benefits of this program is the camaraderie that develops between roommates or among groups that form during meals and round-table discussions. I have found that after our problem-solving sessions, people develop the sort of friendships that encourage them to call on one another for advice or help when they have a problem in the field. It might be something as simple as securing some hard-to-find item for inventory or solving an important customer or supplier conflict. Whatever the case may be, fellow employees seem to come to one another's aid much more readily when they know one another personally.

The most important purpose of AMP is the opportunity for management to share its feelings and plans with the very people who are expected to play a key role in the company's development. We must all be in agreement if we are to attain the kind of budgets and operating goals we have set for the company.

Everyone must rally behind the program.

On the even years when we don't hold AMP, the staff and regional managers spend a week traveling to the headquarters of major suppliers to discuss marketing plans and products. We have been successful in obtaining financial underwriting for this by the manufacturers we visit, so the cost to our company has been nil. A side benefit of these trips is the camaraderie built between district managers and staff.

OUR BEST SESSION YET

At AMP VI in 1989, we had 220 participants from the ninety-seven branch locations, including district managers, district sales managers, branch managers, branch support staff and corporate staff. The instruction lasted a rigorous eight hours a day. The morning sessions were mandatory, the afternoon sessions were electives. Each day started at 6:30 a.m., with buses picking up participants at the hotel and delivering them to the Lake Michigan College campus, where they had a 7 a.m. breakfast, then classes. The day finished at approximately 10:30 p.m., when we returned them to their hotel after dinner and an eventful evening.

I have never seen our employees get so charged up over the company. Our theme was "Leadership in Quality," and the sense of belonging we stirred up was amazing. All members of AMP VI went away feeling as though they truly were part of the All-Phase family. By the last session my theme had become "Reach Higher," meaning we all had to push ourselves to the limit and strive to be the best we can.

Twenty-three management trainees attended, and every one said that this reconfirmed their decision to join All-Phase.

In part, the success owed to twelve months of intense planning by a committee of key people. Although the cost to the company on this project, including time away from the office, ran about $400,000, it's probably the best money we could have spent.

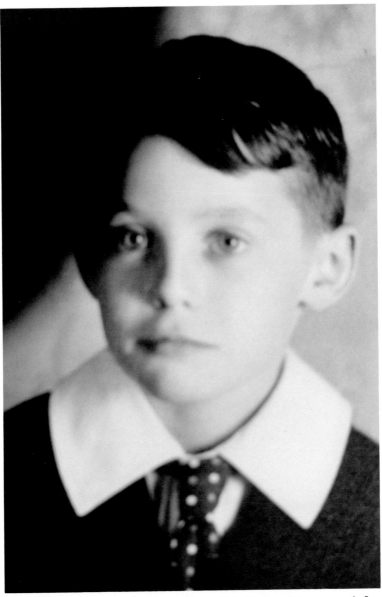

*Ronald F. Kinney around the time of his first entrepreneurial venture--selling eggs door to door with his two brothers. It was a success until a neighbor found blood in the eggs.*

*TOP LEFT: The original All-Phase Electric location in an old A&P supermarket in Benton Harbor, Michigan. It opened its doors on April 1, 1959. TOP RIGHT: Five years later RFK made his first acquisition and moved into grander quarters a few blocks away, going from a $1 million company to a $3 million one overnight. ABOVE: RFK with the first competitor he bought out, Ray Jeffirs (left), and his father, John J. Kinney Jr.*

*Most of the original employees who set All-Phase on its path to success helped christen new headquarters 15 years later (from left): Ervin Bradford, Danny Wegenka, Gino DaDan, John Podras, Len Niemier and RFK.*

*RFK and his father, John--also a self-made man and a successful coal merchant--break ground for new All-Phase headquarters (above left), which opened in 1974. The company expanded into its Regional Distribution Center (above right) in St. Joseph, Michigan, in 1988.*

*The All-Phase look on the road. The truck fleet's logo design won a national award. With a company plane also on call, RFK can make a sweep of the multihouse network in a matter of weeks.*

*"Lookalikes" RFK (right) and Randy Goldrick at a regional convention of the National Association of Electrical Distributors in 1986. Goldrick is NAED president-elect.*

TOP: *Valued industry friends--Andy Anderson and Mike Finn from G.E. Lamp; NAED president Marv Schylling. ABOVE: RFK at one of the inimitable All-Phase open houses.*

RFK has the distinction of gracing the cover of McGraw-Hill's Electrical Wholesaling magazine three times, in 1973, 1982 and 1989. With nearly 100 branches by then, the phone idea just wouldn't work anymore.

*RFK as first recipient of the GEM Award in 1988, honoring distinguished achievement in electrical marketing.*

*The succession management in place: RFK flanked by sons Stephen (left) and Richard, along with Richard's first-born, Gabrielle.*

*The Kinney team after hours--spectating, sharing a glass of beer, or simply resting an arm.*

*TOP LEFT: All-Phase's convention booth during its 25th-anniversary year. TOP RIGHT: An All-Phase employee since he was 17 years old, Fort Wayne manager Tim Culp is recognized at AMP VI for his branch's top performance. ABOVE: RFK and Richard bestow the CEO Award on veteran employee Mike Kmiecik, Northwest District Manager.*

*TOP: RFK addressing the industry's top vendors at the All-Phase 30th-anniversary luncheon at the Ritz Carlton Hotel, Chicago, 1989. ABOVE: The boss with management trainees during the sixth biennial Advanced Management Program.*

*TOP LEFT: Corporate vice-presidents, from left: William Vegter (finance), Dr. Shaz Khan (human resources and public affairs), Richard Kinney (administration) and Frank Wimbush (marketing). TOP RIGHT: Mike McInally (field operations), Jim Cleworth Jr. (materials management) and Richard Lewis (information systems). ABOVE: RFK with Sacramento branch manager Jim Powers, who turned a 21,000-square-foot start-up into a moneymaker in a remarkable five months.*

*RFK clowning with a chimp at the U.S. Open; at dinner with his wife, Eva; and at the slopes during the 1988 winter Olympics.*

*Mr. and Mrs. Ronald F. Kinney*

## The Personal Touch

BACK AROUND 1970 WHEN WE WERE writing our first employee manual, someone suggested that I send a letter to the home of every employee, perhaps once or twice a year, to let them know how things were going. Since then, I've sent such letters at least annually on the profit-sharing contribution, plus another one on the state of the economy or the condition of the company.

It's unbelievable how much these letters are appreciated. Employees often mention how much they value the personalized attention.

The letter dealing with profit-sharing is vitally important because we contribute such an enormous amount of money, such a high percentage of our net profit after tax, to the profit-sharing fund. So I like to get every ounce of benefit due us. My personalized letter tells employees how we fared over the year, how the fund itself did in terms of earnings and value appreciation, and what amount we contributed. It gives me a chance to give the employee an overview of the year, be it good or bad. I think it's very, very wise to keep them informed.

I've always been big on letter-writing. I also send a welcoming letter to every new employee's home. I say something about the company, tell them to whom they report and welcome them into the All-Phase family. If I've met the person before I send the letter, I pen a little postscript or, if I'm due out there soon on a trip, I jot down that I'm looking forward to seeing them.

I sent a letter to every employee as a follow-up to our twenty-fifth anniversary open house. It was a note of congratulations thanking them for their participation and hard work in producing the celebration. I did the same thing after the thirtieth-anniversary celebration.

## BOOSTING MORALE

Any time there's an opportunity to send a letter—not only to an employee's home but also to the branch—I try to do so. If I see somebody's name on the list of top outside sales performers for the month, I send a congratulatory letter. If I'm told about a particularly large contract we wrote, or some job we were able to secure, or a promotion for an employee—I take the opportunity to thank people. Employees have told me they save these letters, particularly if they're addressed to them at home.

I often labor many, many hours in search of ways to keep in personal contact with all employees. Obviously, the purpose is to maintain very high morale within the network. One such instance occurred in June 1983, when *Electrical Wholesaling* magazine ran a cover article on our company. With the financial assistance of three of our four major suppliers who had advertised in that issue, I reprinted 25,000 copies of the article at no cost to us. I then sent a personalized note, in longhand, on the back page of 900 of these reprints to every employee in the company. I tried to be as original as I could in my messages. As I was toiling through the night on this project, I wondered whether it was worth the effort. But when I walked into our branch in Monroeville, Alabama, and saw my longhand message to the manager—thanking her for what she had done to make the company successful—framed and prominently displayed on the wall, I knew it was.

Once I sent a letter to our former senior-citizen telephone man, whose only compensation was his company-provided car. I told him how much I appreciated the fine job he was doing for us—and I really meant it. He worked like a demon. One Saturday, he worked all day installing the telephone system in corporate headquarters. When I arrived, he was hooking up some wires and he stood up, shook my hand and said that he really appreciated that letter. I got the impression that in his forty years previous at the telephone company, no one ever had sent him such a letter.

I also dropped a short letter in the mail to our man in charge of networkwide maintenance on the buildings. He came into my office, shook my hand and said that now he could see why I was so successful—because I really pay attention to people.

I do the same for friends and acquaintances. I always go through my issues of *Electrical Wholesaling*, *Electrical Distributor* and the "Electrical Marketing" bimonthly newsletter, and invariably I'll send a letter to someone I know who is mentioned. When you consider how little effort it takes to dictate a letter on the tape recorder I always have with me in my car, the returns are astronomical. I'll see people at the next convention and they will thank me for the letter; or often they'll write me a letter of appreciation for the one I wrote to them.

It's not that I write any great literary masterpieces, but even a small note means so much.

## IMPRESSING A RECRUIT

The personal touch has even made a difference with new recruits. On a quick overnight trip to Tennessee and Virginia (covering three branches in twenty-four hours), one of my interviews was with our newest outside salesman, who used to work for a very large competitor of ours. I had an opportunity to spend some time with him, riding in the car from Martinsville to Danville, Virginia, trying to arrive in time to watch the Monday-night NCAA championship final basketball game. So I asked him a little about his former employer.

I told this young man that I was a good friend of the president of his former employer and inquired as to whether he had seen him recently. He gave me a quizzical look and said, "I've heard the name, but I just can't place it." I said, "Well, then, surely you know so-and-so," and mentioned the owner's name. Again he said he didn't know where he'd heard the name. Finally I explained that one was the president and the other the chairman of the board of his former company. "That's where I've heard the names," he said. I thought to myself, what a lousy job of communicating with their employees, when this salesman, who had been with them two years, doesn't even know the two top officers of the company by name, much less ever having met them.

Later, as we were watching the game, this salesman told me he was really impressed that after being with our company only two weeks he had received a letter from me at his home. He said he had never received any communication from the superiors at his former company. He further added that I could be assured that people didn't just wad up those letters and throw them away. Anybody receiving a letter from me had saved it, and that made me feel very good, particularly if it had made some impression on this new salesman.

When I asked the man what brought him to All-Phase and why he had left his previous employer, he told me that we had recruited him heavily and really spent some time with him, telling him all the advantages of belonging to the All-Phase team. But what nudged him over the top was his boss's giving him a copy of *Electrical Distributor* magazine, which contained an article titled "All Phase—On the Grow." He said he read about how I treated members of the All-Phase team as I would my own family and that he was very taken by the article. He immediately called our local manager to accept the job.

## A BOSS, NOT A BUDDY

Of course, when you're the boss, there's a limit as to how far you can go to be a friend of your employees. I know firsthand how that old adage "Familiarity breeds contempt" can affect a business relationship.

When we were a small company back in the early 1960s, I wanted all of my employees to consider me their friend and companion. I felt that the greater the friendship, the more they would do to try to make me successful. I wanted to be loved by everyone. So every evening after work, and every Saturday at noon when we closed our doors, I would journey down to Elmer's Colfax Cafe with them for a beer. Of course, I generally bought the drinks, and in a relaxed atmosphere, we would talk about the occurrences of the day and nurture our camaraderie. At least, that's what I thought was happening.

Then I was shocked to lose two of my salesmen who had opened the doors with me in 1959. When I took one of them to lunch and asked why he was leaving, he said that a major reason, though it might seem insignificant to me, was something I had been doing unwittingly—I was literally smothering them with my presence at these cocktail hours. After all, he said, we need time to talk among ourselves about you and about the company, and if you're always there, we can't really express ourselves.

That hurt. While I had been thinking it was just great that I was one of the boys, I was really becoming too close rather than setting myself apart as the boss. Theoretically, that would have made it difficult to discipline people if the need arose. I even went so far as to have poker games with them monthly, both at the company and at somebody's home. The additional negative thing that happens in all of this is the amount of drinking that takes place. Sometimes someone would drink beyond their limits and start arguing with another employee, or even with me. So while it's fine to have your people like you, you should never fall into the trap of being a buddy when you still have to be the boss.

## BREAK PLUS AND BRANCH BREAKTHROUGHS

Once or twice each month we extend the normal ten-minute morning break to thirty minutes for something called Break Plus. We serve rolls, juice and coffee and assemble all of the corporate people in the training room at both headquarters and the Regional Distribution Center. We hold two sessions at each location. We update employees about new activities and give detailed explanations about the functions performed by each department. This is a wonderful way to maintain morale and a high sense of commitment and loyalty to the company.

Nothing takes the place of personal contact. It's such a good way to trouble-shoot and nip signs of discontent. I could fill volumes with the positive results of my walks through the warehouse and interviews with employees, but let me cite just a few that occurred on a recent fifteen-branch visit that spanned two-and-a-half days.

• I handed a profit-sharing certificate in the amount of $51,000 to a salesman who was making more than $40,000 annually. He said he was very happy with his income and that I had been fair to him over his fifteen years with All-Phase, but he complained that he had not been consulted when accounts were reassigned. He didn't expect to get any more accounts; he simply wanted to be asked. I asked whether this had made him look around for other employment, and he replied it absolutely had. I spent a few minutes with him, and as a result we kept an employee happy and squelched a problem that appeared large in his mind but was easy to rectify.

• In Mobile I learned that our credit manager for the district had been unreasonable in turning down current credit applications. The branch manager was so disgusted he simply wasn't seeking new business because he knew he would get a rough time from his credit manager. Had I not found a solution in time, it could have become a chaotic mess.

• At another branch I learned that the sixteen-year-old son of a key employee had gotten his girlfriend pregnant and was going to marry her, although he had a year of high school left and the employee hoped he would go on to college. I reassured the employee she had to stand behind her son and offered to put him on the payroll—even though that went against stated company policy. We put this bright young man to work for the summer to give him some confidence in himself and hope in the future.

*190*

As I dig deep to find out how our people feel about the company and to solicit their opinions on things, I never fail to uncover some problem. That is why I will never give up my branch visits.

## The Profit-Sharing Plan

I CONSTANTLY BOAST THAT WE HAVE the finest benefits in the industry—benefits that set us apart from our competition. Those include profit-sharing (with contributions over $1 million per year) and the 401(k) plan (a tax-deferred savings plan, with contributions of more than $500,000 a year made by the company solely for the employees). These are great plans and a valuable perk to being on the All-Phase team.

We have had a profit-sharing plan since the company first started to turn profits, in 1963. Over the years the fund has grown to a value of more than $10 million, accruing solely to the employees. The 1981-82 fiscal year was the first and only in which the company failed to make a contribution to the program, because we were hurt by the economic recession. Nevertheless, thanks to astute planning and investment, the fund still grew by some 26 percent that fiscal year—an amount that greatly outdistanced any contribution the company might have made, even during excellent economic times.

This fund is noncontributory, meaning that the employee does not pay into it. The profit-sharing success stories include office personnel whose funds have grown to more than $175,000; a counterman with a profit-sharing certificate in excess of $200,000; a salesman in the mid-$200,000 range; and a purchasing agent with well over $225,000 in the fund.

Every employee over twenty-one years of age participates in the program after one year. It is terribly effective in binding employees to the company. If an employee is recruited by another company, generally the profit-sharing fund tips the balance in favor of All-Phase.

The vesting feature of the program—the time they must put in to qualify for the full amount of funds in their name—is the primary holding force, but that runs out after a period of time. Under our original plan, which applied to employees hired before 1978, an employee was fully vested after ten years in the program. Then it became fifteen years to fully vest. Through government regulation this full vesting is now down to seven years. Our hope is that by the time individuals reach full vested rights, they will have the loyalty and dedication to make All-Phase their life's career.

There have been three instances—all, strangely, in the Holland, Michigan, branch—in which employees left the company, took their profit-sharing payment and invested it in a new electrical distributorship, thus becoming a competitor of ours. In one case, although their new company was doing fairly well, the two partners had a terrible falling out, and we were able to purchase their assets and dissolve the corporation. In the other two cases, the companies are no longer in business.

We cannot let these isolated instances deter our commitment to rewarding employees by sharing profits with them. Overall, it's an excellent program and, if anything, doesn't receive the kind of notoriety and publicity to which it's entitled.

## WE PROFIT TOGETHER

I've been asked if we've ever considered awarding profit-sharing based on the profitability of each branch or district. I would resist this because the plan is one area where we draw all of the company's branches and personnel together as a unit. (Also, I believe that it would be extremely difficult, if not impossible, to receive government approval for a profit-sharing plan that singled out a particular portion of the company.)

I love the way our construction manager travels throughout the network doing repair and remodeling, building offices and warehouses. He always carries this message with him: "Look, I need your help while I'm here, because every minute we waste is a reduction in profits that will be available for all of us in the profit-sharing program."

I just wish everybody could be imbued with that type of attitude and enthusiasm. It's a joint effort, and it takes everybody to generate profits so that we have something to share with employees at the end of the year. If we have a losing branch, everybody must try to help make it profitable. We are united in the profit picture.

A more recent benefit at All-Phase is the 401(k), a contributory plan wherein the company contributes 25 cents on every dollar the employee places in the program, up to 10 percent of their pretax income. Although this guarantees them a 25 percent return on their investment to begin with, the investment of the funds, as selected by the employee, has traditionally returned an additional 8 percent to 25 percent per year. Employees can make a total investment up to 15 percent of their income, but only the first 10 percent receives a company contribution. Our tax consultant calculated that if a person were to join the company at the age of twenty-five and spend his or her forty-year working career at All-Phase, making an annual contribution of $3,000 and investing in the guaranteed income plan at 8 percent, they would leave the company with a fund worth more than $1 million.

# Managers as Entrepreneurs

I OFTEN REFER TO OUR BRANCH managers as presidents and owners of their own corporations. I like to see them operate as autonomously as possible, and as long as they stay within the guidelines, benchmarks and performance standards for their operations, they will receive minimal interference from district and corporate headquarters. The better they are, the more autonomy they have extended to them.

The individual must be enough of an entrepreneur to operate a branch or district as though it were his or her own company. Yet he or she also must operate with corporate interests at heart. We need the best of both worlds—the individuality of an independent, locally operated company that supports its community and is made up of individuals from that community; and the team spirit that recognizes that we operate as one network, one entity, helping each other progress within the industry.

Of course, every branch must adhere to corporate policies and standard operating procedures, which is one reason we always change the name of our acquisitions to All-Phase. Just as our central computer system provides billing and payables for all branch locations, so our corporate headquarters acts as a service facility for the network.

It is a very difficult challenge for managers to balance the demand for autonomy with the demand for a corporatewide sensibility.

The ideal branch manager is one who has joined the company rather early in life (perhaps in his or her twenties), grown accustomed to our method of operation and developed into a hard-

*195*

working, aggressive and ambitious manager. These people accept the help our corporation offers. If the person is innovative, it certainly helps, but this is not an absolute requirement for success under our management philosophy. We need to think alike and strive for a common goal.

I doubt that any other company in this industry has extended such responsibility and autonomy to the field. The system has its drawbacks, in that by teaching people to operate independently we sometimes have trouble getting them to cooperate with and support the corporate headquarters staff. They sometimes are reluctant to accept suggestions and direction, particularly in the area of asset management—inventory turnover and accounts receivable.

Sometimes corporate staff members have difficulty asserting themselves with the field personnel, and from time to time the point has to be made that despite their independence, they still have a company to answer to.

## A KNACK FOR NEGOTIATING

We expect every district and branch manager, along with responsible personnel reporting to them, to be excellent negotiators. We want them to obtain the very best pricing levels on purchases that they can find in the field. We also expect them to negotiate the very best sale prices that competition and local conditions allow. In dealing with their own personnel, we expect them to be able to negotiate competitive yet affordable wages, salaries and benefits.

A manager's negotiating ability can sometimes turn on us, and we become victims of our own making, when it comes to the manager negotiating with the company on his or her own salary arrangements. It isn't a major problem, but it does cause some difficulty. The essential thing to watch for is that the person be fair and have the company's interest at heart. That too is an essential characteristic for all managers.

I think that with the hands-on management we expect at the branch level, our managers are listening to their people and exposing themselves to comments and suggestions. I encourage everyone, including staff and myself, to have an open-door policy. I try to make it a practice to walk through the office once a day and perhaps the branch warehouse once a week. Every branch manager should be walking his area once a day. If someone says, "I'd like to see you when you have time," the manager should always say, "The time is right now." A manager should never say he or she is too busy, will see them after hours, or tomorrow, or next week. If you don't grasp the opportunity, chances are that by the time you're ready to talk, the employee may not want to. Take your blinders off, look around and be sure you never give the impression you're too busy for your employees.

Delegating is also part of the manager's job, but there are times when delegating can be overdone. One district manager delegated to the point that he lost touch with the day-to-day operations. He didn't have a finger on the pulse of the operation. I'd ask questions that he should have been able to answer off the top of his head, but couldn't.

## REVIEWING THE MANAGERS

Because we rely so heavily on top performance in all management positions, particularly branch and district managers, they must come under constant review so we can be certain we have the right person in the right slot. This occurs at every month's end, when we review the profit-and-loss statement, as well as the return-on-asset report, plus other criteria. If the performance does not come up to par within a realistic period, the pressure mounts and serious consideration may be given to a management change.

Up until the past few years, my mode of managing these manager-entrepreneurs was to look at certain key items monthly or even weekly. These were telltale signs of how the branch was doing. One such task, irksome though it was, was approving unusual, miscellaneous bills. I hated to let go of it, though, for it gave me a feel for how well the branch was controlling expenses. I routinely kicked back about 25 percent of these unusual items for further clarification. I also approved all expense reports and questioned the business reasons for the expenditures. I no longer have the time to personally do all of this, so I have delegated it to other responsible management people.

If someone's performance doesn't measure up, it's very difficult to keep that person within the same branch, but it is reasonable to transfer him or her to some other branch within the network and drop him or her back a position or two. It is also very difficult to promote someone within the branch to the branch manager's position. Chances of success are much greater if a person is transferred in from a smaller, so-called training branch into a new, larger branch.

That's one reason for training branches. Because it's so expensive to buy and sell a house in a short time, we encourage our training-branch managers to lease rather than own and to remain flexible for relocation.

# The Role of Outside Sales

I F I WERE TO PICK ONE JOB IN THE electrical-distribution industry that seems to offer optimal rewards, it would be outside salesperson. These folks spend their days calling on their friendly customers and making sales that carry with them handsome commissions, expense accounts and a position of respect. No doubt about it, this is the crown jewel of the jobs.

Almost everyone seems to aspire to this job, and I guess I finally understand why. Any inside person could account for just as much gross profit and in many cases much, much more, yet gets paid less money. Even more important, the inside salesperson's level of recognition is almost nil compared to his or her counterpart in outside sales.

I could never figure out why, when we promote people to outside sales, we always seem to change their compensation to a point where they receive an overly generous increase. For some reason they're given a draw, a commission and a car allowance, along with an expense allowance that lets them realize some 25 to 40 percent increase in income. This is not the way it should be.

I would prefer that salespeople be given the same draw against commission as they formerly received in salary. The assigned accounts would generate commission income only if they improved over their levels at the time of the assignment. The car allowance is essential, as is the expense allowance because, of course, the individual needs that as a "pass through" to cover expenses. Guarantees should always be avoided unless we are bringing in experienced salespeople and need to assure them of income similar to what they received at the company they left. I do believe in dip-backs, where a deficit (difference between guarantee and commission earned) must be made up out of future commissions.

There is an ongoing argument within this industry regarding an outside salesperson's compensation. Distributors seem to be in full agreement that the only way to go is a commission based on gross profit.

The total gross profit of territories assigned to salespeople varies so much that it would be impossible to say that any given commission percentage is the right one, but I feel that the 11 percent we have settled on is the fairest arrangement I've ever seen. This is not to say that we won't have some variation in certain parts of the country due to existing arrangements at some acquisitions. We would be foolish and foolhardy to change these, as long as the salespeople and the acquired operation are doing well. Sometimes you just leave well enough alone and live with it, provided, of course, you're making the proper return on assets and net profit after tax. If not, you change things—quickly.

We want to avoid the impression that we're trying to limit or control an individual's income. The arrangement must allow people to be open-ended on the amount of compensation they receive for their efforts, but they certainly must earn it. Unfortunately, within our industry not all electrical distributors use the same criteria for success. Any good businessman, however, knows that the return on investment theory is sound and probably the most common denominator when judging a company's track record.

We have one location where, for some time, all three of the salesmen we inherited from the acquisition were on 20 percent, with a company-provided car and expense account. What really made it difficult was that the employees who were with the small existing All-Phase operation in the same city remained on an 11 percent arrangement. This disparity caused no end of problems among our salespeople and drove a wedge between the two segments of the company, old and new, which now were working under one roof.

I further complicated the issue by announcing at the time of the acquisition that nothing would change, including commission arrangements. I didn't know that the former owner really was paying only 19 percent but was making his salespeople think it was 20 percent. That 1 percent difference could amount to quite a bit, especially considering the increased volume that has been developed under our ownership there. Eventually I was successful in bringing parity to our commission agreements.

As you might expect, there's some fallout when we have to make commission adjustments. One instance occurred when visiting our Southeastern regional manager in 1976, who oversaw the three Georgia locations. We had had a long, difficult day of interviews with existing employees, adjusting some of the commission rates to the point where one or two of the people left the company. As the manager was driving me to the airport, I commented that I needed to "pull the weeds so his garden could grow." That statement became something of a byword in the Southeast, and eight years later our new district manager said to me that he guessed when I visit I pull the weeds so his garden will grow.

## MEASURES OF SUCCESS

I often feel that our reputation for excellence within the industry is due to our good, sharp, service-minded sales counterpeople, aggressive telephone salespeople and good purchasing and follow-up procedures, not to mention routine things like adequate inventory, extension of payment terms, delivery, prompt and accurate billing and so on.

I recently spoke to a distributor in California doing $8 million with one part-time salesman two days a week. That is the most extreme case I have ever seen. I also look at a proprietary report we have, which is an accounting of the salesperson's cost to the company totally as a percentage of the gross profits the person produces, and I believe that fully one-third of our salespeople exceed the cost percentage parameters I have set as a goal.

I'm very proud of that report, which I find unique to this industry. It's rather awkwardly titled "Salesmen's Expense as a Percentage of Their Gross Profit." That simply means that we list on a computerized sheet of paper, spanning some two years so we have some history for comparison, all of the expense items that result from having a salesperson on the road. This includes base salary or draw against commission, commission payment, entertainment expense, automobile allowance, company portion of FICA tax, hospitalization expense, profit-sharing and any other expense. Then it reports monthly and year to date the salesperson's gross profit dollars and the ratio of expenses to gross profit.

We look for something in the neighborhood of 15 percent on this report. There are isolated instances where it's as good as 11 or 12 percent, and I have had cases where it has cost more than 100 percent of gross profit to keep a salesperson on the road. That didn't last long. I would say an acceptable norm is between 17 and 20 percent. Anybody who consistently exceeds 25 percent on this report requires an adjustment—perhaps assigning these people more accounts or changing their territory or taking them off the road entirely.

When I get into the field myself and spend a full day on a sales blitz or individual calls—as I often do—I always can make at least seven or eight calls on contractor accounts (perhaps six if I limit myself to industrials). My visits are more than just a hello and shake of a hand: I bring the customer up to date on All-Phase, go through our brochure and discuss local branch performance.

I become furious when I observe some of our salespeople making only three or four calls per day, because then I know they're not working as hard as they should or are spending too much time in the office. This is unacceptable. There are too many mouths to feed with that gross profit they bring in.

I often ask everyone connected with sales to be aware that they must be responsible for a sale that returns at least three times their salary every day, and that there are no carry-forwards, only dip-backs. A big sale one day doesn't justify taking the next day off, but if you don't make the sale today you must do twice as well tomorrow.

## PHONE AND COUNTER STAFF

We started out in sales servicing the small shop employing from one to six people, and that type of company was responsible for the success of All-Phase for a number of years. Our mainstay was the small contractor who came in to order at the counter. This is why our personnel at the counter and on the telephone have been so important.

Today we are a different company, and increasingly we are developing industrial sales. We have a strong, new market in high-tech products. But we don't want to neglect the project business where the margin might be low but the volume high. Thus, wherever possible, we have developed commission arrangements based on a graduated scale for those individuals responsible for counter and phone sales, because this is where the profit truly is. This is unique to the industry.

Outside and inside salespeople aren't the only employees who benefit from the gross profit. We even have purchasing agents, operating managers and office personnel prospering from the gross profit developed by the branch. My goal is to get to a point where everybody who has a hand in sales, and for all practical intents and purposes that is almost everyone within a branch, be compensated for his or her contribution to the gross profit.

The branch manager and district manager, on the other hand, should be compensated for return on assets. That is to say, if they utilize to the fullest extent those asset items of inventory and accounts receivable, which account for about 95 percent of our total asset investment, then they should be remunerated for their success. But if they have a disproportionate investment in inventory, which will return to them something less than 4.8 turns per year, then they should not be compensated as well.

# Keeping Employee Costs in Line

I LIKE TO SEE OUR BRANCHES OPEN early enough that they can service the contractor trade. I'm talking about the small contractor who wants to pick up his material as early as 7 a.m. We should be open by then and should close no earlier than 5, preferably 5:30 p.m. This requires some staggering of hours so that our employees work an eight-hour day and no longer.

Saturday hours normally are from 8 a.m. to noon—which should always be the case if we have a residential-fixture showroom in conjunction with the sales counter. Some showrooms stay open as late as 3 p.m. on Saturday, and many stay open one evening during the week and on Sunday. In these cases, hours must be staggered so that employees do not work beyond the regular forty-hour week.

On occasion, overtime has to be approved for these people, but normally I like to see two-thirds of the extra-hour workers be salaried employees who are not paid for overtime. In the case of an annual inventory at fiscal year end, we generally send the hourly employees home first and have the salaried people stick around for the clean-up and the price extending and totaling of the items not on computer.

We keep a pretty close eye on something we call the "hours worked" report, a weekly listing of every employee in the company and the number of hours each worked, including overtime, sick time and vacation. These reports, prepared by branch, have helped a great deal to control overtime costs. They are reviewed either by me or by the district managers, then are forwarded for comments to the branch manager. If a branch consistently has excessive overtime, the manager is constantly warned about it, and eventually something will change.

Some overtime is necessary, particularly in the case of shuttle-truck drivers, who can't complete a route in forty hours; fixture-showroom personnel, who have to be there when we are open more than forty hours a week; and month-end accounts-receivable personnel, because it would be folly to try to hold overtime down if it meant we didn't get our receivables done. But I have seen branches with as much as 25 percent of their salary expense in the form of overtime. At that point, the branch should eliminate the overtime and hire more people, full-time or part-time, or get better productivity out of existing people.

GOING BY THE BOOK

We must, of course, meet federal wage and hour requirements. We put as many people as possible on salary, but they have to make a certain amount of money, have a certain number of people reporting to them and fulfill other qualifications to be salaried. The wage and hour law people make the rounds of our branches to be sure we're complying with the law.

Most frequently an audit is brought about by a disgruntled ex-employee who wants to cause problems for the company. The very first time I was faced with this was in 1959 when we had only eight employees, and one of those individuals, our pricing clerk, returned from his lunch hour at 4 p.m. I didn't have a private office, so I took him out into the warehouse and confronted him with the fact that he had taken a four-hour lunch and I wanted to know where he had been.

He said arrogantly that he had been at the Elks Club playing gin rummy. He was very nonchalant about it and commented, "If you don't like it, you know what you can do about it." I said, "I sure do, you're finished. Clean out your desk and get out of my company." He did and promptly filed a grievance with the wage and hour people. I had to reimburse employees and ex-employees a total of $2,000 when I could ill afford to do so, because we had classified some employees as salaried when they should have been hourly. I remember distinctly arriving at his home and handing his check to him with great animosity.

I guess we didn't learn our lesson, because three or four years later we again were subjected to a wage and hour review. This time we had one branch in Kalamazoo, in addition to the main house in Benton Harbor. We were found to be remiss and had to make out checks to employees. But this time I had a different approach. I took the check to each employee, counseled with him or her privately and asked, "Have I treated you fairly? Have you always been paid the wage you agreed to? And have I done anything other than what is fair and equitable to you?" And in every case the individual said, "You have always been very fair with me; I'm happy with my pay." Whereupon I would present the check, turn it face down and ask the employee to endorse it back to the company. Every person did so.

In that instance no ex-employees were involved in the audit, so I got 100 cents on the dollar back. Today, of course, the rules are much more stringent, and I couldn't repeat what I did. But we have been successful in presenting our side of arguments and keeping dollar settlements at a minimum.

TRAVEL EXPENSES

We send a number of our people on the road, and my policy is that employees on an overnight stay should spend money as though they were spending their own. In other words, they don't necessarily have to have the most expensive appetizer. As a matter of fact, they shouldn't have any appetizer at all when ordering dinner, unless they're entertaining a customer. That's also the only circumstance under which I'll pay for a bar bill or any extras. Nor should employees charge the company for dry cleaning. I don't think anybody stays out so long that they can't take the required number of clean clothes to wear on the job.

I also object to long-distance telephone calls charged to the company. If a person is out for one night, he or she certainly doesn't have to call home. If the employee is out for an entire week, maybe one or two phone calls are in order; but they should be short and certainly not nightly.

# The Matter of Confidentiality

I OFTEN ASK MYSELF JUST HOW MUCH of our operation we should reveal to employees, particularly on a branch level. What has to be considered is whether the person would use the information for his or her own benefit. Of course, I am concerned about revealing confidential information that might be proprietary in nature, and then having that individual leave the company and use that information against us.

We have every employee sign a confidentiality agreement, whereby they agree not to divulge anything of a confidential nature if they leave the company. The agreement states that any violation of the agreement will be prosecuted. It does not apply to normal on-the-job training and product information, only the confidential aspects.

I find that the more you can tell your people about performance on the branch level, the better off you are. If you expect them to suffer through the tough times, you have to show them just how tough the times really are. If you want them not to complain about long hours and the fact that they haven't had a satisfactory salary review, you have to share with them how the company is doing.

People also are entitled to know when we're doing well. That sometimes causes a problem, because as soon as the tide turns they want not only to be reviewed for wages but to make up for some of the lost time they experienced over the low period in the economy. It's a fact of life that the company has to keep its overhead down, even when the economy booms, to try to make back at least a portion of what was lost or not made in difficult years. If you start hiring immediately and giving raises and promotions, you'll make a minimal amount of money. It's a fact of business that industry and distribution need to have some golden times during which they continue to operate with minimal overhead and with greater profitability.

# *CHAPTER V.*

## OUR CUSTOMERS, OUR SUPPLIERS AND OUR COMPETITION

# Getting and Keeping Quality Customers

PERHAPS AS IMPORTANT AS quality employees are quality customers. First, of course, we must earn their business. Sometimes it takes years to develop the kind of relationship with customers we like to have.

I am convinced that the only thing that sets one distributor apart from another in this industry is quality service. Of all the value added in electrical distribution, certainly everything comes back to service. No other item could begin to compare to it. I refer not only to giving courteous service at the counter and over the phone, but also to having the product in stock when needed and delivering it promptly and completely the first time.

I often ask myself when I run into poor service, is this happening within my company at this very moment? And I know that the answer often must be yes. But I do everything within my power to be sure we never shirk our duty to service. I have become obsessed with the idea that the phone must be answered within the first three rings. If it rings a fourth time and I'm on the other end, I ask the person who answers, "What happened? Were you too busy? Why didn't you answer the phone promptly?" It does get them on the ball.

To make the point even stronger, I had our telemarketing group call every one of our branches, once in the morning and once in the afternoon, asking for the branch manager, to see how the call was handled. Each branch was rated on courtesy, number of seconds kept waiting before being connected and background music. (All background music while on hold has since been removed, although I do approve of a voice message about the branch or a special sale item.)

## SERVICE ABOVE AND BEYOND

Very early in my career a friendly electrical distributor in the Detroit area shared a short story on extending service after operating hours.

It seems that he received a phone call at home in the evening from a customer who needed something for installation that night. When the gentleman went down to his store, he thanked the customer for the call, but at the same time asked why he hadn't simply gone to a distributor down the block who was still open for business. The customer replied that he didn't want to deal with this man's competitor and had never opened an account there. The distributor serving up the order thanked him profusely and said that he welcomed a phone call at home anytime.

I was a little startled by this story, because at the time I didn't really understand the value in servicing a customer after hours. I had never stopped to consider the importance of true customer commitment. Now I know: There is nothing that can compare to the loyalty of customers who will conduct 100 percent of their business with you. This is something that needs to be earned and re-earned every single day. Such loyalty must be rewarded with an all-out effort to extend the absolute best possible service.

Because of this, we developed our nationwide toll-free emergency WATS line. It is answered by an All-Phase employee (not an answering service) twenty-four hours a day, seven days a week, with no exceptions. Our guarantee is that we not only will answer that phone within three rings but will have an All-Phase employee meet our customer at the branch in question within sixty minutes. We are so committed to this working like clockwork that our telemarketing group calls the customer back the following morning to ask if he or she received satisfactory service, if there is anything else we can do to help and to thank the customer for calling us. We advertise this emergency telephone number on all of our trucks, correspondence and calling cards. There is no one else in this industry who can offer this service. It's just another way All-Phase sets itself apart from its competitors.

## LISTENING TO CUSTOMERS

We have the rather unusual and extremely fortunate situation where in every location we have a handful—maybe just one or two—very, very loyal customers who live and die All-Phase. They don't ask for competitive bidding; we know that if they get a job, we'll get all the material on it. And thank God for these people.

We need to expand that circle of close friends, as they are, beyond a doubt, the most valuable customers we can have. Sometimes I get the feeling that if we extend good service to a customer, we think we've really accomplished something—but good service ought to be the norm. We should be on our toes giving great service at the counter, over the telephone, from the salespeople, on deliveries, all the way through our organization.

A good barometer of our service levels can be comment cards. These are postcards available at the counter and addressed to me, the president of the company. We encourage customers to fill them out with comments on the person who waits on them, the kind of service they get, whether it was courteous, whether we tried to transfer the merchandise in to satisfy their needs, and anything else they want to say. We also mail surveys to customers and conduct phone surveys biannually.

I have received some very caustic comments that have helped us improve our service, such as increasing our level of inventory or improving a truck delivery schedule. I like to feel that we listen intently and regularly to our customers. I welcome a letter to the president and respond the very same day I receive it—that is, if I can get the information from the appropriate manager. I never let a letter go unanswered. What I detest most is an anonymous letter of criticism from some customer who doesn't have the nerve to sign it. I simply throw it away. If I receive an anonymous letter from an employee criticizing his or her boss or another employee, that letter quickly finds its way to the wastebasket too.

Sometimes, when I feel overconfident about the company or even personally, I need only to make calls on our customers with a branch salesperson. I always tell them to take me to the difficult accounts. I don't want their customers to tell me how good they are; I want to hear the other side of the story. If we've got a problem, I need to know so I can help fix it. I must admit these visits are a great neutralizer. Just let somebody tell you about the problems they've had with a certain aspect of service in your company, and you are brought back to earth.

Also along these lines, I'll go to just about any lengths to get a new account. There was the time when I called on Miller Brewing Company in Eden, South Carolina, with our Danville, Virginia, branch salesmen. I was determined to get in to call on the purchasing agent, as I had been told repeatedly that this was the one account in the entire branch that they considered impenetrable. I accepted that as a personal challenge to get the door open to our company.

When I entered the guardhouse and called the purchasing agent, she relayed the word to me through her secretary that she would not be able to see me, even though we had called ahead for this meeting. I replied that I had traveled over a thousand miles on my company plane and committed a day to making this call, but still she refused to come out. I felt that I deserved more than that. I then went up the ladder of command until finally I reached the plant purchasing manager. Even he would not give me an opportunity to meet face-to-face. I was so exasperated after these repeated denials that I started to leave the guardhouse in disgust, but then I turned around and went back into the counter and announced to everybody within earshot that I have never been treated so shabbily in my life and that I would not drink another Miller Light until I felt vindicated for this insensitive attitude.

For that matter, I would not allow any of my 1,700 employees or any of their dependents to drink a Miller beer until this situation was rectified. I told them that surely that had to number some 7,500 people who would be denied this pleasure of drinking Miller brew until I was heard. Needless to say the guards were embarrassed and said that they personally would do whatever they could to relay this message to management.

When I got on the plane, still fuming, I dictated a scathing letter to the plant purchasing manager. I did get a response; the end result is that today it is one of our better accounts. It took some ranting and raving to get us there. But I'll go through that exercise any day if it means bringing an account to our company. I'll take anybody's abuse if it means getting an order.

PLAYING IT STRAIGHT

Something in our industry that has always bothered me a great deal are requests from customers for favors, concessions, lavish entertainment, gifts and sometimes, literally, cash payments and payoffs of one form or another to secure business. I pride myself on our strict company policy that under no circumstances whatsoever will we consider anything that could be construed as an under-the-table payoff.

I am very proud of the high ethical and moral posture All-Phase maintains, and I go to great lengths to protect any erosion of this policy. There is never any real temptation to be any other way, but there are so many propositions thrown at us that it's unbelievable. Recently, we had three such proposals.

The first was a job in Mobile, Alabama, which we had secured in the amount of $23,000 with a $21,000 cost (a relatively typical 10 percent markup). The agent for the product told our local manager that his cost would drop to $16,000 provided that our manager kick back $2,000 to this agent personally. When our Southeast District manager called and asked me what we should do, I told him that he knew the policy of the company. He said yes, he certainly did, and that he had already turned it down, but he just wanted me to know. I was proud that this man had acted on his own. I told him I had no objection to his entertaining this agent and his wife at dinner or even a sporting event, but under no conditions would we ever give him cash or goods.

In the other two instances we were asked to bill two different contractors for tools or materials. But instead of shipping the job-related products, we were to buy the contractors appliances for their homes. Our gain would be in making a sale at something slightly over competitive prices and also in making friends by accommodating these contractors. But I quickly pointed out that if we agreed to such an immoral transaction, the customer would be back again next year for something more, and it would become a never-ending form of blackmail. Once you do it, you'll always have to keep doing it. Besides that, it's illegal and immoral.

There have been times when an extremely good customer has said he would like to have some personal item purchased for him by All-Phase and billed to him as merchandise. The person making this request is the principal and owner of the company, so he's really not taking money from another source but merely trying to avoid purchasing something with after-tax income and to run it through the company as a company expense. Even so, we never went along with it.

We've gotten where we are today by playing it straight, so why in the world would anybody give a second thought to a fast buck through some immoral and illegal action such as this? I'd much rather lose the sale ten times over, and even the customer, if need be.

## CUSTOMER ENTERTAINMENT AND PROMOTIONS

Now, of course, we do entertain customers, and sometimes rather lavishly, and I have no objection to that. We take customers to football games; we fly them back to corporate headquarters and entertain them for a couple of days; and that generally is with the complete blessing of the principals at the corporation, because they know they benefit if their people know their suppliers better.

We used to make an annual trip to the Chicago Bears vs. Detroit Lions professional football games. We started that the first year we were in business, in the fall of 1959, and for the first five years we could accommodate all of our customers in one bus. We charged everyone $5 for the bus ride to Chicago—or Detroit alternating years—just to be sure they would show up. For that they got the round trip on the bus (although for a few it was only one way, as some people never got back to the bus and ended up taking a taxi back to Benton Harbor), the game and dinner afterward. We made the mistake one year of handing everyone a half-pint of liquor as they left the bus. We did away with that after we carried one person back to the bus before the game started.

This project grew until we had three buses going to Chicago, which got a little out of hand and very expensive. A tragedy of sorts befell us on our last trip. My sales manager left all of the sandwiches, which Eva and I had labored to prepare late into Saturday night, in the parking lot at the old A&P store building. I guess that's why that guy didn't last very long with our company.

One time we rented hunting acreage in Texas so that our contractor and industrial customers could hunt for game on our leased property. I was convinced by the then-manager in Orange, Texas, that to be competitive with other distributors in the area we needed to lease some land—I think it was 1,000 or 1,200 acres—so our customers could go there and hunt. I was concerned about the liability if one customer happened to shoot another one. So I told him to go ahead and lease the property under his name, turn in an expense report indicating the charge to him personally, and I would reimburse him. What I didn't know was that, on his own, he somehow obtained company funds and took a small hunting cabin to the site. I understand that he had an accident on the way and severely damaged the cabin, as well as the vehicle, which was borrowed. I'm just happy to be rid of the whole mess, and I will never do it again. But it's amazing how we can get talked into these things.

I have always resisted getting into a competitive situation with another electrical distributor who might be offering trips out of the country, elaborate selections of merchandise from catalogs and so on. It's very difficult to say where the line should be drawn in all of this. I only know that past experience dictates that as soon as a competitor's contest or other promotion runs its course, we're generally able to get the customer back into the fold. In the meantime, of course, we've missed considerable volume with him. And he has quite naturally placed it with somebody who has given him more than just the normal pricing and service that we extend day-to-day.

We've come close to succumbing to this temptation, especially in areas where we're losing money and see a competitor offer a trip to Acapulco or London or wherever, but I just don't want to start it. I'm afraid if we do it in one branch, everyone else will want it.

## ENTERTAINMENT PITFALLS

Sometimes a customer or a manufacturer sponsors a golf outing or perhaps a fishing trip and invites electrical-distributor friends to attend and generally participate in the expenses. But I would much rather spend that money on an individual basis. If you agree to, say, $100 participation on a golf outing, you might get paired up with people you don't even call on, or worse yet, have a competitor in your foursome. Then you end up eating dinner with the same people and playing poker into the night.

I've even had salespeople turn in their poker losses as expenses, expecting me to cover them, and who do you think was sitting around their poker table? It might have been a couple of suppliers, one or two distributor competitors and a couple of customers. And generally, by that time in the evening, they couldn't care less who's spending the money on them—they probably don't even know who's doing the entertaining. So I abhor participation in those kinds of outings, unless they're our own.

Such outings also raise the possibility that you might alienate yourself from some other contractor or industrial account in attendance who resents the fact that you attended as a guest or that you played golf with one of their competitors. This is a particular hazard at the outings the National Electrical Contractors' Association seems to have annually in every city where we're located. There's also the danger that too much alcohol flows freely and things are said from one supplier to another, or one manufacturer to another, that could be extremely damaging.

I remember one golf outing where one of our host contractors lost $90 in a poker game. How do you think he felt about the distributor who may have won that $90? Also, of course, we can't afford the time off during the busy months of summer when this type of activity generally takes place. I'd rather have my employees golfing and socializing with customers on the weekends or in the evenings, not during company hours.

## SALES-BOOTH STRATEGY

I try to keep the company name and image before the contracting industry by occupying a sales booth at the annual meeting of the National Electrical Contractors' Association. I show our audiovisual, distribute literature and have some attractive giveaway items for customers who stop by. Generally, I send a couple hundred letters to member contractor companies within our cities and ask them to stop and pick up this gift. It seems to work very well, and it gives me the chance to shake hands with the principals of a lot of large companies that I otherwise would not see from year to year—for that matter, they might not see anyone from All-Phase during the normal course of business, as our people deal principally with their field-support personnel.

I do this personally, not wanting to entrust such an expensive trip to some other staff member or district manager. Besides, it takes a little bit of boldness and aggressiveness. I literally stand in the aisles and look at the name badges of people as they pass by my booth, and I haul in the ones who are from a city where we do business. If someone stops to talk and I see they're from New York City or Chicago or some other community where we have no branches, I almost ignore them. After all, there is only so much time and so many people you can talk to, and you have a limited number of gifts to hand out. So why waste time on people I'll never see again and certainly never get an order from?

I also avoid large national firms whose business practices are such that we choose not to do business with them. Maybe they are habitually late with payments, or they are famous for bill-backs and endless deducts, or they set a bill aside and don't pay because something is amiss on the job. The margins are so slim to begin with that we can't make any money with such people, and I marvel that anyone is able to handle their business.

# Promotions That Work

PEOPLE SOMETIMES ASK ME HOW WE spend our expense and entertainment monies. I have very definite opinions on this. For one thing, the regularly scheduled weekly lunch with a particular client is for the most part useless. I know our people do it, and I know they think it's valuable. They think that they are the envy of the industry because they happen to have a time slot on a given day with a favored customer. But in my opinion, with few exceptions, our return on that type of investment is not worth the expense. The customer starts taking you for granted, and the salesman stops selling and merely fulfills a social obligation. Of course, there are exceptions, and if it is truly a business meeting to discuss new items and so on, then it is worthwhile.

The way to spend your money and get your money's worth is to entertain a customer in a grand manner. Preferably this means bringing the person to our corporate headquarters, in some cases even using the company airplane to do so, giving a professionally conducted tour of the facility, showing the audiovisual programs and explaining the advantages of our computer system. Then we offer lunch or, if it's a very important client, dinner and an overnight stay. We often spend a half day at our corporate headquarters and then fly the customer on to visit a supplier of ours in Chicago or Milwaukee. Whenever the plane takes me to a branch city for an overnight stay, I ask that we properly utilize this opportunity by returning to our headquarters with customers for the day and then returning with them to pick me up. We do this several times each month.

Also, I believe in entertaining customers at a sporting event

222

that is out of the ordinary—unless he's got more invitations and tickets than he can handle to football and baseball games. Spread the tickets around to people who don't have those kinds of invitations from our competition. We should be sure that an All-Phase employee accompanies the customer to the event—otherwise the customer may not even remember who the benefactor was.

Of course, I encourage every branch within the network to have at least one open house per year. We try to make our gatherings distinctive and meaningful for both customers and manufacturers by conducting them as trade shows. Vendors set up booths and display the latest in their product lines. If it's properly handled and they're assessed a portion of the expense, we generally come out of an open house—with dinner, drinks, door prizes and giveaways—spending very little of our own money. We can push our manufacturers only so far, and there are occasions when some of them won't go along with it. But I have yet to see the case where a manufacturer couldn't at least give us some materials out of his sample account to offset his share of the expense. It depends upon your relationship with the individual, and how clever you are in working with him on covering expenses. We would never ask them to do something that was not within their realm of capability.

We use a couple of items at our open houses that are unique in the industry. One is the blimp with our name and logo on the side. It's about twenty-five feet long and flies at a height of perhaps 150 or 200 feet, kept aloft by helium. It's amazing the kind of attention this attracts, particularly when our open house is held near the main artery of the city. We had one experience where the emergency provision failed and the wind whisked the blimp away, and the last we saw of it was a little dot in the sky at about 15,000 or 20,000 feet. But we replaced it, and now we are a little more cautious about flying it on windy days.

Another regular at festivities is our mechanical robot, Hero I. This little fellow has an arm and a voice and does things like hand out paper cups near the coffee pot during an open house or counter days. Or he stands at the door and welcomes customers. This always gets a big reaction.

Besides entertainment and open houses, we hold counter days, when we feature a particular product and give away hot dogs, along with doughnuts and coffee in the morning. Usually, the tab is picked up by the manufacturer highlighted that day.

From time to time at most of our branches we have run a lottery in which we offer a $2 prize by drawing a name out of a hat at the end of each day. If that customer had signed in during the day, he or she would win the $2. We would add $2 for every day the prize went unclaimed. When it got over $20, we really saw our counter business zoom. Quite frankly, though, I am not sure whether people actually bought something or just came in to sign up for the prize. But it certainly got their attention! Again, it cost some money, but it got people talking.

One time we tried a coupon program. We distributed some 22,000 coupon books to our customers via our "All-Phase Facts" mailing list. All the customer had to do was bring the coupon to the counter to get a discount ranging from $1 to $10. It didn't really work, and we concluded that this is more a retailer's approach to sales than a wholesaler's. When we asked customers about it, they said they didn't want to take the time to bother with such an insignificant discount. Also, the numbers of manufacturers' line items involved were limited, and while the booklet itself had some thirty or forty items, some branches handled only fifteen or twenty of them. It got to be a bit of an administrative nightmare. Our cost, incidentally, was just the production of the coupons, the mailing and the handling of the refund. The refund itself was covered by the manufacturer.

Another thought is to have a special of the day that is promoted only at the counter. The person can't buy it over the phone, can't have it delivered by truck, can't even hear about it from his or her salesperson. He or she must come to the counter, see what the special is, buy it on the spot and take it along. If you make that special attractive enough, and really emphasize fast-moving, daily-needed items, you'll find that contractors will not let a day go by without coming in to check on the special. We must be sure it's handled in that manner, however, and not sold through another avenue.

## GIMMICKS AND GIVEAWAYS

The things that really make a difference with customers are the little courtesies and favors you extend to them. Besides always giving outstanding service at our counters, we should show them how much we appreciate their patronage by doing a little something extra.

I like gimmicks and promotional items. I remember when we had our first necktie made for the company—it had All-Phase logos in black and white on a red tie. It was a ghastly, Godawful-looking thing, but today those few ties we distributed, maybe fifty of them, are like heirlooms. Once in a while at an open house one shows up. I think the tie had ten logos, one for each branch we had at the time.

My trademark in calling on good customers is a pocketknife with a rosewood handle encased in steel and a blade engraved with my name. I probably have distributed 2,500 of these not only to customers but to employees who have done something extraordinary, our branch managers, district managers, district sales managers and staff members.

As far as giveaways are concerned, there is nothing in our history that quite compares with hats. We never have enough to go around. Everybody seems to be a hat collector. I suppose over the years our company has distributed 100,000 hats, and we still have daily requests.

I once had a local potter make personalized mugs with the names of every customer who came to our counter. We hung these from pegs adjacent to the coffee counter, and customers had coffee from their mugs while waiting for their orders to be filled. Our only problem was keeping the mugs clean. That was left up to the countermen, and frankly, they neglected it. I would like to reinstitute that program, even though, instead of the fifty customers we once had frequenting our counters, we now have 65,000 or so throughout our company. But what was good for us once should be good for us again and should not simply be dismissed as something we can't do because we're too big. Of course, the pot of coffee for counter customers has always remained.

We used to have a machine that made fresh, hot, buttered popcorn for customers. Making the popcorn got pretty old to the countermen, so it fell out of favor. The machine is a sizable investment, and we couldn't do it at every branch, but it's still a sound idea for some of the more popular counters, and some do continue with it. We had potato chips or pretzels for a time, but we eliminated them one year as part of an austerity program.

We still have doughnuts in some of our branches once a week, but there was a time when I had two or three dozen doughnuts delivered to our front door every morning of every working day. Sure, it was pretty expensive, but did the customers ever appreciate that little bit of extra attention!

One successful promotion we've used to draw counter traffic is to wash everyone's car or truck while they are being served. We set this up with cheerleaders from the local high school and paid them for each wash job. Not only was this colorful and appreciated by our customers, but we also got credit for supporting a worthy cause.

Not everything works in every branch. One time we sent a cooler with tap beer around to each location, thinking it could be used for a Friday-afternoon happy hour to let customers know how much we appreciate their business. It was well received in about half the locations, and the other half—mainly those in the Bible Belt—absolutely turned the idea down. It really clicked with the small contractor who loves to come to the counter and have that kind of camaraderie at the end of the workweek. As the legal environment changed and our liability exposure increased, we put a stop to this entirely in 1985.

There are myriad other promotions and certainly a thousand ways to spend money. We all need to be original, find out what flies in each city and get the support of our manufacturers to the fullest.

If one branch does something that is unique and clever and results in a profitable venture, it should be shared with the other locations. It's important to bring all of these good ideas together and make them available for everybody's participation. One idea might be an all-inclusive manual covering everything from vendor arrangements to the stocking of the warehouse, counter promotions, spiffs, sales incentives, quotation methods, open houses, sales blitzes, and hundreds and hundreds of other types of operations—similar to our instruction manual on how to operate an open house. This would be a monumental task, but well worth the effort.

## Pricing It Right

I HAVE ALWAYS RESISTED THOSE little charges that might add some profit to the company but are not worth the risk of irritating the customer. I'm thinking, for example, of a minimum on a charge sale, a charge for delivery, a charge for any expediting of an order, UPS charge add-on for handling, and other add-on service charges. There may come a time to institute these types of charges, but I haven't been persuaded yet.

I once noticed a billboard announcing that a local bank would assess no service charges to customers. It sounded like a good idea, so I went to the next meeting of the bank board on which I sit and suggested to the directors and officers that we consider meeting the competition. They replied that if I was willing to give up $190,000 in income, sure, we could do it. But would it be worth that much in good will and perhaps an additional customer or two? I agreed that it would not. Service charges now appear to be universal throughout the banking industry, and I think the same thing may happen in our industry.

We must remain open to changes and suggestions as long as they make good sense, develop additional profits and don't too severely affect our customer relations and growth.

For years we have assessed service charges on past-due accounts. At first, this charge was only 1 percent of the amount outstanding; then we raised it to 1½ percent, and back in 1982 when the prime rate went over 20 percent, we raised our service charge assessment to 2 percent. We have held it there ever since. (There are a few exceptions in states that limit service charges.) This is the source today of considerable income. Of course, we never view it as an income item when it's assessed but enter it on the books only when it's collected. It would be much easier to collect service charges if all other distributors in the industry assessed a similar charge. Some of the largest either make no assessment at all or still assess only 1 or 1½ percent.

Many companies we have purchased have had no service charges, and it has taken us time to establish them because of our policy not to change the operation at the time of purchase.

We make some exceptions to our service charges. One is when it involves an industrial account that we know can pay on time and would be late only due to a discrepancy in the billing. There's no need to irritate that customer with such an assessment.

In matters of pricing, as in all aspects of our company, we pride ourselves on our high ethical standards. I'm reminded of the time back in 1959 when I hired a counterman from South Bend, Indiana, named Danny Wegenka. Danny would spend his next thirty years at All-Phase. During my indoctrination discussion with him, he asked whether I was going to insist that he continue the unsavory practice that his former employer in South Bend had been doing. I asked him to explain. He said that as a counterman, he also doubled as the pricing clerk. His boss had told him that he had to make at least one mistake in favor of the company on every invoice he priced, regardless of whether there was one line item or a dozen. Being a moral individual, Danny refused to do this. However, when the owner found out, he took matters into his own hands and did some of the pricing himself. I am proud to say that we never have followed such a practice, nor would we ever employ anyone who did. In fact, we will do absolutely anything to avoid mistakes. Instead, our mottos are:

- Treat your fellow worker as though they were a customer.
- Make it easy for our customers to do business at All-Phase.
- Do it right the first time, a phrase that has since been altered through our Organizational Quality Improvement program to: Do it right all the time.

**229**

# At Least I Tried like Hell

I DON'T PERSONALLY DO VERY WELL in matters of credit and collection. That's why I am pleased to be able to delegate this job to our national credit manager. But at one time I wore all the hats—sales manager, controller, credit manager. I did just about everything except purchase material—and even then I did much of the negotiating. You might term my early attempts at collections somewhat unorthodox, but I got the job done.

A liquor store owed my company $20. Try as we might, we were unable to collect this through the usual letters and phone calls. So one Saturday evening I stopped at the store and ordered four cases of beer. The man loaded them into my trunk and asked for the money. I told him I would have to send him a check because I didn't have any cash with me. Of course, in Michigan you cannot charge beer or liquor, but the man let me do it. I didn't pay the bill, and some sixty days later when he called and asked for his money, I told him it was a wash. I would wipe out my account receivable and would ask him to do the same thing. He got a little upset, but it worked.

Another time involved a somewhat more serious debt that I thought I had collected, but my effort backfired on me. It happened in Fort Wayne, Indiana, where an account had moved after running up a bill of approximately $2,000 while in Michigan. I stopped by with our lamp representative late one afternoon and told his office worker that I needed to buy twenty industrial heaters for a job at the nuclear power plant. She said her boss was not in and not expected for the rest of the day. I assured her that it would be all right, and we loaded the heaters into our station wagon. We used every square inch of space.

When I arrived at my corporate headquarters in Benton Harbor, I put the heaters out on the floor and sold them at a discounted price. When the man called and asked that I send a check immediately, I told him we were even. I merely took enough heaters to offset his debt to me. Unfortunately, he turned the matter over to a lawyer, who filed suit, and believe it or not, I had to pay the bill.

A still larger debt—about $3,000—was run up by an appliance dealer in Buchanan, Michigan. He told my salesman that he simply wouldn't be able to pay the bill and was going out of business. This was only a few months after we had opened All-Phase and I was still closing out major appliances at Consumers Heating and Appliances. So I jumped right into a truck, drove to Buchanan, loaded up all the appliances I could get my hands on, and cleaned him out of major appliances in two full trips that afternoon. I put them on the floor of the Consumers sales office and sold them out at discount prices. I completely cleared that debt with no repercussions.

When a tavern near Holland, Michigan, owed us a couple hundred dollars for a fan, we worked out an agreement whereby the tavern would pay something like $10 a month. Well, when the balance got down to about $150 and we were in Holland moving our branch into a new building, we decided to enjoy ourselves that evening. Four of us went to the tavern and ran up a bill of $150. We were buying drinks for people around us and splashing money around rather lavishly. When it came time to pay, we told the waitress to send the manager over. We told him that we were not going to pay the bill, as we considered it an offset. One of our people said, "We're going to close you up if necessary."

He excused himself from the table very politely, left and then returned to the table and pulled up a chair. The lights went on, and surrounding the table were a bunch of rough-looking characters swinging their jackknives on the end of chains. The manager said, "Now tell me again how you're going to blow me up." He misunderstood us to say blow up instead of close up. We reached in our pockets and pulled out as much money as we had—we were barely able to cover the bill. We backed out of that tavern with beer bottles in our hands, ready to do combat but hoping we wouldn't have to. When we got to the door, we turned and ran to the car, locked our doors and sped out of the parking lot.

As we were rolling down the highway one of our group said, "It's a good thing you got me out of there! I was just about to beat them up." We all had a good laugh on ourselves. So I guess you might say that some of my collection efforts worked, and at other times I didn't do so well, but at least I tried like hell.

# Spreading the Word on All-Phase

W E COULD BE THE GREATEST company in the electrical-distribution industry, yet if we did nothing to promote our image, we'd never get the recognition and respect that this great company All-Phase deserves.

One promotional activity that gave us great benefits for our investment early on was "All-Phase Facts," a pamphlet issued whenever we had something of major importance to announce, such as a new opening or an acquisition. We issued one approximately every quarter, and sometimes every other month. We generally paid for both the printing and mailing through an ad sponsored by one of our manufacturer friends.

The mailing list for our in-house publications is 30,000, a number that exceeds the circulation of our industry magazine. That list is very exclusive. To keep it well maintained, we send it to our branches annually for deletions, additions and updates on individual names, titles and addresses.

Whenever we have a new opening or an acquisition, I make a point of sending a personal letter to everyone on this mailing list, both supplier and local customer.

## NEWS AND ADVERTISING

I am not so sold on advertising. I have seen so many abuses of advertising budgets that I have to be convinced before I will approve a particular campaign. For example, I think advertising in the Yellow Pages is worthless, except perhaps for our residential-fixture showroom, which has its name in bold letters under that classification. These showrooms deserve to be promoted. We can expect at least 50 percent co-op advertising with manufacturers with all residential product lines. We should spend whatever funds are available to us in this area.

Never under any circumstances will we run a display ad. We've acquired some companies whose Yellow Pages advertising ran as much as $1,000 per month, and this really got them into financial trouble.

As for newspaper coverage, for the first four or five expansions, I notified our local paper and the newspaper in the city where we were acquiring or opening the branch, and as a result had articles announcing the All-Phase expansion. But I realized that, while the recognition for myself and the company might be valuable, it also made me vulnerable to solicitations for advertising, charities and fund-raising events. So I stopped doing it entirely.

Then in the early 1980s when we had some fifty or fifty-five branches, I decided that the positives of such publicity might outweigh the negatives. So we commenced sending news releases to the newspapers in every city where we have a branch. It's surprising the number of papers that run these articles. Quite naturally, it isn't the large cities of Pittsburgh, Seattle, Denver, Los Angeles or Atlanta. But almost every one of the smaller cities, being proud of the growth of a company that has a local branch, gives us a couple of inches. Sometimes we send two different news releases, one tailored to the city or state where we are announcing the acquisition, the other giving background on the company. We also send news releases to the national and regional trade publications.

I like to announce acquisitions because they demonstrate growth and progressiveness to manufacturers, to the trade and particularly to candidates for acquisition. I would like anybody who decides to put a company on the block to think they had missed something if they hadn't had All-Phase take a look. I also would like to make potential recruits aware of our company and its track record, and any publicity brings letters of inquiry regarding employment.

## DEALING WITH THE PRESS

We are always very careful when being interviewed, especially over the phone, for an article in one of the trade magazines or newspapers. When *Electrical Wholesaling* did its three cover articles on All-Phase, I agreed to the interviews only under the condition that I could review the rough drafts before they went to press. The author of the 1982 story had made a couple of statements that would have been terribly embarrassing. For example, she said that it had been rumored that All-Phase had received expansion capital from Arab shieks and the Mafia. When I confronted her with this, I said, "Where in the world did you get that kind of information?" And she replied that she had only said it "had been rumored." Nothing was further from the truth, and I insisted that the editor remove it.

Also, in her opening paragraph, she had written that Ronald Kinney was considered by some to be "ruthless." I thought that the word could be very damaging, so after a little argument, I got that removed also. But the entire article is still mentioned within the industry. Recently in my office a visitor—the chairman of the board of a large wire manufacturer—even pulled it out of his briefcase to show me he still had it.

Often reporters will call and ask for an opinion on some matter related to the industry. I always tell them that I will comment but that I do not want my name to appear in the article. Within the week I'll see my quotes reprinted in our industry newsletter, but attributed anonymously.

Even though it's tempting to accept an invitation to be interviewed by someone in the news media, I find that it's better sometimes to beg off. *Electrical Wholesaling* was trying to reach me to talk about the subject of doing business with the government, and on that touchy issue there's no way I could win. If I spoke my mind and said how I really feel about the government's preference for doing business with small businesses rather than with large ones like us, there might be severe repercussions. On the other hand, if I came out with a comment that was soft, my fellow distributors would wonder what happened to me after all of my vocalizing on the subject at private meetings. At times it's best to say nothing.

# *Working the Conventions*

As IS THE CASE WITH MANY trade associations, our National Association of Electrical Distributors conducts five annual meetings. The national convention is an absolute must not only for me to attend but also staff members, particularly those having to do with marketing, materials management and field operations. The supplier dialogue day, for example, gives us a chance to negotiate cost-savings programs and the like.

There also are four regional meetings, which I and my son Stephen, who will be doing more of the vendor relations in the future, attend from All-Phase, although sometimes I'll take our district manager within that territory. I find they get more out of these regional conventions, where they're able to get into more specific details on a one-on-one basis than they do at the national level.

NAED decided to run these regional gatherings a bit differently a few years ago. Instead of having the manufacturers sit behind a table in a booth and inviting the distributors to randomly select whom they would visit with during this half-day session, they turned the tables, placing the distributor in the booth section and allowing the manufacturers to roam the aisles. I like the idea, as it allows me to meet with almost every manufacturer at these regional conventions without wasting time standing in line to see someone or traveling from booth to booth. I am proud to say that we always have people lined up at our table waiting to see us.

The first time NAED tried this, at the eastern regional convention in Florida, I thought I would do something cute and unusual. I arranged to have several magnums of champagne on ice placed at my conference booth and two showgirls to serve it in long-stemmed glasses. It was a great idea that never saw daylight. The association got wind of it and met me at my conference booth just before the show began and said that, while they thought it was a marvelous, innovative gesture, they just couldn't allow it. They were afraid that it would push other distributors to do something bigger and better—and this was not the purpose of this dialogue day. Of course, I backed down. Still, I'm forever trying out new ideas to attract attention. I even had a boy at my booth once to shine everybody's shoes while they waited to see me.

I make it a practice not to invite spouses to these regional conventions. Occasionally I'll make an exception, but as a rule I think they hinder the freedom that an individual needs to move about and make contacts.

At the national convention, on that one day on the floor dealing with suppliers, we are the first ones to arrive when the opening bell rings and the very last to leave at the end of the day. In addition, as with our sales blitzes, we form task forces of two people each to approach targeted manufacturers in a planned and scientific manner. We never just wander aimlessly about shaking hands and exchanging pleasantries. I always exchange calling cards with the people I speak to and send them a letter within two or three working days after the convention confirming our discussions.

Over the years I have garnered tremendous benefits from these conventions, all the way from contacting prospects for acquisitions to becoming acquainted with distributors from other parts of the country. Probably most important, I've kept in constant contact with the principals of our suppliers.

## HARD-WON RELATIONSHIPS

I don't think anybody else in our entire electrical-distribution industry knows personally more of the principals of the suppliers than I do. I've made it a practice to become acquainted with everyone in this industry who is noteworthy. For this reason, I am very disturbed when I see people leave our industry with whom I have worked so hard to foster a relationship, because it takes a great deal of time to get to know those people well enough that they honestly want to help you succeed. One advantage I have is that people recognize me as the founder of our company, and they respect the fact that I have worked hard over the years to develop a little peanut of a company into a rather significant factor in the industry.

By the same token, it would be more difficult for anybody else in our company, regardless of their position now or in the future, to have the kind of respect and acceptance I do. It's a fact of human nature that no one can take the place of the founder. A lot of people are pleased that they know me on a first-name basis, and of course, I'm pleased with that association too. I feel that I can pick up the phone and call probably the top 500 suppliers in our industry and personally know someone at the headquarters in every case.

It's even become a bit of a problem, because as I try to work my way through the booths at a convention or across a lobby at one of the convention hotels, I run into so many acquaintances that a lot of time is spent on small talk. It's good, though, to shake hands with somebody and keep the acquaintance alive.

I once became so disgusted with the amount of time spent just passing the time of day at a convention that I posted a flip chart at my booth on which I listed all the small talk I could think of. I put down the time of my arrival, how the weather was back home, that Eva was with me on this trip, that the children were doing fine, business was good and we expected another year of prosperity. On the bottom, I wrote in capital letters, "NOW LET'S TALK BUSINESS." People still laugh about it. As emphatic as this message was, however, people still walked up and asked me some of the trivia addressed on the sheet. I guess it's just habit. But my little gimmick worked for the most part, and we got right down to business.

The convention can become burdensome, because with the kind of image we have in the industry, we receive many invitations for breakfasts, lunches and dinners. If you're not careful, you get so tied up that you see only fifteen or twenty manufacturers rather than the seventy-five to one hundred you need to touch base with. So, although I do schedule business lunches and breakfasts, I try to avoid scheduling too many dinners, which almost always turn into nothing more than social events. Instead, I spend evenings circulating to the hospitality suites, immediately seeking out the principal of the hosting company in every case. These cocktail parties provide all the dinner and drinks you need, and yet you make ever so many more contacts than at some private dinner.

It's difficult sometimes to conduct the kind of business at the conventions that you'd like to. About your only chance are meetings in a private hotel room for at least an hour at a time. And you can sandwich only so many of these into the convention. More frequently, you touch base on those items you want to discuss, and then invite the person to visit you at corporate headquarters.

# Tough but Fair Negotiator

ONE OF THE MOST REWARDING THINGS I do in my job as president and CEO of All-Phase is to negotiate terms and conditions with vendors. I have always prided myself on being a great bargainer, or as the Jewish put it, "hondeler." I have worked hard over the years to hone my skills and now, after thirty years of practice, I feel that I have some expertise—and a reputation within the industry as a tough but fair person.

My first lessons in bargaining came from my father. As a small child, I used to accompany him when he bought a pumpkin for Thanksgiving. If it was priced at 30 cents at the roadside stand, he would bargain it down to 15 or 20 cents. I have vivid recollections of Christmas-tree shopping, when he would argue the price down from the $4 posted to perhaps $2.75, then tip the man a quarter for bundling it and putting it in his trunk. It wasn't that he absolutely had to save the money; he simply loved doing it.

I grew up thinking that a clothing store always "threw in" a tie with the purchase of every suit. The reason I thought this, of course, was that my father always pulled it off. I'll never forget buying a suit for the first time at a men's store in Benton Harbor. I convinced them to throw in a tie, and I was surprised that they resisted to some extent. I always got them to do it, however, until I stopped doing this twenty-five years ago.

When Eva and I bought our first automobile in Athens, Georgia, while I was in the navy, our negotiations with the salesman hinged on whether he would throw in the $12 for the license. He resisted and I ended up pulling out of the drive in my old car, with the salesman clinging to the side of my car until we

*241*

finally came to terms. We split the cost.

## IMMEDIATE REWARDS

Good negotiating can return immediate and unbelievably large results. The company income today from tough and constant negotiation for cost savings, dating, deferred payment and return goods authorization from suppliers is considerable. It's obvious that we would not be the successful company we are without these features.

One of the basic requisites for negotiating a good program is to have the reputation of being honest and fair but tough—and perhaps most important, to know the limits of the person with whom you are negotiating. In some cases an executive can give the store away on legally earned rebates but has no authority over extended dating. I pride myself on knowing the limits of every person with whom I have negotiated over the years. Of course, I have been negotiating with these people for more than twenty-five years, and anyone from within the company, even one of my sons, will have a difficult time without the historical background I have.

The thing I so love about negotiating is that you can see the results immediately. As soon as you leave the bargaining table, you know whether you have won, tied or lost. Fortunately, we have won our share. I also like the fact that any agreement goes on year after year, just as long as we continue to treat each other fairly.

The five most exciting days of the year for me are the regional NAED conferences where I can spend half a day in dialogue sessions with my suppliers. This gives me the opportunity to negotiate with a great number of manufacturers within a short time. All of this culminates in the one complete day of conference booths at the national NAED meeting. To me this is Christmas and the Super Bowl rolled into one. It's like a smorgasbord laid before me, with more than 300 manufacturers on the floor at one time, just waiting to have you walk up and start negotiating. I have never failed to pay for the trip many, many times over. That kind of satisfaction carries with it all the rewards I could ask for in this business.

I can give a manufacturer every reason in the book to be part of our program. I haven't missed with many. I can think of only two manufacturers who either have refused a program or left us once they had one, and with one of those I am negotiating once again. I hope to establish a cost-savings program with every one of our suppliers. I have accomplished that in the residential lighting-fixture showroom area and with many commodity items, such as wire, conduit, boxes and fittings, lamps and others, covering at least 75 percent of our volume. I won't be happy until it is 100 percent.

I could call to mind many great negotiations, but one that I am quite proud of was with Burroughs Computer Company when we were installing our third-generation computer. The company had a number that made me absolutely dizzy. I told our people to negotiate every bit of fat out of the price and then turn it over to me when they felt that there was nothing left to gain. As I recall, when it was laid on my desk, the price was still $1.2 million. Because I had been prepared by our people and was psyched to get the job done, I took a hard line. After a solid afternoon of negotiation, I saved an additional amount in the six figures. That's when I feel I've earned my salary.

## NEGOTIATION STRATEGIES

My experience in negotiating cost savings and other matters with the principals of the major manufacturers has led me to develop some effective techniques. Above all, I have come to realize that these meetings must be one-on-one. That is, whenever possible, the meeting should involve only myself and the other company's single top-ranking official. If they have other members of their organization with them, they tend to feel a need to perform in front of them, so they hang tough on negotiations. On the other hand, if alone, they are much more willing to negotiate and leave with the order.

At a meeting in San Francisco at the time of the NAED annual convention in 1983, I had all of my district managers and a few staff members in a hotel room with all of the principals of a certain manufacturing company, their staff, regional managers and marketing and sales forces. It took fully half an hour to exchange calling cards and go through the introductions. The purpose of the meeting was to discuss a delicate matter of a return of some $20,000 worth of merchandise, and it got so out of hand, with everybody taking a hard line to impress their bosses, that both the vice-president of sales at the other company and I felt our relationship took a giant step backward. It took two or three meetings between us to bring our companies back on firm footing.

I will never again have so many people present at one meeting. I now have our people go their separate ways at the conventions, set up their own meetings with whomever they can, and leave the more significant meetings with the principals to me.

## THE PSYCHOLOGY OF NEGOTIATING

Psychology is extremely important in negotiating. You always have to start very high to end up where you expect to be. It's healthy to give in a little. Of course, the vendor has to want to make the deal in order for anything to happen. I try to prepare him by doing a real selling job on the company, including a tour of the facility and a viewing of at least one of our audiovisual programs, so that when he comes into my office, he's three-fourths sold on giving us the best deal he has in his pocket. Any supplier wants to be connected with a winning team and, beyond the obvious reason of personal gain, to see us succeed.

We sometimes encounter people who purposely conduct business on an adversarial basis—using unreasonable demands and intimidation to gain advantage and improve results. I believe

that this approach is ill-advised and counterproductive. Good communication with our customers and vendors does not happen when the environment is antagonistic.

I would prefer to overcompensate and be considered a bit tough rather than a pushover. After all is said and done and the sale is completed, the vendor doesn't necessarily remember how tough we were in our negotiation. If he does remember, it lasts only until the next order. I'm afraid we get some of our own medicine from our customers. But even if their bargaining gets unreasonable, it takes an awful lot before we say "enough" and cease to do business with them.

## THERE'S ALWAYS MORE TO GAIN

Following a great negotiation I have a tremendous feeling of satisfaction—but some doubts too. As I left the office of the president of one of our major lighting-fixture suppliers after a very tough one-and-a-half-hour negotiation once, the first thing that occurred to me was whether I had gotten everything they had to give. Did I leave anything on the table? Did I push to the absolute limit for everything I could get? I guess I shouldn't worry so much—at this meeting I was told that I had negotiated the very best deal that the company had ever given to anyone in the electrical-distribution industry.

That all sounds very good, and I would like to believe it. But there's a side of me that challenges everything and causes me to wonder whether there was even a single element of the deal that could have been improved upon for the benefit of All-Phase.

There is one drawback in all of this, and that is that I tend to want to negotiate even the smallest of items. When it comes to state and federal government, where I'm not able to get much, if any, concession, I become frustrated and furious.

This is particularly true when I negotiate sales tax audits and personal property tax reviews. I really manage to do quite well. I remember one $80,000 sales tax audit that I got down to $18,000,

but that was exceptional. Today we have a professional tax auditor on our staff, and he does a great job. I love it because he does with governmental authorities exactly what I have been doing all my life.

# Deals with Manufacturers

Μy BARGAINING TAKES ME INTO other areas besides negotiating cost savings or deferred payment with manufacturers.

A lamp manufacturer once charged us with $80,000 worth of unauthorized sales rebates. It said we had claimed sales made to day-in and day-out customers against contracts that we had with municipalities. Only the contractual business was subject to the rebate. I asked the branch manager to dig up the figures and help me find a way to have this charge thrown out. We found bits and pieces of information, such as a sale to a shopping center that was financed by a large life insurance company where we did have a contract, so we claimed the end user really was under contract and convinced the manufacturer that this was so. We also found sales to end users that had a relationship with other contract wholesalers, and we managed to get the bill down to $8,000.

Then I told the manufacturer that we were going to audit every invoice with their two field salesmen. If it took a week, we would simply take them out of the field and labor over this until we got to a point where they owed us money, rather than our owing them. In the end, it all was washed out. We didn't pay one penny in this whole episode. It was simply a matter of standing fast, arguing and fighting for what was fair.

I had a similar experience with one of our largest suppliers. It had charged back $55,000 in unearned cash discounts (which had occurred as a result of disputed bills and charge-backs), and I just couldn't convince the company that the matter should be negotiated. I held off for months until it went so far as to refuse to put us on as an authorized distributor when we made a five-

branch acquisition. My hand was forced.

Of course, I thought the supplier was holding me hostage, which I felt was terribly unfair. I really had to put on my bargaining shoes. I calculated that the time use of the money would have been more like $16,000, using a 7 percent rate of interest for an average thirty-day period that the money was used. I decided that before proposing this amount, however, I should cut the time use in the calculation down from four weeks to three weeks, thus leaving a little room to bargain. I offered a settlement of $11,000.

The company wouldn't have any part of this, and after a lengthy bargaining session and a long letter, it offered a settlement of 50 percent, which meant $27,500. I stood fast on my numbers and said plain and simple that I couldn't do it. It would take too much of our profits, we hadn't reserved anything for this contingency, and it had been a rough four years during which our company had never gone over 1 percent return on sales net after tax. Finally, the man sympathized with me somewhat and offered to settle for $20,000. I came up to $13,000 and finally agreed to $15,000.

The bottom line is that I saved $40,000 from the original amount and even $1,000 less than the amount I had intended to offer originally. I slept pretty well that night.

## THINKING THROUGH SUPPLIER CHANGES

Whenever a change occurs, particularly at the manufacturer/supplier level, I like to think through the potential ramifications and repercussions. Recently, a large supplier sold its electrical-products division to an individual, with some of the employees and officers of the company obtaining a very small minority equity position. I notified our regional managers, and in some cases spoke directly to branch managers, advising that if they had any outstanding claims from our cost-savings program, we should withhold further payments until these claims were paid.

We had one claim in Atlanta that amounted to $35,000 to

$50,000, and if it ended up in a lawsuit, as it very well could have, it could have run double or triple that. When I found out, I notified accounts payable to withhold payments until the company settled its suit with a major contractor. We were not directly involved, as these parties were dealing with each other, but I'm afraid that if they didn't reach a settlement, we would certainly have been enjoined as a third party.

I told our locations using this product heavily that obviously the company was not making money with this product line or it wouldn't have sold it. As a matter of fact, the *Wall Street Journal* indicated that the company's telecommunications division made something like $350 million but went on to say that the company itself in that same quarter made only $325 million. It doesn't take a genius to figure out that the electrical-products division and lighting must have lost about $25 million that quarter.

It also stands to reason that the new owners wouldn't have bought this company if they expected to lose money. Now there are many ways they could improve efficiency and cut losses, but the only way they're really going to be profitable is to raise prices. So I advised all of our branches to strongly resist any attempt on the part of that company to change our discount multiplier, and if they would not listen to us, to stop buying their product. It was tough, because some of those officers and employees who remained with the company are friends.

I told the president of the company, who phoned and told me of the sale just before a public announcement was released to the *Wall Street Journal*, that he still owed me $10,000 in the cost-savings program, and I would certainly feel much better about the company if I had that in hand. He was surprised to learn of this, particularly when I told him that it went back a year or two, and he promised to get it right out to me.

The point here is always to look at all of the angles and be sure that you cover all the bases. We can sometimes even work an ownership change or management change to our advantage.

# The High Value of Vendor Relationships

H AVING A GOOD, SOLID RELATIONSHIP with our top-quality suppliers has always been of paramount importance to me. That is one reason I attend all of the NAED conventions and make myself available to serve on distributor advisory councils. For three years in the late 1980s I simultaneously served on the Square D *and* the Allen-Bradley advisory councils. I am the only person in the history of these two councils who has served not only simultaneously, but served on both at all. I was particularly pleased that when I informed the principals of these two companies of the coincidence, they had enough trust and confidence in me ethically to know that anything said at these sessions would never, ever be repeated to their competitor. The point is, I will make personal sacrifices and considerable time commitments both to get closer to and better acquainted with the principals of the companies serving All-Phase—and to help them become better companies. That in turn will make me better.

I make it a point to visit with my top electrical suppliers at least every two or three years at their headquarters. Those with whom we do an extremely large volume of business I visit at least annually and sometimes every six months.

There is nothing quite like visiting a company on its home turf. All are very pleased at your having taken the time, effort and expense to travel great distances to see their factory floor and visit in their offices. I know of many of my competitors who almost never visit with their suppliers. To me, it is an absolute must if you want to fulfill both ends of the bargain. I want our manufacturers to know that I am eternally indebted to them for the fine,

fine support they have shown me through the years. We wouldn't be where we are today without them.

Quality suppliers are what this industry is all about. We always represent the very best quality available in the marketplace. There is, of course, a temptation sometimes to place price over quality, but we never compromise our values. The companies we represent have no equal in the electrical industry. I'm thinking particularly of our long and valued relationship with Square D. No other manufacturer is as closely tied with All-Phase's growth and prosperity. It's the line I probably tried hardest to get, and it has remained an undisputed leader in quality and distribution support.

Putting together a lineup of suppliers is like naming an All-American football team. You have to have the very best to perform well. More important than price is a supplier's product quality, return-goods policy, and sales and marketing efforts. Anybody can make something cheaper. But a reputation in the industry as having the best must be earned over years of hard work. And it means everything. That is why the first question I ask when talking to a potential acquisition is, "Who do you consider your major lines?" If they can't give me some of the top ten, I lose interest immediately. This is particularly true in the case of an industrial distributor.

## APPRECIATE YOUR VENDORS

Whenever salespeople and vendors visit All-Phase, whether at the branch level or at corporate headquarters, whether calling on our purchasing department, making a scheduled appointment with me or dropping in to see me or some staff member unannounced, we always take time to talk. Even if we're very, very busy, we acknowledge that we appreciate their calling on us, even if it's nothing more than to shake hands in the reception area. We can take that minute or so to make them happy that they made the call and happy that they're doing business with All-Phase.

Ignoring such people, telling them you're too busy to see them but you'll see them next trip, or sending some such message by a secretary or receptionist, just doesn't do the job. After all, those salespeople represent an arm of our sales force, and if we expect them to support us, work with our salespeople and bring orders to us, we should treat them with respect and dignity. I fear that sometimes our branch managers are too busy, too rude and too short with some of those vendors.

You never know when the people calling on you might have a more significant role with their company and you'll need their help more than ever. When somebody calls for an appointment, I nearly always fit them in, particularly when they're bringing with them someone from the home office to visit with us. I encourage every one of our top manufacturer suppliers to visit us at least every year. Yet I know of some companies that would rank in our top fifteen or twenty whose principals have never visited us.

Incidentally, it upsets me when I find that the principal of a supplier who's visiting me has scheduled several other calls, either before or after our meeting. The message to me is that I was just part of a regularly scheduled swing. It means so much more when a person makes a trip directly to Benton Harbor specifically to visit our corporate headquarters and then returns to his home base. When I visit a manufacturer or another distributor we might acquire, I make it a point never to mention any other stop.

Visits by suppliers to All-Phase are an ideal time to set the stage for negotiating cost-savings programs or, if those are already in place, some other feature that earns them preferred status. It's much easier to ask for and be granted concessions when you're dealing with people on your home court.

One thing we instituted at some branches is a wall chart, prominently displayed, with a block for every week of the year, in which to insert the names and dates of vendors who call on our branch. We can go to these charts and show some of our manufacturers that their agents or representatives have not called on a particular branch for six months or a year. This shows that we need their help and yet don't get it, and implies that if they don't call on us we'll seek a different vendor. This can be a source of irritation and embarrassment to the rep or agent, but when properly used, it can get his or her support.

We do have to be careful to cross off weeks that have passed to keep the chart up to date, because we caught some people backfilling dates showing that they had been there in certain weeks when they really hadn't. This is a little delicate, as we don't want to be too dictatorial; but if vendors are out there to work with us, we should use every method available to make sure we get their support.

## AN UNDESIRABLE TACTIC

There is one tactic used by manufacturer's agents and representatives that I abhor: In trying to persuade us to take on a new line they will sometimes bring us an order they have secured from a contractor or an industrial user and tell us that if we put the line in, we can have the order, but if we choose not to, they will be forced to take that order to a competitor who might be interested in carrying the line.

To me, this is coercive and an unacceptable way to go to market. I hope that everybody within our company shares this view and never agrees to such an arrangement. If the line can't sell itself and carry its own weight, we surely won't put it in our inventory just to accommodate an order. On the other hand, if the representative has been extremely supportive of our company on all other lines that he or she carries, and if we can credit him or her with repeated and continuous profitable sales, we might have good reason to support this.

## SAYING THANKS

When we had our twenty-fifth anniversary open houses, vendors participated with display booths in the warehouse, which we called a mini-trade show. I made it a point to walk around just before the start of the open house shaking hands with each vendor and thanking them for their participation—and then reaffirming my appreciation as we were closing up. I followed that up with a letter. I sent a twenty-fifth anniversary commemorative knife, plus a jacket and hat, to those vendors who went well beyond the call of duty, either by attending a great number of our open houses or by doing something extra special. For example, in Burbank, California, fifteen or twenty vendors spent many, many hours helping us rearrange our entire warehouse.

One feature I have instituted is the vendor-appreciation dinner. This dinner and cocktail party is hosted by All-Phase at a local country club or stylish restaurant, often in conjunction with a new branch opening and sales blitz. We entertain all of our top vendors, including the local agents and representatives as well as supplier executives. I am told that it is unique in the industry and probably the only time a distributor entertains the supplier at no cost. It seems to be greatly appreciated, and I am sure that we get a return on this investment tenfold.

Beyond face-to-face greetings and acknowledgements, these dinners allow me to address this valued group, telling them how much we appreciate their support and stressing the need for unity in attacking the market. I also update them on the state of the company with our current goals and objectives.

I always make a point of asking them when was the last time they personally heard or met my counterparts (and I name their names) at Graybar, CED, WESCO or GESCO. This always seems to hit home. Not once has anyone said they have met these individuals, much less been entertained by them.

I follow up with a personal letter telling each attendee how much I appreciate their taking the time to spend an evening with us. I also stress that I am personally always available to hear any suggestions on how we can improve our mutual market.

# One Step Ahead of the Competition

THERE ARE DISTRIBUTORS WITHIN this industry who pride themselves on being friendly with all of their competitors, but I am not of that school.

I remember an instance when the principal and owner of an electric-supply company in Lafayette, Indiana, complimented me on the fine operation we had in Crawfordsville, Indiana. He said we had a fine bunch of people who were good competitors. I couldn't wait to return from that discussion at a NAED convention to ask our district manager just what was wrong in Crawfordsville that it had become so friendly with a competitor.

I feel much better when someone asks me how I can be so aggressive and competitive. I liked the comment overheard in a bar in Natchez, Mississippi, where a salesman for our competitor was announcing that All-Phase is literally destroying the market with its competitive pricing. He said this to a group of electrical contractors, and if I were one of those contractors, I would never again submit a bid on a job without first getting All-Phase's pricing.

One friendly competitor of ours in Florida always questions why we find it necessary to be so aggressive. Although I do not always like that image, we don't want to give the store away, either. There's such a thing as ruining a market by getting prices so low that it may take years to return to the proper profit levels. One tactic is bombing a market to get in, and then reestablishing some decent pricing practices. But if you slash prices for too long and cut too deeply, you may never be able to restore the market. I'm not so concerned about the influence this would have on our competitors, as it's a practice of live and let live. But I am concerned that everybody in a particular city becomes accustomed to such low margins that no one ends up making any money.

We perhaps alienate ourselves further from the competition by not having mutual agreements with them on the exchange of merchandise. It's fairly common in our industry to exchange inventory at cost plus 10 percent. My feeling is that the manufacturers' lines we represent are proprietary and highly valued. Why should we share that with our competitor? I say let them wait until they can get the merchandise from the manufacturer. Why give away our greatest tool—inventory availability? I doubt that anyone has the $70 million inventory at their fingertips we do.

We use our shuttle-truck system—that is, the transferring of inventory between branches on a regularly scheduled basis—to augment our already substantial branch inventories. If I let my competitors in on this, I would be going to considerable expense to make them look good. And I'm not just talking about exclusive, proprietary line items, but even commodities that are used daily by our trade. Why should I help somebody out of jam when he or she is servicing my account?

I know there's been some erosion in this policy within our company. Our branch managers and operating people naturally love to get along with the competition, and I suppose there might even be an isolated instance in which I would approve such a transaction. But I always want to know when the rule is being broken. There's a distributor in Houston that sells to competitors at the same margin he does to a customer. He considers these competitor accounts as house accounts and says that his volume with competitors exceeds all of the volume with regular accounts assigned to one single salesperson. In other words, these house accounts result in more gross profit than that developed by one of his outside salespeople. However, his inventory is beyond a doubt the largest investment of any U.S. distributor under one single roof.

He is so possessed with the idea of inventory that it seems he would rather have his money tied up in inventory than in the bank. Even in the mid-1980s, when there was a severe decline in all electrical volume in the Houston area, he continued not only to maintain his inventory but to build it. He keeps both Square D and Allen-Bradley happy under one roof because he carries such huge inventories. I saw his Crouse-Hinds inventory, and it equals the total inventory investment we have for a medium-size branch.

However, this distributor holds the line on pricing. He knows that his inventory and his lines are second to none, and he's adequately compensated for this. He very seldom cuts a price to anyone and certainly never to a competitor.

### GET BIG OR GET OUT

When I look at industrialized America and see the tremendous problems the oil and steel industries have had, I am happy to be in the service business. Best of all, it's the type of service business that has so much potential for improved efficiencies. I just can't wait to get our computer going full-steam, properly train our people and start instituting new ideas on how to beat our competition.

In the farming industry they say get big or get out. In other words, the medium-size farmer can no longer make a reasonable profit. The small farmer, who often has a second income, does well, as does the large farmer (with considerably more than 1,000 acres), with the help of automation and new technology. But there is no room in the middle.

There is an analogy in our industry. The small, family-owned distributorship that does not find it necessary to computerize does quite well. Generally, such a company owns its building, so there is no rent; it does not have the burden of extensive automation; and, in particular, it doesn't have the cost of development. Often the company is living off its capital account, and because it doesn't borrow money, it doesn't pay interest. These people seem to get along just fine.

Next there is the medium-size distributor between $5 million and $20 million. This company generally has grown beyond its owner's financial resources and has to borrow money and pay interest. It probably has moved into a new building for which it pays rent. And, most serious, it has automated at an investment of perhaps $300,000 in a system that still does not allow for inventory control and, if the company were sold, has almost zero value to the new owner and probably no resale value on the open market. This category of company is probably one of our best prospects for acquisition.

Then there is the large distributor, with branches and sales in the area of $20 million to $75 million plus. He has automated and has that horrifying transition behind him. He has operated with interest charges for a long time and knows how to live with them, and he pays rent on all of the buildings he occupies.

There are very few exceptions to these three scenarios. The only one that comes to mind immediately is a company in Florida, whose owner once said to me, "Did you ever stop to consider that if we had to pay interest on our money and rent on our building, we really wouldn't make any bottom-line profit?" I looked at him quizzically and then realized just what he was saying: that he really doesn't view his company as a corporation nor operate it that way, but rather as a tight, family-owned entity.

I have often said that in our industry a company can do well simply with good organization and proper operating procedures and paperwork. So many small companies seem to go aimlessly through their business life without any degree of professionalism—not even the bare essentials of organization, not to mention computers. But organization is what it takes to get ahead. For example, we used to operate our purchasing departments with Cardex boxes holding the individual calling cards of the representatives and agents of our manufacturer suppliers. We relied on our people to develop their own systems of placing orders and reaching the ultimate source for the material.

Then several years ago we developed something for our purchasing department called a Buy Guide. It had a cover sheet listing each All-Phase supplier and the contact's name, address, telephone number, and other essential information. Inside the guide was space for a monthly physical inventory, a box for the quantity on order, and another box showing the amount that should be ordered to bring the inventory up to suggested levels. Of course, all of this has now been replaced by our computer.

This one little example could be magnified a thousand times over. I said to myself at the time, if we just do things halfway right, pay attention to business and try to improve our operation daily, then we certainly ought to succeed in this industry.

## DOING ONE THING AND DOING IT WELL

I feel that we're holding our own as number five in the industry. We're in pretty heady company. We shouldn't feel that we've taken a back seat to anybody. My dream, of course, is to acquire a very large company, which would propel us into the billion-dollar range overnight. But for the time being, I'll have to be content with our $450 million volume and a growth rate of 20 percent or so per year.

I still stick to my principle of doing one thing and doing it well. Many large companies in our industry distribute products other than electrical. Some sell plumbing, heating and ventilating. Others are in industrial supplies. Some are combination electronic and electrical distributors. I think you can do justice to only one thing at a time. I want our people to concentrate every ounce of energy and drive on one product category, and that is why I have been so single-minded on this subject.

I recently spoke to someone with more than 100 branches who is a combination distributor, and he said that if he had it to do over again, he would have stuck to either electrical or plumbing, but not both. He found that his salespeople were spreading themselves too thin and were mediocre at both rather than experts at one. He eventually divided his sales force so that each individual sells one category or the other.

## Staying on Guard

NOT A WEEK GOES BY THAT I DON'T get a phone call from some consultant wanting to come in and give us a hand with running the company. I have always been wary of them. I was shocked recently when a person who worked for a consulting firm told me to be very wary of answering any question at all from a consultant. She said she had worked for a consulting firm that represented itself as being owned and managed by some professors at the Graduate School of Business at Northwestern University. Hearing that put the prospective client at ease, and he felt free to discuss some very confidential and detailed information about his company. Call it what you may, pride of ownership or just plain vanity, these people actually would open up to the consultants and tell them anything. The truth was that the consulting firm had been hired by a competitor to obtain inside information—and got it handed over on a silver platter.

I know of one time when a competitor of mine conducted a telephone survey and represented itself as some sort of institutional firm gathering information for statistical purposes. I understand that the competitor even called some of our branches to get information, and that we were rather free with some seemingly innocent facts, such as number of employees, size of warehouse and so on.

Another time, I received a call from a supposed eastern consultant that purportedly had a do-it-yourself firm on the market and wondered whether I would be interested. When I asked where it was located, the caller said he couldn't reveal that. When I asked the size, he said he couldn't reveal that either. Then he started asking me questions about the nature of our company. I told him simply that I couldn't reveal that information and hung up. I am quite sure that it was more dirty tricks.

All of this just proves that we must always be on guard. When I visited our branch in Burlington, Washington, once, the manager told me he had interviewed a salesman who was working for one of our competitors, and he told our manager that he had been sent by his employer to dig forms and documents out of our dumpster. He also said that he parked his car across the street from us and noted the license plates and names of our customers. He said that he could tell us more, but he was afraid that if he said anything else, we would have him thrown in jail. I guess you just can't be too cautious. At times I look at what a lousy bunch of cutthroats we compete with. To my way of thinking, they should spend their time on more constructive things like selling rather than worrying so much about us.

It's often been said in our industry that we electrical distributors try awfully hard to out-dumb each other, and I'm sorry to say that at times the sentiment seems appropriate. It really isn't a complicated industry, in that we merely buy products in the right quantity at the right price and resell them to our loyal customers at a reasonable profit margin. We collect our bills on time, pay our vendors and get a rather minimal return on our investment. But we manage to screw it up principally by excess competition with one another and cutting the margins down to unreasonable and unrealistic levels.

## TRADE SECRETS

On the surface it might not appear that there could be many trade secrets in an industry that is so simple. But as with any other challenge in life, electrical distribution can be as sophisticated and professional as you want to make it.

I pride myself on taking All-Phase into the realm of the unknown. I like to try things that are different and to experiment, even if the risk is high. As the saying goes, the greater the risk, the greater the reward. Thus I am constantly on the lookout for innovations to make us different and better.

One such venture was our preferred-status requirements that I negotiate with manufacturers. Naturally, I shared this information not only with my corporate staff but of necessity with the suppliers with whom I negotiated the deal. In one instance it backfired in a big way. The president of a nationally prominent residential-lighting-fixture company quizzed me on every element of our plan, even wanting to know the justification for each request. Of course, I accommodated him and spent a couple of hours in private conversation at his office, feeling that I was dealing in good faith, as I expected him to do.

Much to my surprise, this man resigned from his company and originated a buying group that used as its reason for existence all of the programs I had enumerated to him. He built the group into the largest of its kind in the nation, doing more than $2 billion in business with approximately 100 electrical distributors.

I never really figured this out until our Regional Distribution Center's open house, when one of his former executives, who also had left the lighting-fixture company, informed me I had been duped. He asked me if I had ever thought about the fact that the man had dismissed him from the meeting to confer privately with me, quizzed me extensively and then left his company to start the buying group. Indeed, I hadn't thought about it.

I guess I wouldn't make a good lawyer or police investigator, as I simply don't suspect people of this kind of chicanery.

# CHAPTER VI.

## ALL PHASES OF OUR BUSINESS

# How a Branch Makes Money

SIZE OF INVENTORY OFTEN DETERMINES the success or failure of an electrical distributor. I have often said that more companies choke to death on excessive inventories than starve to death on too little.

Regional and national chain houses have the reputation of having too little inventory. The reason may be that as large corporations, they keep a closer eye on the numbers than do small, independent electrical distributors. They operate on ratios, and inventory turns are one of the key ratios in rating their people and their company, so they strive for high inventory turns. Independent distributors, on the other hand, are more interested in gross profit and net profit after tax and not so concerned about return on investment, so they don't pay as much attention to size of inventory. Although this may result in larger inventories than they really should have, they can service the customer better.

I look at All-Phase as a cross between the two. I am sure that our inventories are larger and have lower turnover than other multihouse distributors in the top ten, but we don't have quite as much inventory nor quite as poor a turnover as the smaller independents that I see when considering a purchase. This hurts us on one count but pays back on the other.

Thus, our greatest problem is also one of our greatest attributes—namely, we have good inventories but poor turnover.

INVENTORY TURNS

The benchmark in our company is 4.8 turns per year on inventory. That means selling the entire inventory every seventy-five days. In some locations we don't even come close, but in others, such as northern Michigan, we approach six turns per year (a sixty-day supply). Those are the people who are properly utilizing their inventory asset.

Of course, you can't have so little inventory that you're constantly running out or plaguing neighboring branches with transfers of fast-moving merchandise. You must be realistic and logical and have an adequate stock to service your customers. Far too often, however, we find that some huge percentage, like 10 or 15 percent of our inventory, does not turn during an entire year. If a manager is prone to that kind of a problem, it's very unlikely that he or she will ever get to 4.8 turns per year.

The "turn and earn," concept is very important in judging the viability of a manufacturer's inventory. The higher the "earn," the lower the requirement for turns, or in plain language, if our goal is "120 turn and earn" it means that the combination of gross profit and the number of times we sold the item in the year must total 120. If the gross profit margin is 20 percent, you would have to sell, or "turn," that item six times during the year. If the gross profit margin is only 10 percent, you would have to turn the item twelve times, or every month. Our reports of inventory turns help us judge the profitability out of stock on the manufacturer's lines we represent.

When we look at excessively large inventories, we often find an overstock or perhaps even obsolete inventory. We might have ordered merchandise for a specific customer, only to have it canceled without time to notify the vendor to stop shipment. To correct this situation, it is mandatory that we have a blanket order from these customers agreeing to relieve our inventory of all of a special make or special order item if they turn out not to need it. At least they have to agree to buy everything that we have in stock for them. A verbal agreement or a letter is not sufficient. It has to be on that company's purchase order form.

Our company went onto the LIFO (last in, first out) method of inventory valuation back in 1974, when we had a tremendous inflation of 36 percent in cost of products within our industry. Now anybody who took that 36 percent and used it in valuing their ending inventory had a paper profit that was exorbitant and paid the resultant federal income tax. I just can't imagine anyone not being on LIFO.

We picked the ideal year in which to go on LIFO. As a matter of fact, over the ensuing fifteen years, our LIFO reserve (the amount set aside to offset inflation), which, of course, has no federal income tax effect, amounted to as much as the company's total net worth on a LIFO basis. It's quite astounding that we protected this amount of money from federal and state income taxes—and had the use of that money as working capital to grow.

## TIMELY COLLECTIONS

Accounts receivable make up approximately 50 percent of our total assets. Our goal here has always been forty-five days sales outstanding (DSO). About half the company is able to attain this, and I'd say about 10 percent of our branches are even in the high thirties. On the other hand, there are a few who regularly run over sixty days. This means that they are abusing the credit privilege by extending liberal credit to customers who just plain don't warrant that kind of treatment.

On a related issue, our company has never accepted a request from a customer that the customer pay for all of the merchandise on a purchase order only after it is completely filled and shipped. We have gotten caught once or twice on this, but never again. As you can imagine, there might be one item on the purchase order that takes four to six months to ship, and that would delay the payment for the entire purchase order. This, of course, is ludicrous.

It's amazing to see how a pattern can be set by a particular branch manager and how difficult it is to change it. Once someone gets into a jam on collections, it can take a year or two to straighten out, and sometimes it never changes. But collections affect the branch manager's compensation just as much as the inventory turns do. It's how he or she uses these two asset figures that determines his or her total income. Since the key benchmark for bonus is return on assets, the manager must keep investment in inventory and accounts receivable low while garnering a good profit. This is the manager's all-important ratio.

Corporate headquarters produces a report that lists every branch by district and its return on assets for the month and year to date, and compares these to the budget figures. This report becomes a very important factor in evaluating the success of its people.

SETTING GOALS

I sometimes feel that we are too optimistic when we set our goals at the beginning of every fiscal year and when we work out our operating plan. We let the branches set their own goals, approved, of course, by the district managers and then by the corporate staff and ultimately by the president; and we seldom adjust a goal down. We believe that if they feel so good about themselves and so optimistic about their branch and business conditions, far be it from us to dishearten them.

Perhaps we should do some readjusting, however. Branches sometimes set goals beyond those that could be expected from a reasonable growth pattern. Managers like to be proud of their optimism, but it's equally important that goals be attainable. It's disappointing to the branch manager, the district manager and certainly the staff and myself when our company falls short of its budgets, particularly now that the budget figure appears on every month-end statement for every location and has become an important factor in judging the success of the operation.

Perhaps I cause a bit of a problem, in that I will not allow anyone to have a deficit budget. It's a principle of mine that if we have to budget for a deficit, we shouldn't have the operation. Well, sometimes it's impossible to turn something around within a year and show a profit after a deficit the previous year. Also, I will not allow anyone to budget a net profit after tax of less than $10,000. Again, my thinking is that if we can't make $10,000 in even the smallest of branches, we should be rid of it.

## UNPROFITABLE BRANCHES

In 1981 as part of our strategic plan, the company developed a countdown policy with regard to an unprofitable branch operation. The first step is to send the maximum amount of help from corporate headquarters to help reduce assets. (We are also mindful, of course, that you can get your inventory and accounts receivable down only so far before you permanently maim the company and keep it from ever recovering.)

Next, we continue to monitor the branch closely. If there is no change in performance, the branch manager is replaced. We might even change managers more than once. If there still is no improvement, we start winding down the branch, further reducing assets until finally, after approximately twenty-four months of futile efforts, we close the doors, sell the building, transfer the fixed assets and inventory, and collect our receivables.

This had happened eight times by the late 1980s, where we saw no hope for recovery in a reasonable length of time. We closed three branches in South Carolina—Greenville, Charleston and Columbia—with consolidation into Spartanburg and Anderson. We also closed Kokomo, Indiana; Monroe and Shreveport, Louisiana; and Beaver Falls, Pennsylvania. We closed Martinsville, Virginia, but subsequently reopened there. In Fort Wayne, Indiana, we had two branches for about five years but consolidated them in 1982, turning two mediocre branches into one superior performer.

## FINANCIAL BENCHMARKS

Financial information is provided to each branch within five days of month's end. This profit and loss statement is very detailed in its listing of income and expenses. There are certain criteria that we use as benchmarks. The salaries and benefits as a percentage of gross profits should never exceed 40 percent. The contribution margin, which is the gross profit less controllable expenses, should equal 50 percent. The net profit after tax should be a minimum of 2 percent. The accounts receivable DSO should be a maximum of forty-five days and inventory turns four-tenths of a time per month for 4.8 turns per year. The turn and earn, that is, gross profit on sales for every dollar invested in inventory, should be annualized at $1.20. The gross profit per employee per month should run a minimum of $5,500. While return on assets varies all over the map, 8 percent is satisfactory.

Whenever a branch hits a new monthly gross profit record, I send the manager a mailgram of congratulations on this tremendous accomplishment. I also send a copy to the district manager. Some branches have received this congratulatory message as often as four or five times a year.

I would like to tie some sort of incentive to that kind of accomplishment, but it's difficult because, like anything else, the situations vary. Some branches have one absolutely tremendous month that probably never could be accomplished again. Say a windfall deal goes through, as often does happen. Perhaps 30 or 40 percent of our branches have had such a fluke record month, and I really can't tie compensation to something like that.

It is nice to let the whole network know, through our in-house newsletter, when a particular branch hits a new monthly gross profit dollar record. That way people can honor that branch and feel good about our company's accomplishments.

It would be interesting to develop a program between branches, carefully controlled and monitored, whereby they could compete, one with the other, to prove their excellence and to strive to be the best within an area or a region. Competition between branches is a very sensitive matter, however. You like to see them strive to make the best showing possible, but it's also essential that they work hand in hand within the network—sharing inventories and, in the case of contiguous branches, not competing for customers.

# The All-Important Profit Margin

THE ONE THING THAT UPSETS ME most about the wholesale electric-supply industry is that we have to generate such huge revenues for a very meager bottom line. We consider ourselves very fortunate to realize a 2 percent net profit after tax on sales, and even that has been unattainable at times.

Profit margins differ tremendously from city to city and particularly from district to district. Ours can go from 20 percent in the South Central District down to 17 percent in the Florida District. Or we can go from 28 percent at an isolated branch in northern Michigan to less than 15 percent in a competitive city such as Atlanta. When our average cost of doing business is around 17 percent of sales, you can well understand that the company must average a minimum of 20 percent gross profit on sales.

As a general rule, profit margins vary with the type of sale. A sale out of the warehouse, which means either over the counter or via delivery truck, should be in the neighborhood of 25 percent gross profit, and such sales should account for roughly 75 percent of our overall volume. With factory-direct shipments, which means delivery direct from the manufacturer to the project job site, profit margins are generally bid at between 5 and 7 percent, with an overall average of 8 or 9 percent. These sales account for the rest of our volume.

The reason the overall margin on factory directs is higher than the original bid margin is what we call buying out. This means you bid the job to get it, which may mean less than a 5 percent gross profit and perhaps as little as 1 percent or, in isolated instances, even at cost. Then you must be sharp enough in your purchasing practices that you can build profit back into the project.

You can accomplish this, for example, by getting the specifying engineer or architect to accept an item you can buy at a more competitive price as a substitute for a comparable item called for in the bid. Of course, you would also have to show a savings to the contractor, so you can get a change order, changing the distribution equipment or the type of fixture used or some other aspect of the project, in which case you make your margins by beefing up the profitability of the change. You can improve margins with any product, including commodities such as pipe and wire, where you work hard to obtain the very best price that can be had in the industry on a given day. Thus the savvy of the purchasing department can determine the profitability of the operation.

I have seen some terrible misapplications of these practices, in which a quotation person bid something at cost and then wasn't able to buy it out. More commonly, however, our people are sharp enough to know how far they can go on a job. We have one quotations man in Seattle who bids not only for that city but for all of the northwestern group, and who prides himself on his ability routinely to raise what originally was a 5 percent margin on jobs to almost 15 percent.

The important thing here is to know your limitations. You know that certain manufacturers will not budge from their price, so don't think you're going to be able to influence them. On the other hand, you know certain others just put out what is called a street price—a price from which to negotiate—and you have to know whether the negotiation is going to lower your cost by 5 percent or 20 percent.

The amount of project factory-direct business has a bearing on the gross profit within the branch or district. The reason the South Central District runs at a higher gross profit margin overall is principally that 80 percent of its business is out of warehouse and only 20 percent factory direct. By contrast, the Southeast District has about a 50/50 split. Our companywide split of 75 percent stock and 25 percent direct is somewhat better than the national norm. I guess this is in keeping with our feeling that the true backbone of All-Phase Electric during our formative years was the small electrical contractor, who requires few direct shipments.

## MONITORING ACCOUNTS

Within our company we review every account at every branch every month and year-to-date for their gross profit percentage. If it's below 17 percent, we look further at the customers to determine whether they have good paying habits and, if not, whether they pay the 2 percent service charge. We look at total volume to see whether it justifies the tight gross margin, and we consider other questions, such as whether we someday will improve our gross profit percentage with a particular customer, mainly with over-the-counter and warehouse shipments.

Every district manager sits down with every branch manager and reviews this report on a timely basis. Often we find that someone who appears on paper to be a profitable customer actually causes us so many headaches and problems that we're better off without him. We must make such decisions selectively, however, learning everything there is to know about the account.

I'll never forget the time that one of our major competitors published a statement of policy declaring that any customer who intended to maintain an account had to do a specific volume of business with them, or else they would no longer solicit or accept business from that account. I think the required volume was something like $5,000 per year, which of course drove away many, many smaller contractors. I know that our company has benefited from this competitor's policy.

We would like to have some minimum annual billing, and certainly we would like to enforce some minimum amount per sale at the counter or for delivery. We do publish some specific operating policies such as restocking charges, a minimum of cash sales and, in some cases, delivery charges, and in the case of a one-time customer a down payment with the placement of an order. However, every district and branch manager knows he or she may use his or her discretion to deviate from these policies if justified.

OUR SHUTTLE SYSTEM OF transferring inventory between branches is one of the greatest services our sales and purchasing departments can tout. The idea started out modestly, when we had only two locations. A counterman from Benton Harbor who lived in Watervliet, Michigan, halfway between Benton Harbor and Kalamazoo, would drive a loaded panel truck home at night and leave it in his driveway. Someone from the Kalamazoo branch who lived nearby would do the same thing. They would actually swap trucks in the middle of the night or early in the morning, thereby effecting the transfer. The only cost to the company was the fuel and wear and tear on the trucks. But the labor was free, as we provided transportation to and from work for these two individuals. This system lasted about five years, until we grew to the point that we had to have an official shuttle truck, which picked up and dropped off merchandise as it passed through our small network of branches.

Today the system is a marvelous boon to customers, yet it probably causes more dissension and morale problems than any other single item within the company.

If employees use the system properly and don't abuse it, remembering to treat the person at the other end of the line just as he or she would want to be treated—that is, treat them as though they were customers—the transfer works ideally: getting merchandise speedily to a branch where it is needed because of a temporary outage, or removing merchandise from a branch that has an excess. Problems arise when one branch attempts to attain its inventory turnover goals by drawing all of the fast movers from neighboring branches. The result is a complete breakdown in the system. Also, if the merchandise is not properly packed, treated and cared for, marked and labeled, the transfer can be chaotic. The merchandise arrives at the wrong branch, or a lighting fixture has conduit piled on top of it—the potential problems are endless.

Then there is the case of a special-order item, where a branch places an order for a one-time-only item and delivers it to the neighboring branch that requisitioned it, only to find that the customer canceled the order. Of course, we are unable to return it to the manufacturer, so who eats the loss? The answer is that with any special orders, the branch that originally ordered it should have received payment in advance or a noncancelable order.

When the shuttle system fails, it's the customer who suffers. If a branch calls in the presence of the customer and is assured that the merchandise is in stock and will be on that shuttle, you can imagine the disappointment when the customer arrives the next day to find that the merchandise missed the truck. There is no excuse for that type of customer abuse. To work, the route has to be traveled on a very tight schedule, the merchandise has to be ready and available for loading at the truck dock when the shuttle-truck driver arrives, and he should get help in loading and unloading when needed. Under no conditions should the driver be deterred from his schedule. He should not make local deliveries nor be expected to perform any function other than making the shuttle-truck system work.

## MANUFACTURERS' WAREHOUSES

Among the banes of our business are the manufacturer and agent warehouses. These are designed so that a distributor can pick up inventory items, but if the warehouses are used regularly, they can reduce or eliminate the distributor's need for carrying any inventory at all. Certainly it's much cheaper to run a truck around the city picking up inventory than it is to keep stock on our shelves. These warehouses give the burden of inventory to the manufacturer—but also relinquish one of the values we must add as a distributor.

When we first entered the Atlanta market in 1976, I entertained 175 manufacturers, agents and representatives at a cocktail party and dinner at an exclusive club. I delivered to them just one message, and that was that All-Phase no longer would make pickups from local warehouses. We were going to remove the radio-dispatch equipment from our vehicles and live off our inventory.

This was a radical change that stirred a great deal of interest within the industry. Most of the attention was complimentary, because if our system worked, the manufacturer's agent would be much more profitable without the expense of keeping a warehouse and the required personnel and overhead. As it turned out, however, we were lone pioneers in this area. Not one single distributor took up the cause. Of course, we couldn't talk about it with others, because that could be interpreted as collusion, so we merely had to hope that by setting the example others would fall in line. It didn't happen.

This is also why there are a hundred distributors in the Atlanta metropolitan area, which should support twenty. Think of how easy it is to get into business if all you need is a truck to pick up inventory around town and a roll of quarters to use at a telephone booth. As a matter of fact, some distributors even asked their contractor and industrial customers to make the pickups themselves from the manufacturer's warehouse. It got to a point that the vendor was holding the invoice ticket for several days, a week or even a month to accommodate both the contractor and the distributor. This allowed the distributor to make as many pickups as he wanted and yet receive only one bill after the twenty-fifth of the month. In effect he was receiving the next month's dating, which gave him an additional thirty days to pay.

We tried, but we failed to change the system. I know we'll keep trying. The spreading of our Regional Distribution Centers throughout our network will move us to take up this campaign once again.

In 1984, when we joined 260 other electrical distributors in the Los Angeles market, we found the problem of local pickups even greater than in Atlanta. One manufacturer, and not a major one at that, told me that his firm had 600 pickups per month—or twenty-five to thirty a day. He said that his company was absolutely choked at the shipping dock with distributors and contractors picking up merchandise.

I asked why he didn't simply close that shipping dock to that type of traffic, and he replied that if he did he would be committing business suicide—someone would step in and take his place. I disagreed, pointing out that his product is unique to the industry, with a tremendous share of market, but he still felt that he had to stay with his present policy.

If ever I am in a position to influence our industry, this is one area that I would like to concentrate on. I'm proud that we were a little ahead of the times on this issue. Finally, this swing away from manufacturers' warehousing appears to be happening.

# Regional Distribution: A Giant Step

$A$ CROWNING ACHIEVEMENT OF THE 1980s was our first Regional Distribution Center in St. Joseph, Michigan. Opened in 1988, this 140,000-square-foot facility has 20,000 square feet of corporate offices and 120,000 square feet of warehousing. It accommodates $10 million in inventory for distribution to the thirty-four branches in Michigan, Ohio and Indiana.

The advent of the RDC has given me and our entire purchasing group the opportunity to negotiate a new deal with every one of our suppliers. Our confidential, yet expressed goal with these vendors is to make the RDC break even. It may seem unusual to talk about a "break-even center" rather than a "profit center," but truly, all we want to do is come out at the end of the year with a balanced set of books. We don't intend to make money on this facility, other than what would accrue to us through better service and improved inventory turns.

As far as actual profits go, we are happy to see it be a wash. That means if we budget the RDC to have an operating cost of 5 percent of volume, then we had better be sure that we average a 5 percent improvement in cost. We generally show this in our cost of goods shipped, as compared to the invoiced price to the branch or in the form of a rebate, preferably at each month's end.

I look forward to the day when the product managers in the RDC, as well as all of the other people connected with the procurement and distribution of inventory, are paid on a percentage of the profitability, if there is such a thing.

When calling on a customer I always point out that while our $70 million inventory is marvelous to have, unless we can access it readily at every branch it doesn't mean a thing. What sets All-Phase apart from the competition is that at every one of our 1,300 CRTs, with a touch of a button, we can look at inventory throughout all our branches and Regional Distribution Center and draw on it with ease. No other distributor in the nation can make this statement.

The single reason that a Regional Distribution Center makes sense is to raise our level of service to an all-time high by backing up local inventories with a huge, readily available, centrally located inventory. Our service level must be such that 95 percent to 98 percent of orders are filled the first time through.

We are shipping a number of manufacturers' products nationwide to our branches out of the RDC, thus going beyond the "regional" concept. Of course, we assure the manufacturers that we will give them complete reporting for commission purposes on where the sale takes place. We also protect any limited-distribution policy by making it impossible for a branch to draw inventory on products they are not authorized to distribute.

Our inventory turnover goal is four times per year out of the RDC and ten from the branches, for an overall company turnover of six. One added bonus of the RDC is our ability to identify and close out slow-moving and excess inventory. We now have the ability to assemble this category of material in one place under one roof and to deal with it in an orderly and professional manner.

*Electrical Wholesaling* magazine has recognized this concept as an important innovation. "If 1989 is remembered for one new idea in our industry," the magazine said, "it would be the regional distribution center developed by Ron Kinney and All-Phase Electric."

Since the Michigan RDC is the first of several, it is extremely important that it be successful. That is why I am personally expending so much time and energy to help secure its future.

*The Physical Plant*

I GET A REAL KICK OUT OF OUR branch managers who think they need additional warehouse space to get the job done. They.don't know what living within a really confined space is like. In our first location, the old A&P store building in Benton Harbor, we were doing $1 million in volume out of 10,000 square feet in 1959. In today's dollars, that would probably be $3 million.

I recall being so desperate for space that we actually used the cubic footage over the stalls in the restrooms for storage. We would lay our slower-moving eight-foot fluorescent lamps across the tops of the stalls. The countermen didn't have any particular problems with this in the men's room, but it became a little embarrassing when someone filled an order in the ladies' room.

The size of our buildings today falls generally within three categories. The smallest is approximately 10,000 square feet; the intermediate is 15,000 to 18,000 square feet, and the largest is 30,000 to 50,000 square feet. A service center, which draws inventory from a larger supporting warehouse, is 3,000 to 6,000 square feet.

The company has a policy of investing as little as possible in fixed assets. We have a minimal investment, with no buildings or properties, because All-Phase Real Estate Company handles that end of the business. The only thing we end up with is the office furniture, fixtures and equipment as well as the warehouse shelving, pallet rack and materials-handling equipment. The largest single item is our computer. This amounts to less than 5 percent of our total assets.

Our ideal would be to lease a building for one year with about ten one-year renewal options. Of course, this never happens. More practically, we lease the building for three to five years, with at least two five-year options, so that we can tie the property down for ten to fifteen years with minimal increases in rent. We never, ever have agreed to tie an increase to the consumer price index. I'd rather give the landlord 10 or 15 percent increases at the end of each five-year period.

All-Phase Real Estate has built probably fifty buildings for All-Phase Electric. (I hope someday we can have our own construction crew.) We have a rather typical floor plan, with approximately 2,000 square feet of office space, 3,000 square feet of residential-fixture showroom (if we decide to have one) and the rest in sales counter and warehouse.

Despite our standardized plan, we find it necessary to employ an outside engineering firm when we build, usually for three days. The first is spent at the job site, which the engineer studies to make recommendations about the location of the structure on the property. The second is spent writing specifications and drawing a rough floor plan and schematic of the building. The third involves travel to the job site to accept bids once the branch manager has sent the plans and specifications to half a dozen local contractors.

After bids arrive, we meet with each contractor to discuss them, generally meeting with the highest bidder first thing in the morning and the most competitive later in the afternoon. Then we attempt to negotiate extras and deductions to arrive at the best possible price for the best possible building. We try to leave the city that evening with a handshake and an agreement as to the contractor and the price. The formal contract is drawn up later.

The branch manager and district manager are responsible for site inspections and approvals of payments. The final payment is not made until I personally do a checklist of the completed facility—along with the branch manager and construction principal—typically in conjunction with the facility's grand opening.

We now have our own construction supervisor on staff, so we will be much more self-sufficient and more professional in our approach to construction.

## ALL-PHASE REAL ESTATE COMPANY

All-Phase Real Estate Company originated in 1967 when we built our first branch building in Holland, Michigan. Rather than use corporate funds, which would have limited the amount of money we had available for investment in the vital assets of inventory and accounts receivable, we decided to form a partnership to invest in the brick and mortar to house our branches.

Today All-Phase Realty owns more than fifty buildings and has a net worth in excess of $5 million. It is an arm's length transaction—which means that the rental rates are competitive with anything found in the marketplace. Our rule of thumb is to pay to the realty company 1 percent per month on the investment.

Over the years we have built some beautiful facilities and purchased others. Our crown jewel is the Regional Distribution Center in St. Joseph, Michigan, which opened in 1988.

We eventually formed a second and even a third real estate company.

## ATTENDING TO COSMETICS

We recently have had the time and inclination to improve the physical appearance of our buildings. We're sending our construction and maintenance supervisor throughout the network to give some attention to the cosmetics. He is remodeling the front entrance and the sales counter area as well as any lobbies or showrooms or, for that matter, any part of the building that is exposed to the public.

We have been somewhat remiss in the kind of image we portray through the physical appearance of our branch locations. This became apparent with the acquisition of Wholesale Electric in Huntsville. It has a recessed area, lovely landscaping, a board room and a formal office for the manager or the principal of the company. The facility is just magnificent. That has led me to believe that appearance has something to do with the success of a branch, and if we're going to be a winner, we really ought to look like one. Of course, it's up to the manager and the employees to keep it looking good once we make the improvements. To me, a neat warehouse almost always indicates a well-run, profitable operation. When I visit a branch I try to set an example by picking up bits of paper that might be lying around our entrance.

## BUILDING SECURITY

Our security officer has in his possession a complete list of every single person at every branch in the network who has been issued a key or the entry password. Any time somebody on that list leaves the company, we change the locks. Shuttle-truck drivers often are given a key to certain branches for making pickups and deliveries—particularly if they must do so before or after normal operating hours—so they must be trustworthy.

I dislike using a janitorial and cleaning service to work in the building after everyone else has gone home. We've had occasion to suspect some of these outsiders of theft. As a matter of fact, we once even caught one in the act. I would rather pay one of our own truck drivers or warehouse people time and a half to work overtime to clean (provided they do a good job). I also prefer to see two people working together, not one person in the building alone.

Although it may not be practical, we also suggest that when entering the building after hours—generally to provide some emergency service to a customer—the salesperson or counterman be accompanied by a second individual, usually somebody from management. Certainly one of the key features we offer with a local counter and warehouse is the ability to service an account twenty-four hours a day, so we don't want to restrict entry into the building. The very fact that our employee is there with a customer should be enough to assure honesty.

# Wheels and Wings

IT'S FUNNY WHEN I CONSIDER HOW long I went without buying a new car. My first automobile, other than the used cars I drove in high school and college, was a new Ford I purchased in Athens, Georgia, when I was in the Naval Supply Corps School in 1954. This and a station wagon we purchased after I started All-Phase were the last new automobiles we bought for years. I used to buy good secondhand Cadillacs from a friend until about 1970, when I felt that the company and I could afford to own new cars.

We have had a corporate airplane since 1981, and I often marvel that we went for more than twenty years, growing to more than fifty branches, without owning one. I think back on April 1980, when we had four acquisitions in one month, in four states (Virginia, Kentucky, Alabama and Texas) and traveled to each by commercial airline. In each case I brought along the transition team and did so with relative ease, spending almost the full week in each city. I also find it difficult to believe that I traveled to each of those fifty branches to distribute profit-sharing—and did so by commercial airline or automobile.

Today our airplane is indispensable. We now have two pilots on staff, and that plane is in the air 87 percent of the available workdays. I can make my swing through the entire network in about four weeks, whereas commercially it probably would take a couple of months.

When I'm not using the plane, the corporate vice-presidents spend a great deal of time flying their staffs to remote districts. Like anything else, however, we must cost-justify the airplane. We never allow it to deadhead, for example. If it's going to a branch to pick up passengers, as often is the case when we bring a group of customers to corporate headquarters for a day or two, we fly corporate people to the branch to run an audit program, work on inventory conditions, deal with personnel problems, help with sales efforts or whatever needs to be done. They stay there until we return with the customers. Also, I almost never allow the plane to go with less than three of the six passenger seats occupied. This seems to be the break-even point if we compare the cost of the flight to commercial travel for the three people.

Of course, safety prevails over all else. We absolutely never allow any risk, be it ever so slight. If weather prevents us from flying, we rearrange the appointment, no matter how important it is.

# Living Through the Computerization Nightmare

THE DECADE OF THE 1980s WAS OUR TIME to invest in the future. Specifically, it's when we decided to fully automate the company. It's a decision that has cost us several millions of dollars per year.

I never dreamed it would require so much effort, not to mention heartaches, sleepless nights and serious second thoughts. Sometimes I think of this period as the "horrible '80s." I really think I've lost some hair over it. And one reason it's been easy to keep my weight under control is that those computers have actually caused me to lose my appetite. What a horrifying experience it really was. One has to live through it to appreciate it.

In mid-1983 we installed our B6900 Burroughs computer, with all of its peripherals and software. When we purchased it I thought the system would be a source of happiness and joy and would solve many of our problems. It took about two years for staff members and the Management Information Services group to reach this decision, and while we knew the adjustment would be difficult, we looked forward to it. The one benefit we most hoped to achieve was an improved return on our inventory. We expected it to take no more than two years to get the system fully implemented at all locations and operating properly.

At the time we were turning our inventory about three times a year, with a goal of 4.8 turns per year. We reasoned that if this computer gave us the means to improve a moderate one turn per year, considering that our inventory was approaching $40 million, we could reduce our inventory investment by some $10 million. It's not difficult to realize that even at a modest interest rate of

10 percent, this would equate to a million-dollar savings per annum for the company, and of course, that would help pay for our investment.

Besides giving us an outstanding two- or three-year return on our investment, the computer would provide better control over our processing, more current information, a fast way to produce a vast array of reports, and that all-important feeling that we control our own destiny. Previously we had depended on a service bureau and shared computer time with other companies. The bureau dictated when we would close out our accounts for the month, when we would send invoices and statements, and even whether or not we had down time. Now, at least, it would be in our hands.

Once we had installed our billing, accounts receivable, inventory control, general ledger and payroll programs, we could look for additional benefits. We could, for example, place purchase orders direct from computer to computer with our suppliers. And we could allow our customers to access our computer for inventory information, price quotations and direct-order entry. It would be a tremendous selling point that could open a whole new frontier of opportunity for All-Phase Electric. Although at least one national and one regional chain had already placed CRTs at customers' business places, it had not been well promoted, and with our image and extensive customer base, I thought we really could grab the lion's share of that market.

I came up with what I thought was a tremendous idea on how to get national attention for this and create an immediate market: We would approach the editor of *Electrical Wholesaling* magazine and suggest it do a sequel to the two cover stories it had done on All-Phase in 1973 and 1982. Instead of the large number of telephones (one for each branch) on my desk shown in those cover photographs, we would suggest a picture of me seated at my desk with a simple CRT—the latest and most efficient means of linking our branches. Then we would go on to explain how this function spells success in sales and marketing for the customer. I hoped we might be ready for something like this by mid-1984. (The sequel article ran as a cover story in April 1989 but the magazine did not use my idea. We may use it in our own advertising at some later date.)

Further, the computer would shift some jobs to individual branches from corporate headquarters, where we had our main billing center and accounts receivable, and from our other billing centers at Dothan, Alabama; Seattle; and Bethlehem, Pennsylvania. The branches, in the normal course of business, would perform the functions previously performed at these billing centers. That is, they would enter into a CRT all of the information necessary to create the packing slip, the invoice and the statement. Eventually, this is what did take place.

Six years later, here's where we stood with automation:

• The B6900 was obsolete within two years, and the resale value dropped from the purchase price of approximately $750,000 to $37,000. We still had it on the books for more than $500,000.

• We were only just getting the customer remote-order-entry system and had yet to place a manufacturer's purchase order computer-to-computer.

• We were just beginning to think about that *Electrical Wholesaling* article on "Dumping the Phones for the CRT."

• Our inventory turns were still under four.

• We had poured millions of dollars into our Unisys system.

I guess at the outset of computerization we simply set our sights too high. We thought we were better and smarter than anyone else and could avoid the pitfalls, but I found that we were human and as subject to errors as anyone else. I can remember invoices for the prior month going out as late as five days into the new month, with statements going out on the eighth or ninth of the month and still expecting our customers to pay by the tenth for cash discount. There were times when an employee over the age of fifty-five or so would simply feel that it was not worth the aggravation to learn the computer and would take early retirement instead.

Thank God we had the resilience and total determination to make it work. Still, I would do it all over again pretty much the same way. There is no such thing as burying your head in the sand and not computerizing. Maybe we did it the hard way, but it made us appreciate our success all the more.

Sometimes when I start to wonder whether we did the right thing by computerizing early in our business life, I look at one of our major competitors and see that it still works with the old Cardex for inventory control. That's a throwback to the dark ages. The last time we maintained a Cardex was in 1965. That competitor has a long way to go to catch up and might never even attempt it.

I know of another company that literally went out of business by trying to automate too rapidly. Its chief executive officer, who came from a large computer manufacturer, decided to computerize the company in one year. He hired a huge staff of people who were very expensive, invested heavily in hardware and attempted to build a software package from scratch. The end result was that he took this $475 million company down to $350 million. Then it was put on the market and sold. It was the fifth-largest distributor in the nation at that time.

Now our investment in automation exceeds $10 million, and in 1989 we celebrated the installation of our 1,300th terminal. Three out of four employees have terminals at their work stations. We overcame every obstacle known to man, but today we have the finest system in our industry—thanks to an awful lot of hard work by a great number of people.

One recent event that showed the effectiveness of our system was the 1989 earthquake in the San Francisco area. Although it was impossible to get through by telephone, we sent a message by CRT and within an hour of the quake had received messages back from all eight of our northern California locations (including San

Jose and Oakland) that they had come through unscathed.

I get along quite well with the computer these days. I simply turned this monumental headache over to my son Richard. I approve the expenditures and attend the key meetings, but at least I no longer have to fight the daily battle of trying to understand the computer itself. By mid-1989 we had enjoyed 18 straight months of 98 percent up time, and response times in the branches of three to five seconds.

I still am very much involved when it comes time to buy yet another new generation of equipment. These expenditures, which seem to come all too often, generally come in $500,000 to $1 million increments.

BLESS OUR PATIENT CUSTOMERS

Not long ago I returned from a lengthy automobile trip visiting branches and met my family at our favorite hometown restaurant for dinner at 7:15 p.m. It had been a rather tough Friday, and I was exhausted from the pressures of the day and from driving through a rainstorm.

You can imagine my total frustration when at 9:15 p.m. my dinner was served—two hours after we had been seated. I was so upset that I told the waitress simply to put my food in a doggie bag so I could take it home with me, as I had lost my appetite. Because we're regulars at this restaurant, the owners came to the table to explain the problem.

It seems that they had just converted to a computer—as was evident by the adding-machine tape I received as a bill—and they were experiencing extreme difficulties in coordinating the orders with the production in the kitchen. The problem was compounded by the presence of a large group who had come for the Notre Dame game the following day. There was nothing but mass confusion over trying to get the proper information out of the computer.

Were it not that this is the only good restaurant in our area, and that we are such long-standing customers that we receive personal attention, I certainly would have been reluctant to return any time soon. I even suggested to my wife that we boycott the restaurant for a month or two, but of course that would only have penalized ourselves.

The point is that if I had had some other place to go that was equally as good, this restaurant would have lost me, at least for a period of time.

I couldn't help thinking that this is exactly what we subjected our customers to during our computerization, and it is only through extremely hard work on our part, good loyal customers who keep coming back and a system that in the long run has proved excellent that we have been able to salvage our business relationships. We sometimes felt that we were exposing ourselves to a potential loss of 40 percent of our customer base when we went through the automation process at a branch. We came dangerously close to losing many, many customers in the same way that restaurant almost lost me.

Thank God we're through the worst of it.

# How Banks Have Helped Us Grow

OUR BANKING RELATIONSHIPS HAVE evolved in much the same way that the company itself has matured. As the company became larger and our financial requirements greater, we developed greater capability and sophistication in banking.

I remember how grateful we were in the early days merely to have a local line of credit at the Farmers and Merchants National Bank. Then we progressed into our first acquisition, which required a correspondent bank to supply a portion of the funds. That worked fine until the participating loan portion became greater than the amount provided by the primary bank, at which time the participating lender started to dictate terms. Those terms were not always acceptable to us, and I blame the fact that the bank was not local and had no personal commitment to our relationship. At that point we moved to our second bank, the American National Bank in Kalamazoo.

We had a fine relationship. American National introduced us to the Prudential Life Insurance Company, which wrote our first long-term commitment at 8.75 percent interest over a fifteen-year term. This long-term loan was subsequently rewritten two or three times for greater sums of money, but also at higher interest rates, so the blended rate had been raised over the years to something in the neighborhood of 9.5 percent—still very competitive in comparison to the long-term rates available in the marketplace.

Eventually we left Prudential in favor of bank long-term lendings. The Prudential had continued with its rather restrictive covenants even as the size of the loan diminished, and we wanted to deal with a bank that was a little more lenient in its policies.

When we found that a larger bank in the state of Michigan could be more competitive, we moved from American National to the Michigan National Bank in Grand Rapids, where we were paying approximately 1 percent over prime, with very little in the way of compensating balance requirements. Then, becoming more sophisticated about financing, we put out our feelers for bids and received a fine proposal from the Continental Illinois National Bank and Trust Company of Chicago. After negotiating once more with Michigan National Bank, which mistakenly failed to take us seriously about the need to be competitive, we moved our line to the Continental.

After about two years, negotiating with Continental became more difficult, and, while the rate of interest improved slightly, its requirements for compensating balances on the commitment and the usage of the money became more stringent. Continental had fallen on hard times as a result of some poor loans in Texas and actually took bankruptcy and reorganization to continue in business. So we again started to shop. We rediscovered the National Bank of Detroit, which had been our very first correspondent bank back in our formative years. Finding NBD extremely cooperative and more competitive than previously, we moved half our line to that bank.

When we required a larger amount of long-term money for expansion, we converted approximately 30 percent of our total line to a three-year-term loan at NBD at a rate lower than the going prime rate.

We found it rather difficult to do business with the Continental Illinois, because at the time it had a very high number of poor-quality loans and had been victimized by an unbelievable number of bankruptcies, some related to the oil and energy problems in the Southwest. Continental received national attention for its huge losses and write-offs. As a result the bank became very conservative in its requirements. It found two rather insignificant areas in which we were not in compliance and told us that while we could continue using the money we had already drawn from the bank, we would have to fall into compliance before we could pick up some $3 million or $4 million more we expected and needed.

One area of noncompliance was that Prudential had not given us permission to report our ratios as though we were operating on a LIFO basis. We obtained this permission in writing quickly. The other area was that we had not delivered the required projections for some three to five years into the future. Neither condition would come anywhere near warranting the withholding of funds. Feeling that the bank had overreacted, we became leery of continuing with it. We severed our relationship.

The lesson we learned here was never again to do business with a bank solely on the basis of the individuals involved. We must look at the culture and ethics of the bank as well as the terms and conditions it offers. Continental changed every person assigned to our account overnight, and the new people, of course, had no understanding of All-Phase Electric. They were too busy protecting themselves from criticism or worrying about their jobs to be concerned about the customer.

I lost confidence in financial institutions one other time, in 1975, when we were in the midst of the largest single acquisition in our history, that of W.W. Electric in Springfield, Ohio. At the eleventh hour, our long-term lender, Prudential, decided against loaning us the acquisition money, and it was only through sheer hard negotiating with the Michigan National Bank on a small, relatively short-term loan of two or three years that we were able to swing the deal. Otherwise, we would have had to pass up what has become one of our finest acquisitions.

In a way, though, the long-term loan from Prudential was a fine thing. Our very large and long-standing agreement served to assure our short-term lenders that their agreements with us could be brief and perfunctory. They knew that Prudential was extremely thorough in its dealings, so where Prudential had a presence, other banks could relax their requirements.

One unusual aspect of all our banking relationships is that not a single loan is secured by any asset. That is to say, we do not pledge our inventory or accounts receivable against a loan. Prudential seemed to do business more on the basis of track record and personal guarantees and did not keep a watchful eye on assets. It makes a lot of sense to do business this way; it certainly allowed us to minimize paperwork and reporting. I am told that fewer than 1 percent of all companies have an arrangement as fine as this one, and it continues with NBD. In addition to NBD we also have lines of credit at Northern Trust of Chicago, Bank One of Columbus, Ohio, and Ameritrust of Cleveland.

## HOW TO TALK TO A BANKER

Over the years I have come to realize that bankers are not as sacrosanct as I thought they were back in 1959. I used to stand in awe of a bank's strength and power, but after the Continental Illinois National Bank fiasco, I gradually came to realize that some bankers have the principles of a used-car dealer or a Mississippi riverboat gambler. Their goal is to make money for their bank, and they sometimes sacrifice ethics and business morality to do so.

The experience with Continental was one we'll never forget, and in retrospect I'm pleased that it happened, because we learned from it. I also learned that when you meet with bankers, tell them only what you must to answer their questions. Never expound or offer further details. They seem always to listen to you with a blank stare, then run out to their car, grab their tape recorder and record everything you said for posterity.

I was amazed at items thrown back at me by Continental that I had mentioned over a cocktail or just in casual conversation. Bankers are always looking for your vulnerable spot and probably have files that are detailed beyond imagination. So now I record every single conversation I have with any banker, and I refer to these notes always in preparation for meetings with them. Of course, my direct meetings are rather infrequent today, because our vice-president of finance now handles banking negotiations.

The fact remains that the only time it is really easy to borrow money at a very competitive rate is when you don't need the money. Like lawyers, bankers have a narrow viewpoint. They fail to recognize the very basic precept of business: selling. They have no concept of how to go about making a sale, without which no business is conducted.

I am quick to recognize, however, that our four present lending institutions, and particularly NBD, are some of the finest people to do business with, and I do consider them true partners.

## FINANCING FUTURE GROWTH

Despite our ins and outs with bankers, we have never had a problem securing adequate capital for expansion, and there's no reason to think we can't continue the same type of growth. Assuming we are careful, we can tackle just about any acquisition that is reasonable. If, however, we got into a gigantic acquisition, we would need to come up with some sort of creative leveraged buyout. Either the seller would participate in the deferred payment or a lender would be brought in who might want some return on investment beyond normal interest charges—a portion of the profits or, in an extreme case, an equity position.

That also raises the possibility of All-Phase going public to raise funds for expansion. My opinion is that we would rather have 100 percent of a relatively small, growing concern than only a portion of a huge, rapidly expanding, publicly held complex. I feel extremely secure in what I'm doing and where the company is going, and I see very little need or likelihood of taking the company public. Of course, this could change if estate planning becomes a major concern, or if we were absolutely driven and compelled to rapid expansion and felt that it was worth giving up equity to do so. There aren't many companies in this industry whose acquisition would be worth that step.

# The Value of Planning

T HE GROWTH OF THE COMPANY HAS continued uninterrupted for thirty years, with only two exceptions. One was in 1975,
when for the first time we had a slight decline in sales; and the
other was in the 1982 and 1983 fiscal years, when we lost in the
neighborhood of 5 percent of our volume, and much more in
profits.

I felt bad about this, of course, until I started looking at industry figures. In fiscal 1983, which was calendar year 1982,
General Electric Supply Company reduced its number of branches
from 180 to 160, with a considerable loss of overall volume.

More startling, between 1972 and 1977, a five-year span, the
four largest electrical distributors dropped from 18 to 13 percent
in market share. And this was at a time when the fourth-largest
company was growing rapidly. Presumably the contraction of
Graybar, Westinghouse Electric Supply Company and GESCO accounted for the severe shrinkage in market share. During those
five years we doubled our volume, despite the bad year in 1975.
Today I estimate the four largest electrical distributors' market
share to be back up to about 15 percent.

No question, our rapid growth of the late 1970s and early
1980s was stalled temporarily by the recession of 1982 and 1983.
At that time we were using almost our entire line of short-term
borrowing; we did not particularly want to go back for long-term
lending when the rate was 15 percent, which would have made it
very difficult to make any money in this business. This was one
reason we chose to open new small branches from scratch rather
than acquire existing businesses. We located them in small com-

munities where we felt that we could expect larger profit ratios than in larger cities.

Despite those two setbacks, we have maintained our status as the fastest-growing electrical distributor—a fact that has immensely enhanced our image in the industry.

## A TURNING POINT

Someone recently asked me what I would consider a turning point in the growth of the company. I responded that our move into the South in 1976 was one of our most significant expansions. Until that time, we had grown only in the midwestern states of Michigan, Indiana and Ohio. Each branch city was contiguous. We didn't even leap-frog cities but stuck to neighboring towns so that we could shuttle merchandise between branches and exchange people as needed. We were considered a small regional multihouse operation with a nationwide network. With the move into Atlanta we became a multiregional network and caught the attention of large suppliers and customers who had considered us a minor force in the industry. However, we still weren't—and never have become—what I consider a chain. To my way of thinking the only "chains" are Graybar, WESCO and GESCO. I much prefer being labeled a large multihouse operation.

From our base in Atlanta, of course, we expanded rapidly into Alabama, and within eighteen months had a Southern District with nine locations.

Another significant expansion was our move into Seattle in 1978 with the purchase of a two-branch company, which we parlayed into a four-location network within two years. Then 1984, another great expansion year, was topped by the acquisition and opening of five locations in California in addition to another five acquisitions and start-ups in other parts of the country.

Our subsequent major moves into northern California, eastern Pennsylvania, Florida, Colorado and New England further enhanced the "nationwide network" image of the company.

## STRATEGIC PLANNING

The term has become a buzz word, but I started my own strategic planning in 1965, when I first forecast the growth of All-Phase. I have continually updated these forecasts, which I view more as a matter of goal setting than of predicting the future. We now hold formal strategic-planning committee meetings with everyone in management.

My first forecast, written in 1964, covered the fiscal year 1965. It set a goal of increasing sales to $3.8 million at a 19 percent gross profit margin. Some additional objectives were to keep competition out of Benton Harbor, so that we would remain the only electrical distributor, and to institute an "Inventory and Buying Guide" for our first two locations. We met all of these objectives on schedule.

In the same month I set forth a long-term goal covering the next five years. That called for a 1966 volume of $4.75 million and the addition of a third location, which I specified could be either Holland-Muskegon, Grand Rapids or South Bend-Elkhart. (It turned out to be Holland-Muskegon.) The 1967 objective was to increase sales to $5 million with the same three locations. For 1968, I predicted sales of $5.5 million, and for 1969, $6.7 million with the addition of a fourth location. In 1970, the final year of my forecast, the volume was to be $7.5 million with four locations.

As it turned out, we did even better. We had seven locations by 1970, with a volume of $10 million.

In December 1967 I prepared an updated forecast for 1968, predicting a volume of $7.5 million for the five locations we had by then (including Michigan City and Battle Creek), and for 1969, with a sixth location, forecast sales of $9.2 million. At this point we adopted the slogan "Seven by Seventy," a goal we reached August 1, 1969, when we opened our Sturgis branch.

## LONG-TERM FORECASTS

I wrote my first truly long-term projection in December 1968.

I did both a conservative and an optimistic forecast. The conservative called for sales of $20 million by 1986 at 17 percent gross profit, and a $325,000 net profit after tax. The optimistic forecast called for a 1986 sales volume of $28 million at 17 percent gross profit, with a net profit after tax of $450,000. As it turned out, my optimistic forecast wasn't optimistic enough. By 1974, actual sales volume was $26 million, with a net profit after tax of $665,000, so we exceeded our most optimistic goals twelve years earlier than expected.

Other aspects of that 1968 long-term forecast included a gross profit on warehouse sales at 20 percent and on direct sales at 10 percent, for an overall average of 17.7 percent. Operating expenses were thought to run about 14.1 percent, for a net profit before tax of 3.6 percent. Our sales per employee were set at $110,000, with a gross profit per employee of $20,000. Wages and salaries were to absorb 48 percent of the gross profit.

Today, a few of these figures would seem unrealistic. Of course, the first one that jumps out is the net profit before tax—today we're fortunate if it runs 3 percent. Also, sales per employee today should be at least $330,000, and the gross profit per employee should be at least $66,000.

## THE NEXT DECADE

In 1984 I completed a forecast carrying the company through the year 2000. It has two pivotal years—1990 and 2000. This time I did three projections: conservative, optimistic and realistic.

The conservative one projected 1990 sales at $250 million, with seventy-five branches; and the year 2000 sales of $500 million, with 100 locations and 2,225 employees.

The optimistic forecast placed 1990 sales at $500 million, with ninety-five branches and 2,175 employees; and the year 2000 sales at $1 billion, with 200 locations and 4,000 employees. In between, the realistic forecast called for 1990 sales volume of $350 million, with eighty-five branches and 1,500 employees; and 2000 sales volume of $750 million, with 150 locations and 3,000 people. It is my hope and dream that we can fulfill the optimistic forecast. By then I will have reached the age of sixty-nine and will be ready to accept some form of retirement and turn the last of the duties over to my sons.

At the time of this writing the company volume is at the running rate of $450 million per year. That's with a 100-branch network with 1,700 employees. So, once again, we are pretty much on target for our most optimistic forecast.

By 1990 I plan to start stepping out of the fast lane. I could then devote almost all of my working time to acquisitions, as well as vendor relations. I would travel extensively, attending all NAED functions, and try to become even better known within the industry than I am today. My job would be to improve the image of the company to the point that we would have an opportunity every time an electrical distributor was offered for sale. We also would have the best terms available to anyone in this industry from our suppliers.

Also by 1990 we hope to realize 20 percent compounded growth over the previous five years through a combination of internal growth, inflation, acquisitions and new branch openings. More important perhaps than growth itself is the ambitious plan of profitability, taking the company from its current 1.5 percent on sales to 2 percent. Along with that is the attainment of 4.8 turns on inventory, and accounts receivable days sales outstanding at forty-five. All of this is important, but perhaps the key item is the 10 percent return on assets.

If we could reach $2 billion in sales by 2000, we would be among the top three electrical distributors in the industry. While we are number five today, the climb over numbers four and three—GESCO and WESCO—will be long and arduous. The only way that this company will get there is to grow at a 20 percent rate compounded annually and attain the benchmarks we have set forth.

MARKETING PLANS

Strategies are valuable, and certainly we should pay them a great deal of attention. But when we're so busy fighting in the trenches and working just to get our share of the business, it's hard to worry about long, arduous planning and strategic meetings for the future. The banks require that we project our operating results for some five years in advance, and I'm convinced this is a good discipline.

However, developing a marketing plan is something entirely different. At All-Phase, it receives at least annual attention from every person in management. That is to say, at the beginning of every fiscal year, each branch manager submits a budget and a marketing plan to the district manager, who in turn submits it to headquarters for approval. This is the way we develop the overall company marketing plan and operating budget.

Our marketing plan deals more with market share than any other aspect of growth. We must be sure we are growing with the markets and not losing position. A branch could be growing at an annual rate of 10 percent and still not keep pace with the market.

We probably should have more confidence in our marketing plans and strategic planning. At one point we decided not to bother with any operation smaller than $1 or $2 million in sales volume. Whereupon we promptly opened new branches in Orange, Texas; Kirkland, Washington; and Escanaba, Michigan. None will ever attain sales volumes exceeding $1 million—or at least, the chances of doing so are minimal. I suppose my justification for contradicting myself in this way is that I can rarely pass up an opportunity, and when branch managers present a sound and well-thought-out expansion program, I find it very difficult to resist. This isn't all bad, because it does show confidence in our people, and they go away feeling very good about the company and their ability to influence so major a decision as that of opening a new branch. On the other hand, to be practical about the matter, we can have only so many small branches soaking up our management efforts and time. It takes almost as much corporate effort and district manager's time to operate a little $500,000 operation as it does a $4 million one—although we also have the advantage that they serve as training branches.

Our strategic planning portion of the business must have some merit, for I was recognized as Man of the Year for Strategic Planning in 1983 by a survey conducted by *Electrical Wholesaling* and based on interviews with 200 of the top manufacturers and 200 of the top agencies within the industry. We were the only company so recognized.

# CHAPTER VII.

## MUSINGS

# What Would I Do Without My Tape Recorder?

THE ONE THING I WISH FOR IN MY BUSINESS life is more time for thought and planning. Usually my only chance to put my thoughts together is while flying. That's when I reach for my tape recorder and start my mind wandering. The same happens when I'm driving alone in a car. I always keep a tape recorder in my briefcase, in the glove compartment of my car and on the company airplane. I have become so dependent on my tape recorder that I carry a back-up wherever I go, just in case the battery wears out or a tape is bad.

I have been doing this for the past twenty years. I even have a tape recorder and a note pad on my nightstand so I can capture my thoughts in the middle of the night.

I don't know what I would do without this hand-held tape recorder. It seems to make me much more creative than if I had to write everything in longhand. Just knowing that it's close at hand makes me want to pick it up and dictate a letter or a memo or a directive that I wouldn't otherwise be inclined to do. It's like seeing a telephone at the airport and having five or ten minutes before departure to call the office, just out of curiosity. I can never resist that temptation.

When I drive to work, I never allow myself to turn on the radio until I've searched my mind thoroughly for anything I can record. It might be a memo or a letter or just a reminder. I can't remember the last time I drove to work without making some note. Sometimes the resulting letters are very choppy, because I weave in and out of traffic while composing them and occasionally forget where I am in the dictation process.

I often take a trip by myself in the car or plane just to spend some creative time recording. One time I flew home from Pittsburgh on a Tuesday night, arriving at 10:15 p.m., and the next morning flew back to Pittsburgh for a meeting. The plane was bringing some of our people back home anyway, but I could have stayed overnight. Still, I wanted to pick up my mail and have time on the plane to review my files and do some recording.

That same week I drove to Battle Creek, Michigan, for a branch open house, leaving the office at 3:30 p.m. and returning at 7:30 p.m., having spent an hour and a half at the open house. The point was not simply to make an appearance there but also to have some time alone to dictate memos, letters and directives.

The best time of all is when I'm home alone, able to wander through the house with a tape recorder in hand, as I did while writing this book.

A great time for original thought is over that evening martini while I relax at home. Sometimes it's a little difficult to wind down from the day when I continue dictating like this, but the thoughts that result often are well worth it. Of course, thoughts are worth nothing if they're not put into action, so it's important to have enough time when I get back to the office to execute them.

## DULY NOTED

I am a copious note taker as well. Any time I conduct a meeting in my office or talk on the phone, be it with an employee, a customer, a vendor or an acquisition prospect, I write as fast as I can. I usually record these notes on a tape recorder and have them typed and inserted into the file or distributed. I always keep a tape recorder at my side, but out of consideration for the other party, I never record a conversation over the phone or across the desk.

My wife becomes quite upset when I make notes at Mass on Sunday. I always carry paper and pen with me, and invariably I make a note, usually during the sermon. I tell Eva that I am jotting down inspirational thoughts God sends me, but it is a little difficult to explain to her how this message from "on high" deals with the prosecution of a dishonest employee, or perhaps a needed firing at one of our branches. I've yet to convince her that it's God's providence and will that I make these business notes so I can be a better servant to the Lord. Strangely enough, though, these are the times when many original thoughts enter my head.

I've even thought how wonderful it would be to make a note underwater as I swim my laps in the morning, for I have many good ideas then too. Thankfully, they stay with me until I can dry off.

Any time someone meets with me and the discussion turns serious, I open my drawer, pick up a pad of paper and start scratching notes. It got to the point recently that a computer supplier simply stopped taking notes and asked me to photocopy mine for him when the meeting ended. This inhibited me slightly, but I decided to go ahead and let him read everything I was writing so he knew exactly how I felt about his product and services. Some things weren't very complimentary.

One of our major suppliers told me that it makes him very nervous when, at the start of a meeting, our people whip out a pad of paper and pen to make detailed notes. I told him that this should make him happy, as we are taking the meeting seriously and want to be able to recall everything that is said. We're not trying to "catch" someone in what they are saying.

There also are times that I'll be walking through a warehouse with a purchasing agent or branch manager and, after making perhaps my third point, I'll ask why he or she isn't taking notes. If they say they're committing it to memory, I'll say there's no way they're going to remember everything I tell them. I'll send them back to the office for a pad of paper. This doesn't happen much anymore, because everyone comes prepared.

One of my staff members asked me how I came to take such copious notes. My very organized wife made me realize early on the wisdom of careful notes for verification and reminders. Today I would be afraid to trust my memory to retain everything without notes.

I believe that writing a note is a better way to remember what was said, even if you don't later refer to the note. It seems to make an indelible impression on your mind. As a matter of fact, I seldom refer to my notes, but I like knowing they're there.

# My Love Affair with the Telephone

My WIFE, EVA, TELLS ME THAT I have such affection for the telephone that I can never pass one at an airport terminal without picking it up and calling in for messages. Realizing that this phone is my only link to the action at All-Phase, I can hardly resist the chance to be brought up to date. Also, I have made a commitment to my employees, customers and suppliers to be in touch with my office two or three times a day in case anything requires my input.

One time I was calling from the boarding area and Eva became concerned that I'd miss my flight. She walked up to my telephone stand and laid my ticket on the shelf. I nodded to acknowledge it and went on with my conversation. A few minutes later, I looked up and saw that the door to the boarding ramp was closed. I hung up the phone, rushed to the door and started pounding on it, hoping to attract the attention of the attendant on the other side. The ticket agent approached and said, "What in the world are you doing?" I replied that I had to get on this plane—my wife was already on board, and I could not miss the flight. "Sir," the agent said, "we have not yet boarded the plane."

I turned around to observe a crowd of people sitting there, looking at me in astonishment. Eva was staring at me with her arms crossed, wondering just how ridiculous one can get over this obsession to wait until the last minute to board the plane. I admit I was pretty embarrassed and slinked away to a chair where I hoped to go unnoticed. Needless to say, I didn't get back on the phone to utilize those last few moments.

Given my infatuation with the telephone, you'd think I would have one at my elbow constantly. I do have a phone on my airplane, but I have resisted installing one in my car. I know I would run up astronomical monthly phone bills while making numerous unnecessary calls. More important, I would give up the solitude I find in an automobile.

I also feel that car phones are a needless expense for our employees. I imagine nine out of ten car phones are abused and are not really essential. The rare instance that one might make sense is in a place such as southern California, where it is not unusual to get tied up in a one-hour traffic jam. What better way to use your time than to do some telephone work?

I might add that I think there is some hazard to placing a phone call while dodging in and out of traffic.

VOICE MAIL

When I call someone, I want a genuine, real live person at the other end of the line, not some mechanical equipment that tells me how to route my phone call. I detest voice mail so much that I have not allowed my phone to be programmed, even though the rest of our corporate headquarters has it.

The argument, of course, is over economy of operation versus personal service, and no doubt there is a need for this equipment, at least internally in our organization. After hours, for example, I want to be able to call my executive assistant and leave a message for her, knowing that it will be acted on the first thing the next morning.

But I never want a customer to have to deal with this type of insensitive, mechanical equipment. And even internally, we want to treat all of our fellow employees just as though they were customers.

## Pet Peeves

To MY MIND, CERTAIN THINGS HAVE no place in business.

I have always strongly resisted solicitations from customers, vendors or friends for charitable organizations, political campaigns or other fund raising, no matter how worthy the cause might be. I also become annoyed when charitable organizations or agencies contact our customers' purchasing agents and ask them to apply pressure on us to make a contribution. It's taking advantage of their position.

Nor should our own employees be lured into asking for funds from fellow employees, customers or vendors who call on us. No matter how convinced a person might be of the merits of a cause, he or she should not ask anyone to support it during work hours. It gets in the way of business, and we run the risk of upsetting someone. However, I feel that supporting something as important as the United Community Fund is our obligation both as a good corporate citizen and as a supporter of the community. I personally tout the merits of this program and am proud that we have hit more than 100 percent of our goal for eleven straight years.

Our company is continually receiving requests for contributions. We do donate several hundred thousand dollars in material annually to worthwhile causes such as Habitat for Humanity, as well as supporting worthy local causes such as the Community Economic Development Corporation, to which we contributed $100,000. But we want to choose our charities, not be dictated to by customers who might be offended if we don't back their favorite causes. That should not be the way a charitable fund is administered.

Also, no one should display political affiliation at work. I don't care if they're Democrat or Republican. I will not allow a sticker or sign on their desk indicating some allegiance to a political party, nor can I condone involvement in anything political that could lead to controversy. You never know what the sentiments of your customers, vendors and fellow employees might be, and we don't want to offend anyone.

We've learned that it isn't even a good idea to display a decal or bumper sticker supporting some college or professional sports team. One time in Greenville, South Carolina, we were planning an open house and were going to use a tiger in the announcement to represent the Clemson University Tigers. When I discussed this with a customer, he said we sure as hell hadn't better do that, because half the people in town supported the University of South Carolina and detested Clemson. We quickly changed the theme of our open house.

## ANONYMOUS LETTERS

I have no respect for people who write anonymous letters.

While attending Mass recently, I noticed that our assistant pastor was very somber and long-faced, and I turned to my wife and asked if something tragic had happened in our parish. Later, I found out that somebody had written this bright, young, friendly, smiling priest an anonymous letter telling him that he was too high-spirited and casual for some of the senior citizens in the parish and that he should act more godlike. When I heard this, I thought to myself how tragic it is that one anonymous letter can have such an impact on a young man.

I wrote him a letter giving my philosophy on anonymous letters. I told him I always look at the signature first when I receive a letter on plain stationery. If the note is not signed, I tear it in half and throw it in the wastebasket without reading it. If someone has no pride of authorship and hides behind anonymity, it isn't worthy of my concern.

## LITTLE DISCOURTESIES

I lose patience with people, particularly employees, who cannot remember names. It's a cop-out to say, "I'm not good at names." If you concentrate, you can remember a name; there is no secret to it. People think I have some special ability to remember names, but actually I just give it lots of effort.

I once attended an introductory Dale Carnegie session on this subject and, after going around the room, I remembered thirty-seven of the forty first and last names of the twenty people present. I tried to associate the face or a catchy phrase with each name, and sometimes I still do that. They called me in front of the class and asked if I had been through the course before. When I replied I had not, they said it was the best score they had ever seen from a first-time attendee, and the first time in memory that they could tell someone he didn't need the course. Still, I think anybody could do as well by paying attention.

Another pet peeve of mine is someone who knows what you're talking about but pretends not to in order to humor you. It's frustrating to go through an explanation and then find that the person already knew all or most of what you said. Some people seem to think there is something cute about saying they don't know when really they do. One should express as much knowledge as one has and not wait to have it explained a second time. Time is too precious a commodity to squander.

A small thing, but sometimes irritating, is to have messages or notes written for me on fragments or small pieces of paper. Any message or note that might become part of our records or files should be written on an 8 1/2-by-11 sheet of paper. Small slips of paper can too easily become lost.

I also find it frustrating to call on an industrial plant and find that the prime parking spaces are reserved for management personnel, with their names posted on a little sign or on the curb, while vendors must park as much as a quarter-mile from the entrance. I've always vowed that I would never allow any All-Phase branch to list the name of an employee on a parking space. I do, however, allow the posting of the word "visitor" so that a vendor or customer has space to park.

Although I enjoy a good time after business hours, in the office I insist on discipline and efficiency. Consequently, I absolutely abhor for people to bring their babies to the office to show fellow employees. We once had two baby demonstrations in one day, and three or four that week. It is infuriating to have a crying baby be the center of attention in a busy office—people flocking around, wasting precious minutes. We now have a policy against this. I even once asked my daughter-in-law to leave the office with her baby, although I love them dearly.

## BUSINESS CONSULTANTS

I have never been an advocate of business consultants. Here's an example of why.

The Community Economic Development Corporation was formed in Benton Harbor in 1988 to revitalize the city and surrounding area. One of four projects recommended by the engineering firm of Harland Bartholomew & Associates of St. Louis was to open the old ship canal from the mouth of the St. Joseph River to the turning basin in the center of Benton Harbor. I looked through my archives and found a headline in a 1958 newspaper article that stated that the canal was being closed upon the recommendation of, you guessed it, Harland Bartholomew of St. Louis. It is amazing that this company proposed spending millions to close the canal and then proposed spending millions to reopen it. It just depended on what the local administration wanted to hear.

## LITTLE SECRETS

I don't like to have things kept from me, even for a short time. I want to be informed of anything that's going on that affects the company, or for that matter, my personal life.

I'll never forget the morning fifteen or twenty years ago when

# LIGHTNING STRIKES ONCE

I was driving the children to school and heard on the radio that the Central Docks had burned to the ground. This was a complex of buildings on the St. Joseph River ship canal owned by our family for many, many years. I couldn't believe my ears, and I asked the children to be quiet and listen. They said, "Oh, we forgot to tell you. Mother received a phone call last night from Uncle Pat that the docks were burning."

I asked why Eva hadn't told me, and they said I was sleeping so soundly that she thought I needed a good night's sleep. I still couldn't believe it. But as I crossed the bridge, sure enough, there was the burned-out superstructure of these buildings. I've thought about that often and regretted that my wife didn't tell me that something so important as this was happening—especially knowing my love of fires.

# Governmental Nonsense

I COULD WRITE AN ENTIRE BOOK on the government's interference in business, so I'll scarcely get into it here. It only gets my ire up.

I will say that the rule that favors small business in government contracts is one of the most unjust I have ever encountered. All-Phase is no longer a small business, and it seems to me we're being punished for our success. We've lost the opportunity even to quote some jobs, and we have lost some traditional business with military bases.

Gulfport Electric had been servicing the Naval Air Station in Biloxi, Mississippi, and when we bought the company we had great difficulty in retaining that account. We succeeded only through the cooperation of the people at the base, who convinced their superiors we were still operating the company as a private corporation. We got away with it until my competitor blew the whistle on me. I thought that was an underhanded way for him to try to secure more business. (Subsequently, he was purchased by a large French company, so he too is no longer a small business. I suppose I should inform the government of this, but I don't want to play the game that way.)

I find it totally and unreasonably unfair that we are not permitted to service much of the government. We have worked all of our lives to become larger and more successful, only to find that the federal government chooses to penalize large corporations. We have paid taxes, hired people, kept people off the unemployment rolls, progressed in the good old traditional American way, only to find that we've grown beyond what the government considers acceptable limits of doing business. I fail to understand this restriction.

I wrote to the United States government—my letter was reprinted in *Electrical Wholesaling*—and said if the government wanted me to become a small business again, I could lay off half our people, force them to go on unemployment, and close half our branches. Of course, I would never do it, but I wanted to make the point that the law is unfair.

To give another example of government interference in business, I was surprised and disappointed recently to find that we now are required to keep our books of record on a computer tape for IRS audit. What would they do if we didn't have a computer system? We must keep this information intact for the IRS for whatever years we are open to audit. Now, that's what I call forcing a company to do the government's work at our expense. It's bad enough that we're subject to harassment in the audit, but now we must help them do their job.

Some of the laws on worker's compensation, vacation pay, unemployment liability, COBRA and so on in such liberal states as California and Washington drive me crazy. There is no reasoning with these people. We have to accept their decision, and that pains me greatly when I can't even argue it. But that's the way business is conducted today, and I certainly don't want to grow old fighting the system.

The other rules under which we must operate are too numerous to list here. Suffice it to say that we have an entire staff who do nothing but defend our company against government intervention.

WHAT TAX BREAKS?

My father made me appreciate the finer things of life by putting me to work at a very early age. He taught me the value of a dollar and how hard work pays off. The government has done me a similar favor by making me earn everything I get, with no tax breaks. I guess this just makes me want to work all the harder to prove that I can do it on my own, with nobody's help—much less the government's.

I saw what a handout could do to a community. I sat back and observed the millions of dollars that the state and federal government poured into my hometown of Benton Harbor, only to see it frivolously wasted on welfare benefits and programs that netted not one single ounce of community growth. As a matter of fact, the money acted as a cancer that ate away at my city and finally brought it to its knees. I am not saying that it cannot recover, but if and when it does, it will be on its own merits and from within, rather than because of outside help.

When I heard that Sears had accepted a $60 million tax break to keep its 6,000 employees in the state of Illinois, I really began to wonder. Now, mind you, I do not blame Sears for accepting this offering. I blame the state of Illinois for making such gigantic concessions to keep a company within its borders. I myself would not have accepted such a gift on a silver platter. I would have been so ashamed to expect my fellow taxpayers to support me in business that I would never have been able to save face in the local community.

The government made it easy for me because it never offered my company any money. You see, we fall into a distinct class as a wholesaler. We are discriminated against because we are not a manufacturer and, generally speaking, only manufacturing firms get tax breaks. We have never, in our entire business life, been granted any tax concession, to my knowledge.

While I might sound bitter over this, truly I am not. I do wish, however, that the government would stay out of my hair. I do not need its financial assistance; but I sure do not need its regulations either. I ask only to play on a level field, and being discriminated against by the government because I have been successful and have been fortunate enough to grow seems to me to be a total miscarriage of justice.

My revulsion toward government interference in my business is kin to the disgust I have for a thief, an arsonist, a union organizer and the legal system. All five seem determined to destroy the independent businessman, but only if he is successful. If he goes the other way, he is protected by every bankruptcy law imaginable. Bankruptcy is another thing that makes me see red, particularly when companies can declare bankruptcy on Friday and open up under a new name on Monday. These laws absolutely must be changed.

This world at times seems so turned upside down that I sometimes worry about my grandchildren and their children and wonder what God has wrought for us. Will we somehow pick ourselves up by our bootstraps and make something of this business world, or will we let all of the negative elements overpower us? For my money, there is no question in the matter. We shall overcome all obstacles, but only because of our self-determination and heritage; and no thanks to that withering, crippled, helping hand that someone extends to us.

# The Greatest Threats to Business

THE THREAT OF LEGAL ACTION IS THE single greatest pitfall the businessman faces today. At issue might be age or race discrimination, sexual harassment, unfair labor practices, restraint of trade, price fixing—the list could go on and on.

What surprises me is that for the first twenty years of our corporate existence, from 1959 through 1979, not one single suit was filed against our company—not by an employee, not by a manufacturer, not because of a product failure, not by a competitor or a customer—nothing. Then the roof caved in, and now we have suits at the rate of perhaps one every month. I just don't know or understand what has happened to our society.

No hour of any business day goes by that we (or any company) could not be susceptible to some sort of suit. This is the case because in complying with some laws to the letter, you actually end up breaking other laws. It is so grave a problem that I have to ask myself whether we really want to grow to the point where we draw more attention to ourselves, have more employees, have greater sales and represent more manufacturers, thus risking greater exposure to lawsuits.

I used to be proud that our volume grew so quickly and that we're the fastest-growing electrical distributor in the United States. But size today seems to be a detriment when it comes to the law. The bigger you are, the more vulnerable you are. People naturally think that big corporations make a lot of money, that they should share it with the have-nots, and that a lawsuit is the best way to make that happen. This is commonly called the "deep pocket" theory.

If this litigiousness isn't corrected, our entire society will decay. The Supreme Court someday will have to straighten out the situation. Until it does, all we can do is advise our people to do the right things, say the right things, conduct themselves properly and avoid potentially damaging situations, even if it costs us some sales and profits. I do caution people, though, that the only way not to have exposure is to take no risks and, in the end, do nothing—but we certainly don't want that either. If we ever are faced with a suit, we are committed to fighting it in the courts to the very end.

## CASES IN POINT

We have had many experiences that justify such a policy. One involved a female employee in Seattle who was a prime suspect in the case of two thefts of cash, both exceeding $300. She worked in the credit and collection department and was the only individual who had access to a deposit on the day the money had been stolen. When confronted, she agreed to take a polygraph test, but when she arrived at the polygrapher's office, she claimed nervousness and claustrophobia and refused to take the test. She returned to work, and of course there was nothing we could do to influence her to take the test.

After two or three months, her frequent absenteeism gave us cause to let her go. She then went to the state human-rights agency and filed a grievance against our company for sexual harassment, stating that our quotations clerk had told an off-color joke to our credit manager in her presence and that the credit manager should have stopped the clerk from telling it.

What she requested was rather nominal, but it's the principle of the thing that bothers me. She asked for $1,000, plus one month's back pay, plus—and this really hurts—a letter of recommendation. We lost the case and had to do it. In effect the state of Washington was saying to us, "Look, even though you may suspect her of stealing, we want you to give her not only a cash settlement but a letter of reference so that she can victimize some unsuspecting company again in the future.'' To me, this was ludicrous.

We faced a race-discrimination suit in Muskegon, Michigan, where we placed a minority person in an outside sales position. When he didn't work out, he asked to return to his inside job. Because it had been filled, we offered to transfer him into another area. He refused and finally left the company. Contending that we forced his release, he asked for a settlement involving money and back pay. We had to pay.

The granddaddy of them all, the one we'll always remember with horror, is the suit we lost in Louisiana to a bankrupt company by the name of BECO, of Monroe. The suit was for defamation of character, unfair business practices and breach of contract. It all centered around the fact that we had been misled by a corporation that was headed for insolvency, and when we proceeded to evaluate its assets, we found it to be in a bankrupt condition, and we did not complete the purchase agreement.

Even though we obtained a release from BECO's attorney, which we thought absolved us from any future problems, the BECO owner claimed breach of contract. In my mind, the jury was unbelievably biased in favor of its local company. We lost the case. The cost: more than $1 million. I could fill a chapter on this incident, but it is such a dark hour in the company's history that I would prefer to forget it. Suffice it to say that no one, other than the plaintiff and the jury, felt that All-Phase was guilty of any action that merited a suit. We have talked to local customers, ex-employees, vendors, even competitors, and to a person they have agreed that All-Phase was victimized by the judicial system, particularly as it is enforced in the state of Louisiana. Even the judge said to me, "It appears to me that this lame-duck company was flying overhead and someone finally decided to shoot it down." This suit is by far the greatest miscarriage of justice that I have ever seen or heard of in my life.

It appears that at least in some states a corporation has almost no chance of surviving when pitted against an individual. It's so much easier to swallow your pride and principles and settle with the individual rather than risk an expensive lawsuit. It's ironic indeed that the courts make it so easy for a company or individual to file for protection under the bankruptcy act. It seems as though the pendulum has swung so much in favor of the consumer and the employee that many people are going to ask themselves whether it's really worth the hassle to continue in business.

ANTITRUST LAWS

I certainly don't want to give the impression that I am opposed to all laws. I wholeheartedly support the Sherman Antitrust Act as it deals with monopolies. The government's enforcement of this act in our industry came to the forefront in 1983 when five Dayton, Ohio, electrical distributors were indicted for price-fixing activities between 1972 and 1978.

It is rumored that the principals of a company we later purchased were the instigators of this entire matter. It seems they intended to revolutionize the industry and called all of the distributors together with the express intention of putting some profit back into the business. As I understand it, due to the statute of limitations, these gentlemen no longer could be indicted; therefore, they had nothing to lose by telling all, and as a result, the other five distributors were indicted. One pleaded guilty to all charges, and the other four were found guilty and sentenced. This is a very serious offense, for the maximum penalty can be a fine of $1 million and three years' imprisonment.

This type of thing is not new to our industry. It hit the manufacturers back in the late 1960s, when several people from such prestigious companies as Cutler-Hammer, General Electric and others had to serve jail sentences for price fixing. In 1980, the wiring-device people were found guilty of price fixing, and some of our good friends spent three months in a minimum-security prison. Nothing, absolutely nothing, is worth the risk.

All of this brings to mind my one exposure to a similar situation when in 1963 I was asked to attend a meeting of electrical distributors at the Randall Inn in South Bend. I was quite flattered that they would invite a fledgling thirty-two-year-old electrical distributor with only one location to sit in with such an august group. After a pleasant lunch everyone retired to a motel room, which struck me as rather strange, as there certainly were other meeting rooms in the motel that would have been more comfortable for a group this size.

The conversation immediately turned to recent jobs that had been bid and the prices and margins that had been used in the quoting process. I remember vividly that one man stood up, telephoned the manufacturer's representative of one of the key lines and discussed his pricing policies on a recent bid. It didn't take me long to realize that I had been invited to a conclave of electrical distributors who had the singular intention of price fixing.

I couldn't wait to get out of the room. I don't know what happened eventually with this group, whether they ever did organize or have subsequent meetings; I only know that I never again attended this type of affair. It just goes to show how easy it is to get sucked into something unwittingly. One must always be on one's toes to avoid implication in any way with anything illegal. For that matter, today you have to watch every single thing that is said and every inference that is made, regardless of how much faith and trust you might have in the audience.

We must continually advise our people of the potential pitfalls they face every day. In the case of the Dayton indictment, I publicized the matter to all locations the very day I knew of it.

## PRODUCT LIABILITY

In terms of product liability, we do have protection, for customarily we do not purchase from any manufacturer who does not have a vendor/vendee product-liability endorsement policy. But product liability has become a very big issue in the last few years, and we must be cautious. Although the rulings rendered by judges and juries are somewhat more reasonable today than they were a couple of years ago, it's still an area of grave concern. We have to be very careful about what we say or do regarding merchandise sold to our customers.

We even have to be careful in moving merchandise into a customer's car or truck; the ideal situation is to carry the merchandise to the vehicle but not place it inside. We recently had a customer who claimed that a fluorescent lamp broke in transit and that phosphor got into his eyes. He said it could have been the result of faulty packing within the vehicle by our clerk.

We also have to be practical and careful about how we recommend things, including product substitutions. If we suggest that a customer use another product—assuming, of course, it's equal to the one ordered—we have to be careful not to say it's the same, because generally it just isn't. I would rather be overly cautious, even to the point of losing a sale, than lay ourselves open for a product liability suit.

One thing that really bothers me on court cases and trials is that in product-liability cases the trial lawyers retain 41 cents of every dollar awarded in judgments. To my way of thinking, that is ridiculous.

There was a $6 million verdict against the Eli Lilly Company in which the plaintiff's attorney argued that punitive damages were necessary to punish Lilly because that was the only message that "a lifeless, bloodless corporation could understand." It is a real shame that anybody would feel this way about a company; but sadly enough, the jurors bought it. If that kind of thinking is allowed to prevail, we don't have a chance. That is why it's so important to support business and corporations whenever the opportunity arises.

We should particularly try to educate students of today on the need for profits and growth in the corporate life. It's the only way that the great American enterprise system can survive.

## EMPLOYEES GONE SOUR

Another threat we face is the awesome one of employee theft and malice. It ranges all the way from the disgruntled ex-employee who caused a $1 million fire in Grand Rapids, Michigan, back in the early 1980s to the ex-employee in Monroe, Louisiana, who has shot out our bay windows five times. We know who he is, and we fingered him to the local authorities. They provided us with some surveillance at taxpayers' expense, but it continued to happen until we finally closed the branch.

In the case of the arson in Grand Rapids, we knew who the guilty party was, as he told us at the time we let him go that he would be back to "burn us out." Although I reported this to the arson squad, they were unsuccessful in meting out justice because the man, when confronted at his home, refused to come to the police station for questioning.

I don't know why employees think they can get away with stealing from the company. Although we hold each case up as an example of unacceptable behavior from an All-Phase employee, and we highly publicize the fact that we will and do prosecute every single theft, it still happens. How can anyone steal knowing that they could spend many years in prison as a result?

We seem to face approximately one theft every quarter. The perpetrators have been not only warehousemen and truck drivers but also branch managers—people who absolutely have it made in this business life. I guess greed and cheap thrills could be the cause. Some of the same people also turn to booze, drugs and women for the same reasons.

Our system is somewhat to blame for embezzlement and theft. We simply grew faster than our system would allow. Only now are we becoming sophisticated in our internal-audit department. Our policy is that whenever we know we are in the right in a theft or embezzlement case, we prosecute to the fullest extent. Generally this elicits a signed confession and an agreement for restitution. I've always maintained, however, that when a person is confronted with a theft and coerced into signing a confession, the amount to which the person actually admits is probably one-tenth of what he or she actually stole.

Our security officer uncovered a theft ring in Huntsville, Alabama, involving three employees. One of them signed a confession for $12,000 and did, in fact, make restitution. The other two also signed and made restitution for a minor amount. My guess is that the theft must have amounted to $100,000 to $150,000. They were selling merchandise out of the back room—that is, opening the back door without anybody noticing and selling merchandise to favored customers for half the normal going price. They also were coming in after hours, getting merchandise for the customer and charging it to their own personal accounts. We subsequently had an additional theft of $100,000 by another Huntsville employee. I guess they just didn't learn their lesson.

To prevent this type of thing, our security officer travels throughout the network. We also use what we call shopping services to spot-check sales at the counter.

## Problems Mean Opportunities

I AM REACHING THE CONCLUSION THAT in my job there really is no end to the work. I am sure that I could work twenty-four hours a day, seven days a week, and still find something that needs to be done. It's just a question of setting priorities.

The same holds true for problems. If I dig deep enough, I could find a whole new set of problems to address at every one of our branches, district offices and corporate headquarters.

One characteristic I'm proud to possess is that I look at even the largest problems and try to find some opportunity. As someone once said, our opportunities are so great that sometimes they seem overwhelming.

I love trying to look at things from different angles. I received a phone call from an executive search firm in Chicago looking for an executive from an electrical distributorship who would work for a bank to give guidance and direction. The caller said this position would pay six figures plus bonus. He actually wanted to know if I would be interested. I told him that this would not fit anyone in my organization, but I directed him to an executive of a competitor of mine—one that I wanted to get out of the marketplace. When any situation appears, you need to look for creative ways it can benefit the company.

### CREATIVE SOLUTIONS

I believe that a great deal of my success in this business has been in looking at problems and never giving up until I have exhausted every viable solution. In South Bend, Indiana, we had a potential bad debt. We discovered that a lighting agent selling merchandise to our branch was a 10 percent stockholder in a company that owed us a great deal of money and was filing for bankruptcy. At my suggestion, we reached this man, told him we were going to look to the lighting manufacturer that he represented for satisfaction of this $30,000 debt if he didn't make some arrangements to pay us, and that I personally would contact the president of his company. He immediately contacted his president, told him he would be working out a payment schedule with us, and proceeded to make arrangements to start satisfying the debt. He certainly had no legal reason to do this, and his only moral and ethical reason was that he wants to continue writing business with us. We found a way to get this debt taken care of.

I get excited when I'm struck with a solution to a problem that I can implement immediately. One such idea had to do with billing. Before All-Phase became automated I was so concerned about errors in our billing that I dictated a memo authorizing the payment of 10 percent of the gross profit on all errors found by our personnel, up to a maximum payment of $500. I asked each branch to organize a work evening or weekend when they would bring in pizza and beer and all the employees would pore over the billing. I had nothing to lose and everything to gain. All of these invoices had been put to bed, and there would be no further checking or auditing of the results. Therefore, if we found $50,000 a year through this process and I paid out $5,000, I'd have made a handsome profit.

One August a man found a $24,000 error that had occurred the previous May. He got his $500 in his next paycheck. This one correction happened on Saturday morning immediately after I had discussed this idea with my staff. By Sunday afternoon we had made $23,500 profit on the project.

Another time I was very concerned about theft by some of our employees, yet I couldn't afford a shopping service. And we certainly weren't established enough (we had ten or twelve branches) to pay for the luxury of a security officer. Instead I found another way to dramatize and emphasize the point.

I hired a young man who aspired to be a detective and moved him through three or four of our branches, putting him in the warehouse and paying him $200 per week. He didn't turn up much, so I decided that on his last day we would play-act a scene at the Battle Creek branch. We arranged that he would take a pair of pliers out of the building when he went to lunch and would leave them on the seat of his car.

Shortly after lunch I arrived at the branch and had the manager walk me through the warehouse to meet new employees. I had him introduce me to this man, whereupon I asked him if it wasn't alcohol I smelled on his breath. Yes, he replied, it was. I reprimanded him severely for drinking at noon, because that was against company rules. Then I asked him if it was his car in front of the building, and again he said yes. "What are the pliers doing on the front seat?" I asked. He told me he had taken them and felt justified in doing so because his compensation was so low.

As we had arranged, this turned into a shouting and pushing match in front of the branch manager and the other employees. I scuffled with him and literally threw him out of the building. I guarantee you that word of that incident spread through the company that same afternoon.

# Ingredients for Success

EVERY ENTREPRENEUR SEEMS TO HAVE a list of ingredients for success. Mine looks something like this:

1. *Sense of urgency.* Every morning you must look forward to going to work. I compare it to sitting on the bench and waiting to get into the football game. The start of the day is similar to the first play. You look forward to it, and you can't wait to get started.

2. *Decisiveness.* Make a decision and stick to it. That is not to say that you won't keep an open mind to suggestions, but demand sound arguments before you consider changing your course.

3. *Ability to see problems as opportunities.* When things seem the darkest, you may be making the greatest strides. You make more progress through losses than through gains.

4. *Appreciation for details.* The big picture gets plenty of attention, but it's the details that make or break a company. "Watch the pennies and the dollars will watch themselves."

5. *Independence.* Do your own thing. Don't let your concern for competition consume your time.

6. *Ability to cope with stress.* Turn this energy into a positive. Be keyed up but don't get nervous. Turn your stress into aggressiveness.

7. *Positive self-image.* Have confidence in all of your decisions. Feel good about yourself. Act on what you feel.

8. *Willingness to be imperfect.* Do your absolute best, but try not to strive solely for perfection. Make mistakes, but learn from your mistakes and correct them quickly. The need to be right causes alcoholism, depression and drug abuse. After all, 90 percent of the time that you're on a commercial flight you're off

course, but you still get to your destination.

9. *Willingness to take risks.* There's no such thing as sitting back and waiting for things to happen. You have to plunge in. Always be on the brink. Remember: the greater the risk, the greater the reward.

10. *Good timing.* The economy of our country rides its peaks and valleys, and knowing when to make a move is critical. An entrepreneur also must live within the constraints of his financial capability, and this means easing off from time to time. That's just what we did during 1985-86, when we had a net reduction of two branch locations, having added only two and closed four. It was the best thing we could have done from the standpoint of accumulating capital and restructuring the stock ownership in the company. We got ready for the push of the late '80s when we added a branch per month over three years.

11. *Passion.* Pour every ounce of energy and all of your emotions into your work. Always ask, did I do enough? Did I do my best? Do every job as though it might be your last act on this earth.

12. *Communication.* Always be available to your customers, suppliers and employees. Never let them feel that their problem is too small to bring to your attention. Look for the opportunity for conflict resolution.

13. *Recognition of people's accomplishments.* In addition to a congratulatory mailgram sent to each branch manager on the occasion of a new record month, I also send a number of six-foot submarine sandwiches so they can celebrate. This type of thinking must be a daily, ongoing thing with management.

14. *Compulsion to pay your way.* Make a minimum of three times your salary every day. Maybe you did something to influence the gross profit on a sale or a cost savings. Everyone connected with sales or management must have this as their goal. And if you account for $10,000 in gross profit or cost savings today, you can't say it covers tomorrow's obligation as well. If you

can't claim this type of success today, tomorrow your obligation is doubled.

15. *Good luck.* Of course, no matter how thoroughly one plans, one also needs good luck. Some people seem to have a tremendous amount of it. True, sometimes you make your own luck. I guess part of the meaning of good luck is that you're always looking for opportunities. If you are aware of everything going on about you, you are ready to seize upon good fortune when it presents itself.

# The Blessings of Good Health and Energy

I HAVE READ MANY LISTS OF the qualities shared by successful executives, ranging from loyalty and dedication to ambition and drive. But I heard a new one from Elisha Gray, former chairman of the board at Whirlpool Corporation. He told me of a study of more than 5,000 executives that found that the single attribute most necessary for success was good health. A person cannot have the drive it takes to get ahead in the business world unless he or she is in good health and is strong. Only two of the 5,000 successful businesspeople interviewed had poor health.

(Incidentally, it was Elisha Gray's grandfather who, along with Enos Barton, founded the largest electrical distributor, Graybar, over 100 years ago. I am pleased to say that I have his grandfather's original desk in my office.)

I am blessed with an immense amount of energy coupled, thank God, with good health. I never feel quite satisfied unless I've put in one hell of a day's work. Very seldom is that day less than ten or twelve hours, and when I'm on the road it often stretches to fifteen or eighteen. I would never think of returning to my motel room in the evening to watch television or read a newspaper. I'll stay with my employees or customers until it's time to go to bed. I make every second count.

I have no tolerance for employees who leave work early or don't give me the fullest day possible. They tell me I'm difficult to keep up with, but I still expect the same from everyone. I get a euphoric feeling of accomplishment as the day progresses and seem to pick up momentum later in the day. (I never drink regular coffee, only decaffeinated, because caffeine makes me feel like I'm flying too high.) Eventually, of course, sheer exhaustion might set in and I'll have to stop.

I have very little sympathy for illness, since I have never been sick a day in my life (to date I have never missed one single day of work or, for that matter, school), with the exception of the time in 1983 when I had a serious operation. I find it impossible to understand how people can miss work because of illness. Of course, I worked many days when I shouldn't have, and perhaps I even contaminated those around me. I know that this isn't a good idea, but I still expect everyone to be at work every day.

I also have been very lucky in avoiding catastrophe. Although I am a fast driver, I have never had a serious accident. Once I was passing through Holland, Michigan, during a snowstorm with my children, on our way to an indoor circus in Grand Rapids, and a whiteout completely blinded me. When the snow cleared I saw a red light but had no time to stop. I hit the car coming through the intersection and totaled our convertible. Luckily, the children were buckled in, and we received only bumps and bruises, not even a broken bone. When I returned home to St. Joseph, we stopped at the Catholic church to thank God for seeing us through this ordeal.

Another scare came when I walked through the construction site at our new Danville, Virginia, building, leaned over to look through a window and caught a protruding jagged-edged board in my upper right cheekbone. One and a half inches higher and it would have gone through my eye. God certainly has taken good care of me and my family.

## MINOR AILMENTS

Besides that operation, which was open-heart surgery, only a couple of things have really given me trouble. The first was my five-year bout with torticolis, a condition that caused my head to shake and draw upward to the left. This illness was diagnosed at the Mayo Clinic in Rochester, Minnesota, where I have an annual physical exam. It became particularly noticeable when I was under stress or when I became conscious of it. I can look at pictures taken in the late 1970s and see my head tilted and drawn in an awkward position.

I dreaded getting a haircut, because my head would shake when the barber tried to shave my sideburns. Any public speaking engagement or even an informal talk before my own employees became extremely painful to contemplate. I had to fight against withdrawing from society entirely. I had moments when I felt that I just couldn't face people, but I always overcame them and fought hard to look natural and remain calm.

Finally, with the help of biofeedback and instruction from an oriental doctor whom I met at a Young Presidents Organization meeting in San Francisco, and who urged me to try some mind-over-matter application, I whipped this disease. Mayo Clinic has told me, however, that it could return. I do head and neck exercises religiously in hopes that it never will.

The second thing that continues to bother me is insomnia. Again, I try to conquer it with mental relaxation, but there are times when I absolutely cannot remain in bed any longer. I throw off the covers and bolt out of bed at all hours of the night, often after only one or two hours of sleep. Sometimes I become so nervous about my wakefulness that I can't even read, but usually I can overcome my sleeplessness by lying on the sofa in the study adjacent to my bedroom or walking about the house.

At times my insomnia works to my benefit, because I get up and do some work, think, read or watch television—things I sometimes don't have the leisure to do during daytime hours. These middle-of-the-night activities never seem to affect my work the next day. As a matter of fact, I feel that I do better work when I'm keyed up, although if I've had a very bad night I do feel it the next afternoon.

Of course, adding to my sleeping difficulties are the pressures of the day that creep into my mind, no matter how hard I fight to keep them out. I find it particularly difficult to stop thinking about business if I've worked late and retired shortly after trying to tackle some problem.

A few things do seem to help the insomnia—taking a couple of aspirin or an Alka-Seltzer or both, and sometimes honey with hot milk. More often I can put my mind at rest by thinking of something soothing and relaxing, usually involving my wife and children.

Recently I found something that helps a great deal. It is a wave machine, which provides the background sound of waves crashing against the surf. This is slightly ironic, since I live on the shores of Lake Michigan, but the machine comforts me and often lulls me back to sleep. Sometimes I turn it up a little too loud, and it awakens me during the night.

# An Unexpected Ordeal

ONE OF THE MOST TRAUMATIC EPISODES in my life began in early May 1983, on the eve of my annual physical at Mayo Clinic. I had just spoken to my landlord for the Atlanta branch building—a man who had befriended me during negotiations for this building—and he mentioned casually that since I had last seen him he had had bypass surgery. He had little suspected that he needed this operation but was very grateful that he had taken a stress test, which revealed the problem. He said I should have myself checked out in the same manner. Because I was going to Mayo Clinic the next day, I decided to have a stress test too.

When I arrived at the clinic, my internist said he was happy to schedule the test but saw no need for it. All of my electrocardiograms taken during previous physicals had shown no problems in my circulatory system. At my insistence, he went ahead with the appointment.

The next day, about ten minutes into the fifteen-minute stress test, the doctor stopped me and told me to rest. I thought I had pretty well completed the test. I was perspiring and fairly tired. The doctor told me to return to the internist the next morning for my results and to take my wife along. I thought he wanted to speak to Eva about some problem she may have had. You can imagine my surprise when he and the internist told me there had been some irregularity in my stress test.

Because it appeared that insufficient blood was getting to the heart, they recommended an arteriogram. This is rather minor surgery in which a dye is inserted into the arteries and heart. I said I had a very busy schedule ahead and couldn't have it done for a couple of weeks.

After I got some travel out of the way distributing profit sharing to my branches, we returned to Mayo Clinic. I checked into St. Mary's Hospital in the evening and had the arteriogram the next morning. What bothered me most was that after the operation I had to lie still in bed for six hours to allow the blood to clot.

At the very minute the sixth hour was up, I got out of bed and walked down to Eva's room, where she too was recuperating from minor surgery. On returning to my room I was visited by the doctor. He said I must be one of the luckiest people in the world because, while there was some blockage, blood was flowing through some auxiliary arteries and no operation was required, nor further medication. I went to the chapel that evening and thanked God for the good news.

But the next morning at my internist's office I found not only the cardiologist but a heart surgeon. They showed me the films of the arteriogram and were quite alarmed that the left anterior descending artery was 100 percent blocked, the right artery was 70 percent blocked and the circumflex was pinched. This meant there were times when the only blood my heart was getting was what traveled through the 30 percent opening in one artery on the right side. Then the blood had to travel across to the left anterior descending artery through auxiliary arteries (developed because of my exercise program, particularly swimming), and then feed blood into the heart.

They told me this was an extremely dangerous situation. One treatment to consider was balloon dilatation, in which they would inflate a balloon in the artery to flatten out the blockage. They didn't recommend that because the blockage was so severe that I could have a massive heart attack on the operating table. Another method was simply to go on medication, always carrying nitroglycerin tablets, but that concerned me because I spend so much time away from home or from my office. I could just see myself having a heart attack in some small, remote city and being unable to get proper medical treatment. This left only one alternative: triple bypass surgery.

Once again I had some commitments that would take ten days to two weeks to complete. The doctors allowed me the time to go to our national NAED convention in San Francisco. I also had committed Eva and myself to go to the Kentucky Derby with our G.E. friends. The doctors told me both would be all right, as long as I didn't get excited. It was quite a feat not to get excited at the Kentucky Derby, particularly when I had picked a winner, but I used restraint, considering the alternative.

## A SUCCESSFUL OPERATION

I checked into St. Mary's Hospital on Tuesday, June 14, 1983, for my evening meal and indoctrination. That is one part of the ordeal that I wish I had skipped. The movie showing what I was about to go through bothered me more than anything during the entire operation.

I was given a sedative and I slept well that night. I was particularly pleased that the hospital granted my request to be the first in the operating room the next morning. Not only did I want to catch the doctor when he was fresh but, more important, I wanted to get it out of the way, without the anxiety of waiting half the morning. I also asked the doctor to forgo his evening cocktail the night before. He said he would.

I was awakened at 5 a.m. for a complete body shave. Nurses plastered my body with a hair-removal cream, then had me lie in bed for ten or fifteen minutes to let it take effect. Then I went into the shower and, with the help of a wooden spatula, removed the ointment and hair. I took so long that they finally asked me to come out. They were afraid that the shot they had given me would take effect before I reached the operating room.

I was very pleased to receive a telephone call from our friend Elizabeth Warren at that point, reassuring me. Then, just as I was about to be wheeled out of the room, Eva arrived and we had a moment together. I reached the preparation room shortly after 6 a.m. I was hooked up with the necessary catheter and intravenous tubes, through which I was fed water with a liquid tranquilizer. The last thing I remember for the next twenty-four hours was being wheeled toward the operating table.

I'm told that the operation itself went quite well. However, after returning to the recovery room at about 8 p.m. (roughly ten or twelve hours after the operation), they discovered internal bleeding from the vein that had been taken out of my leg to use for the bypasses. Doctors had to unravel the stainless-steel wire that was holding my chest together and tie off the loose ends on the veins now being used as my arteries. In effect, I had a second operation. Eva said that the first sign of life from me was a thumbs-up motion that meant "I made it" twenty-four hours after the surgery. I don't recall this.

Immediate members of the family were allowed to visit me in intensive care once every two hours, and as I became more and more cognizant, I remember receiving a telephone call from my daughter Maureen, who was working in the Grand Tetons National Park. I don't remember much of the conversation, but I was delighted that the call was allowed to come through.

## A SPEEDY RECOVERY

After a couple of days of recovery, I was taken to a room where I made spectacular improvements. Daily they would remove some instrument that had been inserted into my body, or some coil of wire, and finally the intravenous feeding tube. I remember the delight of taking a wheelchair ride with Eva and my daughter Marla and her husband, Jeff, who maneuvered me around in the courtyard on our anniversary, June 20, five days after the operation.

Then I convinced the doctors I was well enough to go home, and on the sixth day they released me. Originally they had said recovery would take nine or ten days, so I felt I was three or four days ahead of the game. I almost overdid it after returning home, as I went right out into the yard. I was pulling a hose around to water the flowers when I realized I was being foolish.

I spent the next three or four weeks recuperating at home in the sun. When I was able to, I started going to Mass every morning, and as soon as I could I started walking along the bluff in downtown St. Joseph. The first time I tried I could barely make it to the bench a quarter-mile away, but I quickly built that walk up to a mile, then a mile and a half or two.

It was during this period that I really built my strength. I started to gain a little weight, although not much. I had dropped from 164 pounds to 144. It's amazing how a salt-free diet can affect you. Not only does it hold your weight down, but it also kills your appetite. I was pleased that I had been able to talk the doctors into allowing me one martini per night, but even then my nights were sleepless and long.

My son Stephen returned home from his assignment with All-Phase in Lake Charles, Louisiana, one month ahead of schedule and was able to keep me company after I returned from the hospital. We spent many evenings walking on the lawn and playing chess until 2 or 3 a.m., a great way to pass the night.

It was during this period of recovery that I decided to dictate these memoirs. Now here it is, six years later, and I'm still putting them down on tape. Although 60 or 70 percent of the work was done within the first couple of months, I still like to pick up my tape recorder and add items to the book.

## BACK TO NORMAL

I'm proud that I was able to keep my illness relatively quiet. I told only staff members and department heads and those closest to me in the company. I am sure that even today there are branch managers, corporate employees and industry heads who are not aware of my operation. I didn't want people to think I was vulnerable because of something like this, and I certainly didn't want them continually asking me how I felt or if I was getting better. I couldn't have tolerated that. I could just see myself walking across the lobby at a convention and being stopped by every person I knew, wanting to inquire about my health. Instead, I simply told those around me that I had been in Europe and had gone on a diet and lost weight. Some took that with a bit of skepticism, but I pulled it off.

A true test of my recovery was a trip to the U.S. Open tennis tournament in New York a little less than three months after the operation, then catching a plane that same evening and flying to Paris for a fiftieth-birthday party for my friend Bob Warren and a two-and-a-half-week European vacation with our son Ronnie and daughter Maureen. I came through that trip without feeling a bit of pain, and at the same time I built up my strength through lots of walking.

When I reflect back on this entire matter, I thank God for protecting me. I also have a great deal of appreciation for and dedication to regular, regimented exercise—particularly a daily quarter-mile swim in my indoor pool at home. That pool (which, incidentally, was featured in a November 1984 issue of *Forbes* magazine) has been a godsend. Swimming is probably the single thing that kept me in good-enough shape to save my life.

Finally, my appreciation goes to Mayo Clinic, not only for pulling me through the ordeal but, most important, for telling me convincingly that I was free to do anything I wanted with the rest of my life and for recognizing that I would anyway, no matter what they told me. I could work just as hard as I had previously and even participate in sports with the same fervor that I always had.

Although the clinic has told me that my triple bypass may last only fifteen years or so, I am comforted by the idea that if and when I need surgery again, laser surgery will be perfected to the point that one good shot in the artery system will hopefully clear any plaque. If it doesn't, I'll have another bypass. Having gone through it once, I certainly am confident it can work again.

## A CLEAN BILL OF HEALTH

At the time of my 1989 annual physical at Mayo, I was euphoric to find that all of my readings, such as pulse, blood pressure, cholesterol and triglycerides, were, for the first time ever, within the acceptable range of a person fifty-seven years old and weighing 167 pounds. I was taken off almost all medication that I had been receiving since my heart problem six years earlier.

On the stress-test treadmill, I was able to sustain 12½ minutes of vigorous activity, which was 30 percent better than the 9.3 minutes that would have been expected of a man my age without a heart problem. I was told that my daily at-home workout of swimming, stationary bicycle and Nautilus would be par for a man of thirty-five to forty years of age.

Since health is so important as we play the back nine of life, I was thrilled to be getting better with age. A bonus was that Eva was getting the same good reports.

# Four Men in One?

I ONCE ATTENDED AN NAED SEMINAR where the leader had us describe everyone in the audience in terms of one of four categories: friendly, thorough, enthusiastic and forceful.

The friendly person always has a smile on his face, wants to be loved by everyone and is pleasant to be around.

The thorough person is extremely accurate and detailed in everything he does; everything is in perfect order and very neat—he's the type who would have every pencil in the top drawer of his desk facing the same way.

The enthusiastic person is excitable, emotional and persuasive, uses a lot of hand gestures and has great ideas and confidence.

The forceful person represents Type A behavior: He comes on strong, is a leader, has great determination, knows exactly where he is going and will do anything within his power to get there.

We spent a half day determining where each person in the audience fit. The leader started by describing how these four personalities would check into the hotel where this seminar was being held. The friendly person would smile and say to the receptionist, "I'll take any room that you have in the house, and for that matter, if you sold my room to somebody else, just put me in another hotel close by. Go ahead and wait on others if you'd like. I have plenty of time."

The thorough person would say, "I understand your check-out time is 11 a.m. Can I have until 11:05? Here is my credit card. I believe you will find everything in order. I want now to discuss room rates and be sure we have an understanding on any extras."

The enthusiastic person would bounce up to the desk, saying, "Let's get checked in so that I can get to the meeting, where I can learn something to better myself. This sure is going to be a great day!"

The forceful person would start out, "Can you get me checked in quickly? I need to get on to my meeting. Just send the bags up to my room. You take care of the details; I have to move on."

This made me recall my check-in. I asked one clerk, who was busy on her computer, if she would take care of me. She told me I would have to go to the next clerk, which I did. I then looked back to see her finish her work and take the next person who came to the desk. She did not ask me to step back to her position. This upset me, because it was going to take me longer to check in.

The clerk I got couldn't understand who I was. She thought I was one of my sons who also had reservations there, so I finally let her check me in as Richard Kinney. Then she charged two of us the $350 suite rate, for a total of $700, rather than a one-time $350 per night. I became so exasperated that I asked her to call the manager, because I figured she certainly must be a trainee. I demanded that the manager straighten out the problem immediately. When I got to the room, I wasn't happy with it, so I called down and tried to get it switched. Finally, the bellman said, "I certainly hope, Mr. Kinney, that the rest of your stay goes better than the first half-hour." This, of course, would put me in the forceful category.

But as the seminar went on, I realized there are times when I certainly am friendly. I can put on a smiling face and appeal to a person who likes a friendly type. I most assuredly am thorough as well, as I like my desk and credenza top cleared every night before I leave the office. I even do my own filing of important documents, to be sure it is done right and I can find them. I often lay out my clothes for the next day the night before, and if I'm going on a trip I'll pack a couple of days in advance. It's my German heritage, I suppose.

I certainly am enthusiastic too, as I exude a great deal of emotion and persuasiveness in getting things done. I motivate people through leadership and excitement. I get behind every project and push it through with a great deal of energy.

Yet, again, I am definitely forceful. If I set my mind to accomplish something, I do it relentlessly with verve and determination and make it the most important thing in the world, until I have exhausted every ounce of my ability to get the matter resolved.

I guess I'm a rather complex person. I am never satisfied with the way things are, nor with my performance in the business world. I always strive for perfection—and that, of course, disturbs me, because we all know there is no such thing as perfection on this earth. It causes me anxiety and unrest. I cannot think of a time in my career at All-Phase when I have been completely at rest.

I concluded by the end of the seminar, as did the leader, that I seem to be all four categories wrapped into one. Of course, I use this to my advantage in influencing people. I turn on the personality that seems to appeal to the person I am trying to influence. I am not saying that I am a chameleon. I have very definite ideas, and those around me know that I have the courage of my convictions. But I am able to sense what approach is best for a particular individual. As was said in this seminar, "Do unto others as they would like to be done unto." That's easy for me.

# An Entrepreneur's Personality

SOME TRAITS OR CHARACTERISTICS of an entrepreneur can be less than pleasant. For example, I know that I have been guilty of vindictiveness. Yet I can defend it. A good businessman and manager must be a poor loser, to the point that if he has been victimized by a person or a situation, he wants revenge. Anything less would indicate weakness and acquiescence. Nobody can or should sit by and allow himself to be trampled, beaten, pushed into a corner and treated unfairly or unjustly. One must let people know that when such things happen, retribution will follow.

I am the first to acknowledge that the days of ruling with an iron hand are gone forever. But I also feel that it is essential to take a strong stand on issues, acting sometimes from principle rather than pocketbook. These personal characteristics become the personality of the company, and that's as it should be.

I become most vindictive toward ex-employees who have caused hardship for my company after leaving. In my mind there is no greater display of wrongdoing. One example is when people accept the All-Phase training, schooling and job preparedness only to leave and use their profit-sharing funds to go into competition with me.

I don't fault people for their entrepreneurial spirit, and certainly this is a free country in which everybody is entitled to try it on their own in the business world. But if they choose to do so, they should not take advantage of a company that has provided their livelihood and training. It's only fair that they move out of the area into a non-All-Phase city or out of our industry entirely.

## SEEKING THE ENCORE

I can never be satisfied with the status quo. What I most dislike in business is boredom. I'm fortunate that there is little chance of this happening to me, thanks to the challenges and pressures this industry offers.

Within twenty-four hours after a record-setting month, I start asking myself and those around me, "What can we do for an encore?" I expect everyone to do everything in their power to shoot for a new record, and of course I expect the same of myself. An acquisition is much the same. As soon as we complete one I refer to my book on electrical distributors, pick up the phone and start calling around the country to see if I can make another connection. I literally thrive on success.

# The GEM Award

IN 1988 I RECEIVED THE HIGHEST HONOR in my business career—the McGraw-Hill GEM Award at the annual meeting of the National Association of Electrical Distributors in Boston. The GEM (Ganzenmuller Electrical Marketing) Award, the first of its kind presented, was conceived in honor of my friend and business acquaintance George Ganzenmuller, who was the managing editor for *Electrical Wholesaling* and the "Electrical Marketing" newsletter for 41 years before his untimely death from cancer. The presentation is made to the outstanding individual within the electrical-distribution industry for the past year. (Formerly it was called the "I Did It My Way" award and for fifteen years had been given to electrical manufacturers.) I was overwhelmed at the marvelous, flattering manner in which the presentation was made. The Tiffany glass trophy serves as a tribute to every All-Phase employee.

I got a kick out of the fact that, when I was introduced at the awards ceremony, I was twice called a genius. Although I am a long way from that, I do apply every talent God gave me in driving my company forward. Through determination, I have maximized every ounce of my ability. If ever there was an overachiever, it certainly had to be me as I powered the growth and prosperity of All-Phase Electric.

Speaking of honors, I was pleased to belong to the Young Presidents Organization (YPO) for a half-dozen years. This was a very unusual and prestigious national organization whose requirement for membership was to be president of a million-dollar company before the age of forty. YPO is a fine organization that provides many opportunities to discuss problems or events with your peers. It sponsored some great trips and educational experiences such as the Advanced Management Program at Harvard and other domestic as well as offshore universities. We once even had individual pictures taken with President Reagan.

# A Sporting Chance

I DECIDED LONG AGO TO FORGO the male companionship of the golf course or racquetball court, although at times I envy those friends who meet regularly to play. Truthfully, though, the sports I most enjoy are those I play with my children, particularly golf or tennis with my sons. I enjoy those moments and the memories of them most of all. About the only other time I participate in such sports are events involving suppliers or customers.

For the past twenty-five years we have held an annual golf outing with the Square D Company and our friends from Tri-State Electric in Maryland. The SQUARE-TRI-PHASE event, as it's called, is a home-and-home event, meaning we host it every third year. We were doing so at our local club in the mid-l960s when I was seated next to the Square D president and CEO, Mitch Kartalia. He asked if I was still playing my usual lousy game that he had witnessed as my partner the year before, whereupon I responded that my game was vastly improved. I said I was playing at least three times a week and had a weekly lesson from the golf pro. (All of which was a fabrication, as I absolutely never take time out of my business to play golf or any other sport.)

Mitch gave me a disbelieving look, so I told him to check the handicap board when he was in the locker room to see just how much I had improved. Meanwhile, I had gone down and removed the two from my thirty-two handicap, leaving only the three on the board. It convinced Mitch, who said he was amazed that I had accomplished such a feat in just one year. Then, unbeknown to me, he proceeded to make a $20 bet with each of our two opponents, Walt Clarke and Jerry Thorpe, both from Square D.

On the first hole, a par four and relatively easy hole, I took a seven. Mitch asked me what in the world was wrong with my game and how I could possibly have used up my entire handicap on just the first hole. When I laughingly told him that it was all a joke, that I really still did play a lousy game of golf, he stopped the game in the middle of the green and demanded that I pay in full the two bets he had just placed. He was dead serious. I swear that if I had not paid them, he would have taken drastic action that would have affected the relationship between our two companies. Mitch is a great guy but a very determined individual. The last thing he ever wanted was for someone to put something over on him. Needless to say, my practical jokes on Mitch Kartalia ended that afternoon.

## ALL IN THE GAME

The only kind of event that completely takes my mind off business is an exciting spectator sport. I find football most absorbing, with college ball taking precedence over the pros. Nothing compares to a Saturday afternoon at the Notre Dame stadium, particularly when the team is having an undefeated season and I'm entertaining some customer. Then I am not only doing my job for All-Phase but also enjoying myself tremendously.

I have always wanted to spend more time on football. Among our branches we probably have a block of season tickets to six or eight NFL professional football teams, and I have yet to use one ticket for myself. However, I have attended an occasional professional baseball game using All-Phase tickets. The primary purpose of these tickets is to entertain customers, and always in the company of an All-Phase employee. These arrangements generally are made well in advance—far before I think to work a game into my schedule.

I would like to reach the point in life where I could spend a great deal of my time attending the top sporting events in the country. I have listed ten such events, and I hope that some day

I might be able to negotiate with different suppliers to make annual trips to each of them. I've attended them all already, but my goal is to do so every year:

- Rose Bowl football game.
- Super Bowl football game.
- NCAA final-four basketball championship weekend.
- Masters Golf Tournament.
- Kentucky Derby.
- Indianapolis 500.
- Stanley Cup hockey finals.
- NBA final playoff game.
- U.S. Tennis Open.
- Baseball World Series final game.

Of course, I would also like to attend the winter and summer Olympics every four years.

The reason it is so important to negotiate these with suppliers is that without the proper contacts, it would be impossible to get tickets for these events. I would consider it the epitome of my negotiating career to be able to attend all of them. The ones I am presently attending almost every year are the Rose Bowl, Super Bowl, Kentucky Derby and U.S. Tennis Open.

# *CHAPTER VIII.*

## BUILDING FOR THE FUTURE

# *Our Silver Anniversary*

W̲E OBSERVED THE TWENTY-FIFTH anniversary of All-Phase Electric in 1984. It was a marvelous opportunity to ballyhoo the hell out of the company. I gave my secretary and our personnel administrator three double-spaced, typewritten pages of ways I wanted to celebrate the event. Most of them centered around customer appreciation in the form of an extra-special open house at every branch—perhaps a dinner that I personally could attend. I spent most of 1984 traveling throughout the country visiting branches and celebrating the anniversary.

Just as important as acknowledging customers was the marvelous opportunity to let our employees know how much we appreciated their service to the company and their dedication to duty.

I actually developed a calloused hand in 1984 simply from shaking hands with so many people. I calculated that in my visits to the seventy branches we then had, the one national and four regional NAED conventions, the nine new branches added in that year, the NECA convention, the vendor-appreciation dinners and the many, many other events that year, I shook hands with 25,000 people.

Never in our history had we received the kind of exposure we did in our twenty-fifth year. I have been told many times that we carry the highest image in the electrical-distribution industry. That, of course, is what I have strived for all these years and is probably the single most important thing to me in building a future for this company.

# Our Thirtieth Anniversary

ONE OF THE THINGS I ENJOY MOST is motivating our people to do the very best they can and to be the very best person they can be. I like to think I bring out the best in them.

So I was especially pleased when at AMP VI in 1989 one of the highlights was a surprise thirtieth-anniversary party for me. Unbeknown to me, my staff and family had put together an audiovisual program detailing the origin and growth of the company. What made it extra special was the participation of each of my six children in the video. They related fond memories of their youth spent with me and All-Phase Electric. To cap the event, my daughter Maureen pinned a thirty-year service pin on my lapel.

It was a great evening that inspired me to refer to all of our employees as family. We adopted that theme for the balance of the conference and, in my final address to the assembly, we ended with the song "We Are Family" playing in the background. Everyone gave me a standing ovation—it was an extremely emotional moment.

I showed the anniversary videotape to our employees at a subsequent Break Plus. I could see many of the employees had the same emotional reaction as I did. I told everyone that while this piece honored me, it truly was honoring all employees, because it paid great tribute to the company. I said all of the employees have more than a job at All-Phase and even more than a career—they are members of our family, part of a close-knit group who depend on one another for success. I received rousing applause. At the end of the session I shook hands with everyone and gave each one a copy of the current *Electrical Wholesaling* in which we had been featured. I also took that opportunity to distribute profit-sharing certificates as well as service awards. It undoubtedly was the best Break Plus ever.

Two weeks later we had our first President's Ring Club award trip, where we recognized fifty-seven of our top salespeople and their spouses by taking them on a five-day trip to Phoenix. I was amazed at how enthusiastically our people accepted this award. About half a dozen wives had never flown before, and almost no one in the group had been in Phoenix. They had a tremendous time, topped by the ring presentation on the final evening.

The ring itself has a diamond for each year that the salesperson hits a certain volume level. We recognized one salesman for a truly outstanding accomplishment: For the first time in the history of the company, he personally had accounted for more than $1 million in gross profit in a year. Considering that a typical All-Phase branch in its entirety reaches only $1 million in a year, it was an amazing personal achievement.

People have raved about the trip ever since. Our plan is to raise the bogey for the President's Ring award trip, making it increasingly difficult for a salesperson to capture the prize. That spurs them on to bigger and better things. We have seen sales accomplishments never before dreamed of. I credit much of that to the fact that the spouses got behind our program and urged their husbands and wives to get out there and make those sales calls.

Also as part of the thirtieth-anniversary year, Eva and I hosted many of the district managers, district sales managers, branch managers, management trainees and district staff members with weekend celebrations in several of the districts. Typically the event involved a sporting event such as golf, tennis, deep-sea fishing or snorkeling plus sightseeing on Saturday afternoon, then a rather formal cocktail party and dinner followed by theater or dancing. We all stayed overnight at a deluxe resort hotel and concluded the following morning with brunch.

We find that including spouses in a relaxed and elegant atmosphere contributes greatly to morale and enthusiasm within the company. This was the first time we had the opportunity to meet many of the spouses of our "heavy hitters," and it was a real pleasure to thank them for the sacrifices they have made over the years.

## "TWO BY TWO"

As part of our thirtieth anniversary, we hosted an elaborate luncheon that coincided with the NAED National Convention in Chicago in May 1989. We rented the cocktail lounge and main dining room at the Ritz Carlton Hotel and entertained 193 of the principals of the manufacturing firms we represent. It was the hit of the convention, and people said only All-Phase could have gotten such a turnout. We figured that this assembly represented more than $35 billion of the $40 billion in sales throughout the industry. It was such a success that we plan to repeat it periodically at future national conventions.

We have never spent so much money on entertainment in the life of our company as we did in 1989, but I believe that it was a very sound investment. We certainly garnered more than our share of good publicity and recognition with these promotions.

It was around this time that we coined the phrase "Two Billion by 2000," which means that our illustrious goal is to reach a sales volume of $2 billion by the year 2000, or "Two by Two" for short. We plan on doing this with 200 branches.

All of this hoopla has gained tremendous exposure for All-Phase, and it benefits us in every way possible. It helps us attract acquisitions, gains the confidence of our customers, instills in our suppliers the feeling that they are dealing with the finest and most professional distributor in the nation and, last but not least, gives our employees a sense of pride and participation in our growth and prosperity. Everyone comes up a winner.

# The Woman Beside Me

I WAS PLEASED AND COMPLIMENTED once in San Francisco when a supplier called me "predatory" after he heard me explain my plan to capture a certain market in northern California. I was so taken by the label that the next day I went out with Eva looking for something I could identify with, either a painting or a sculpture of a bird of prey. At Gumps we found a brass figure of an osprey mounted on Plexiglas. It was perfect: An osprey is also called a bone crusher. This work of art stands on the credenza in my office today.

I also felt that the bird symbolized a Bette Midler song lyric I like to paraphrase about my wife: "You are the wind beneath my wings, and you provide the power for me to soar to great heights."

While I consider myself a professional, Eva is more professional in her field—that of a homemaker—than anyone I have ever seen. She excels at whatever she puts her mind to, making a point of learning all she can about a given area of interest, be it travel or cuisine or a particular author.

Raising our six children, providing a warm, loving family atmosphere for all of us, keeping me on the straight and narrow in earlier life and looking out for my health—all are elements of the job she does so very well. The wonderful thing is that she has never wanted to do anything other than this. Despite my constant encouragement to enter other fields, such as running a travel agency or writing a book on good restaurants, lodging and travel, she continues with the full-time job of running the house and assisting with my personal affairs. From a business standpoint I depend upon her to review my correspondence and speeches, make

362

travel and entertainment arrangements and decorate offices, as well as many other important duties. I even bounce some business ideas off her and usually get a very analytical response.

An excellent judge of character, she is the person who can most influence my opinion of people. For the most part I like people. I tend to see their best side and overlook their flaws. This is a bit of a problem for me, as I am not objective enough in first impressions. If Eva doesn't take to someone, she always has a good, insightful reason. If she does like someone for some accomplishment or trait, I tend to like that person all the more.

Eva makes sure I keep my feet on the ground. She never lets me get a big head, and if ever I'm feeling the least bit boastful, she tells me to take out the garbage. That seems to bring me back to center.

One incident that indicated our individuality and independence occurred when we built our home on the shores of Lake Michigan in 1980. We had waited so long for it that I gave our builder and architect a deadline: I was going to move in on November 1, come hell or high water. And move in I did.

Unfortunately, the home was not quite finished, and Eva said she would under no conditions move until it was totally ready for occupancy. I moved with just a bed, sofa and chair, and she remained in our old home for an additional week.

As we reflect back on this, we get quite a laugh out of the fact that I called her every evening and even took her out to dinner a couple of times. She also invited me over for breakfast every morning.

## THE ROCK

I know that I have made a great number of sacrifices in the interest of my business over the past thirty years. I calculate that I probably spent eighty hours a week on it early on, sometimes ninety. Even so, I never fell into that chasm of family neglect. Again, the person I have to thank for this is Eva. Our children call their mother "the rock."

When the children were small, she would have them all fed and ready for bed by the time I got home, but they always waited for me before they retired. Although I rarely traveled when the children were young, I still returned home rather late. I never had dinner with them during the week, but we always had our weekend meals together.

I'm glad I spent as much time with them as I did while they were growing up. Thankfully, Eva insisted on it—even when I didn't feel up to the challenge. Every Sunday afternoon I would take the children off her hands until evening. We would go to the YMCA or the House of David Amusement Park or some other such place. Today the children hold those memories among their fondest. And every summer evening we held neighborhood football games in the back yard under makeshift lights I had put up. They still remember those vicious games of tag football, when winning meant everything. Further, on practically every convention Eva and I attended early in my career, we usually took two children along, in their turn.

Our six children have never, ever said they felt neglected by me because of my long workweek. That was because Eva was holding it all together and often doing the work of both parents. It was also because I never developed outside hobbies or a regular golf or tennis outing with buddies, but instead devoted all of my spare time to my wife and children.

# Our Children: Our Proudest Achievement

ONE OF OUR FAMILY RITUALS ABOUT which I smile today was the Family Council. Every Sunday morning after breakfast and before Mass, we gathered everyone together for a little program. I would read something from the Bible and then ask the children to comment on a current event they had read about in the newspaper, heard on the radio or seen on television. My intention was to get them involved in world activities and news. Of course, the overriding effect was to foster interaction in a warm, lighthearted atmosphere.

Two or three of the children always had to scramble to get some news out of the morning paper when they heard the council was about to begin. I then gave them a little talk on something like good Christian morals, and we closed with everyone kneeling down for my blessing. At this point they always thought I was acting a little too godlike, but events like this did a great deal to mold the character of our children.

When you consider that Eva was nineteen years old and I was twenty-one when we got married, it's quite astonishing that our marriage has prospered and grown over so many years. A lot of that can be attributed to the fact that we both are strong Catholics and always have respected each other enough to work out our differences.

We had our first child, Lisa, ten months after our marriage. Eleven months later we had Marla, who was followed by Ronald Jr., Richard, Stephen and Maureen, all born within ten years. With five children in the first seven years of our marriage, it truly is a testimonial to Eva's strength that she kept her sanity and good nature. She did all of this while I was starting a new company and devoting all of my time and effort to its growth and development. For the most part she went it alone. I guess that's why she weighed only 108 pounds in those days.

Eva has done the finest job imaginable in steering our children toward excellent private colleges. With her encouragement and guidance, all of them selected the type of college that best suited their personalities, goals and abilities. Most of the children also went on to receive advanced degrees. In this day and age it's quite an accomplishment just to get six children through four years of college, let alone private schools and graduate schools. Most important, our children had the proper home environment and education to prepare them for today's world.

Perhaps an even greater accomplishment is that they get along so well as brothers and sisters and support each other as they do. They are the best of friends. I observe them when they get together after an absence, and they shake hands and embrace—and tease. I truly love the affection they show to one another.

Of course, I would like nothing better than to have every one of them return to All-Phase. From the time they were old enough to sharpen pencils and empty wastebaskets they were at the office with me on Saturdays. During summers on through high school, every one helped out in various capacities—counter and lighting showroom sales, filing, data entry, warehouse stocking. Today each have individual talents that could contribute to the success and growth of the company.

But maybe things are best the way they are, with each having found his or her own career niche. I'm eternally grateful for the two hard-working, effective and successful sons who have joined me in the business. Richard and Stephen will carry on the tradition. The other four are enmeshed in challenging careers involving marketing, clinical developmental psychology, journalism and art.

I think of my friend who sold his $75 million company rather than make the tough decision as to who among the seventeen relatives working for him would succeed him. At All-Phase, the strengths Richard and Stephen bring are destined to be a winning combination.

## Passing the Torch

AT ONE POINT IN THE MID-1980s, I returned from an eight-day trip to the West Coast and found that my theory of spending one hour on paperwork for each day absent was shot to hell! I must have spent three hours for each day I had been on the road. That's how crazy my job had become.

All that week I arrived at the office no later than 7:30 a.m., took a half-hour for lunch and never left before 8 p.m. The only salvation, I guess, is that I took no work home at night. Because I was so exhausted, I literally fell asleep on the sofa right after dinner. Not only that, but after spending seven hours in the office on Saturday, I took a banker's box full of work home with me. (There was so much paper it wouldn't fit into my briefcase.)

It was a week like this—and they were the norm through the early 1980s—that made me long for the time my two younger sons would enter the company. After graduating from Stanford University, Richard received his M.B.A. from Northwestern University, as well as one year of law, and, after some travel and adjustment, was firmly entrenched in the company by early 1986. Stephen, also a Stanford grad, spent his formative years in the field training as salesman, branch manager and district manager. He joined the company in 1982. He too plans to pursue an M.B.A.

As all of us know, it takes a great deal of time and effort to learn this business. I see these two men accepting major roles in the company by the early 1990s, at which time I will be in my sixties. We then will work through the decade of the '90s together, honing their skills and giving them increasing responsibility. I plan to be winding down over this ten-year period until full retirement at the age of sixty-nine in the year 2000. Let's hope that's in accord with God's plan.

I don't know if I'll ever fully retire from the company. I would like to continue attending NAED regional and national meetings, as well as traveling across the country on the company plane, looking for acquisition opportunities. I've made so many friends in this business that I would thoroughly enjoy that type of activity. I would like to stay just busy enough to keep attuned to what's going on in the industry. Ideally, I would work perhaps half a day, from midmorning to midafternoon. We'll see if it all works out.

## MY SUCCESSOR'S DILEMMA

I was twenty-seven years old on April 1, 1959, when we opened the doors to All-Phase. At the time I certainly could not have begun to manage the size company we are today. We grew up, developed and matured together, All-Phase and I. Our philosophies and personalities evolved together. There's a special feeling when you start with nothing and build, but it's far easier than the awesome responsibility of taking this multimillion-dollar company today and developing it into what we hope will become a $2 billion corporation. Unfortunately, it's human nature that the successor to my job will never get the kind of credit his accomplishments will deserve, no matter how successful All-Phase becomes. People will always say that it got its running start under Ron Kinney. This myth will be impossible to combat.

# The Second Thirty Years

THE YEAR 1988 MARKED A TURNING point for All-Phase. We would have been good candidates for a Harvard Business School case study involving transition from the old entrepreneurial management to the new, second-generation professional management.

I am not saying that I stepped aside, nor did I work any less hard. In fact, I actually traveled more and worked harder than ever. But it was a transitional period in that many of the day-to-day operating decisions were made by someone other than myself, namely my son Richard and the other six corporate vice-presidents.

I had appointed seven corporate vice-presidents—in charge of administration, marketing, field operations, materials management, human resources and public affairs, finance and information systems—and relinquished much of the decision-making authority to them. As is sometimes the case, however, I spent a great deal of time handing over the reins of some of these departments to the individuals while at the same time doing my own work. I placed this additional burden on myself to continue to set a good work-ethic example for all employees.

The decade of the '90s and the twenty-first century offer so many opportunities that I am thrilled for my sons and their generation. This company has distinguished itself as one of the true leaders in this industry. No one can approach the professionalism and quality that we at All-Phase have attained. We are a half-billion dollar company with the management team ready to do $2 billion in volume. Everything from here on in should be incremental, with an ever greater portion falling to the bottom line.

## PERSONAL CONTACT

I have continued to distribute profit-sharing to every individual within the company—although I am slowly turning that over to my sons Richard and Stephen as well. For that matter, they covered a couple of the districts for me in 1988 and 1989. I will still always make the rounds of the branches. This is valuable because it means I continue to know personally all of the key people in every one of our branches. And it enables me to keep my finger on the pulse of the organization.

The employees also seem to treasure this time together, and I make a point of letting them know that there probably isn't another company in our industry employing 1,700 people whose president still keeps personal contact with every single individual.

## WATCHING THE PENNIES

In addition to the seven vice-presidents, we have had many other changes within the company, every one of them beneficial to our growth. For example, we now have sales managers within each of the twelve districts; a professional telemarketing program; a long-awaited remote order-entry system; a new 140,000-square-foot Regional Distribution Center that provides all of the inventory shipments for the thirty-four branches in Michigan, Ohio and Indiana; a state-of-the-art computer system so complete that 1,300 of our 1,700 employees have their own CRT assigned to them; human-resources emphasis on new management trainees, of which we have hired fourteen in the past year, bringing the total to thirty-six trainees; the movement of the company into the high-tech field and the hiring of seventeen high-tech specialists just in the state of Michigan; an emphasis on industrial automation in southern California, Rhode Island, Massachusetts, Ohio and Georgia; the addition of such new departments as Traffic Control,

Internal Auditing and the new promotion and advertising programs that received nationwide recognition recently.

These changes and our emphasis on professionalism cost money. I guess that's what bothers me more than anything—the fact that while we go through this transitional stage, it's still my responsibility to account for a good bottom line. We are spending money on the future, and yet we can't forget today. If we want to continue to grow, as most assuredly we do, our bankers and financial institutions have to see a good return on investment and reasonable growth. That's not always easy to attain when we spend millions on computers, software, expensive executives, travel and training.

I sometimes have trouble convincing people that the company no longer is run by the seat of the pants, and that I no longer shoot from the hip. I'm afraid that our managers had become accustomed to my tirades and demands that things be done a certain way and then my never following up. Of course, the reason was that I simply got busy with something else and had to move on. I couldn't come back to something to check to see if it was done and done right. They knew, therefore, that they could let it slide and they probably wouldn't be found out. With our added staffing, even if I can't follow up personally, a staff member or department or field manager certainly does. However, I do retain my reputation for attention to detail, and I think I surprise people from time to time by asking them about the smallest detail on something I had asked them to do.

## THE CASUALTIES OF PROGRESS

As the company makes this transition from one generation to the other, it does so with considerable hardship and grief. I certainly wouldn't take back any of the changes we've made, but I see some twenty- to twenty-five-year veterans deciding they just don't want to change their style. Some simply have been unable to accept the computer as a key element in business. I don't like to see people retire early or leave for another career, but I must admit that in every case the company was better off for the change. I can't let All-Phase be anchored with people who won't change with the times.

I never feel bad about a true veteran's leaving, as he or she takes an immense amount of money in the form of profit sharing. In many, many cases it exceeds $100,000, and in some instances $200,000. I feel that I have treated these employees very, very well over their career at All-Phase, and they too have stood by me. It's a mutual benefit to them and the company.

I worry a little about the work practices of the new generation. I am not speaking of my own sons who are in the business and do work terribly hard. I'm referring to the new core of people between the ages of twenty and forty, the so-called baby boomers. There is no doubt that they work smarter and make their time count a little more than my generation did, and they certainly make decisions that deal in multiples of dollars much greater than I did at their age. What bothers me is their demand for a private life and leisure time.

There are still a few diamonds in the rough out there who work almost every Saturday and take work home on weekends and never leave the office until 7 p.m. after putting in a ten- or twelve-hour day. But for the most part this new generation does not look favorably on those kinds of hours. I'm not saying that any of them works only a forty-hour week, as I am sure it would be rare to find someone within the All-Phase management group who puts in only forty hours, but I am saying that the days of sixty- and seventy-hour workweeks are pretty well gone. There is that school of thought that if employees really apply themselves and work to the utmost of their ability and can get their work done in twenty-five hours a week, why would you expect more of them? My response always is, "If they can do well and get by on a short week, think how great they could be if they put in a fifty-hour week."

During a visit to one of our largest contractor customers in South Bend, Indiana, I met with the retiring senior executive of the firm, who wanted to turn the company over to his son. He had a message to tell.

He had worked hard all of his life to build a thriving enterprise, and he fully expected his son to take over the business. He noticed, however, that this boy was working from 8 to 5. He told his son he would never be able to get the job done in that time, that to be successful in this industry you must work long and hard—well beyond 5 p.m. and even some weekends.

The son replied that he had his lifestyle to think about and was not going to make such a sacrifice. The father, in turn, started selling off the assets and finally lined up a buyer for the major portion of the corporation. Then the son said that if he had known his father was so serious, he would have worked harder. He wanted to begin doing so, but it was too late. His father went through with the sale.

The moral, of course, is that you can never get the job done by working only from 8 to 5.

## THE ALL-PHASE FRANCHISE

When I see people franchising any kind of enterprise, from landscaping to children's toys, I think surely there must be room in this world for the franchising of electrical distribution. Someday, if I have the time, I would like to investigate this possibility.

Although some of our manufacturers' lines would not be appropriate for mass distribution—because of their narrowly defined territories and basic requirements—there are enough others out there who would welcome this type of added volume.

Over the years, we have developed an excellent array of operating procedures and professional performance that I would love to share with hundreds of other distribution points, and franchising is the only economical and practical way to do so. We have some very marketable features, such as our excellent training programs and recruitment practices. Of course, the name All-Phase Electric is becoming well known nationally within the industry, and an operation would gain tremendous credibility by being affiliated with us.

The first step in analyzing this opportunity would be to assign a corporate vice-president the task of producing such a program. If we could drive the operating costs down through the use of our computer and other proven systems, I would think the economies we could effect would be tremendous.

It would be a lot of fun to take up this challenge, along with the opportunity to spread our name across the face of this nation.

# The Ultimate Satisfaction

BUSINESS IS A VERY FRAGILE THING that is susceptible to change. Like a baby who at birth requires an immense amount of attention and care, so does a company in its formative years. In one's teens one requires discipline and direction, and so does a company. In one's twenties one reaches maturity, and so does a company. It is also important at this juncture to be sure there is a meaningful goal in life.

In the thirtieth year of All-Phase, we set out to find new sights and strive to become many times over the company we were.

I am proud that we have been adding branches at the rate of one per month. I hope this kind of growth will always continue, and that by doing so we will be able to hit our $1 billion goal by the mid- to late 1990s. We certainly have the staff in place, as well as the computer and systems, to carry us to this level. We have raised our total volume goal to $2 billion by the year 2000, and 200 branches by that time too. I'm not saying we definitely will make that goal, but we most assuredly are pointed in the right direction, with all the tools it takes. This is exciting!

As I sit here on my patio looking out at Lake Michigan, I feel a great deal of satisfaction and fulfillment in my work. For many, many years I felt that the entire burden of this half-billion-dollar company rested on my shoulders. Even with 1,700 people out there sharing some of it, I just wasn't getting enough feedback on ideas and solutions to our problems. We seemed only to be performing the day-to-day tasks and not really planning for the future. But with a professional staff now in place, that is changing.

I still miss a few things, such as time to read a novel or just plain relax. As my wife said to me recently, she can never remember a single day in my career at All-Phase where I simply did nothing, not even dictate or write something down about the company. Last Saturday at Mass I had so many ideas that I thought about carrying my tape recorder with me and discreetly dictating notes, but I guess that's going too far. I stuck with my usual note pad.

You might say that my business has become everything to me—my hobby, my sport and my life—other than my wife and six children and my faith in God. Business will, thank God, never take their place.

It is time to set this tape recorder aside and consider these memoirs complete. Because I constantly feel an impulse to dictate something more, this could be a never-ending project. One New Year's Day, for example, I promised my wife that I would do no work. I wouldn't even read any of the business articles I brought home. I would not discuss business, nor would I do any recording. But then I found myself with a full thirty-minute tape to record my thoughts.

I enjoy recording these memoirs, but it has to end some place. So after six years, today is the day, and this is the final chapter. There could be no finer time to do so than 1989, when on April 1 we celebrated our thirtieth year in business. Since I am fifty-eight years old, this amounts to more than half of my life. It has certainly been the happiest thirty years anyone could hope to have, filled with accomplishments, financial rewards and complete satisfaction. As I look at the brilliant future this company has, I wish I were thirty years younger.

I am proud of our accomplishments, and I'd like to list a few:
- We are the fifth-ranking distributor in the nation.
- Our annualized sales volume is $450 million.
- Our compounded annual sales growth has been 20 percent per year.
- We have been recognized by McGraw-Hill's *Electrical*

*Wholesaling* as the fastest-growing electrical distributor over the past twenty-five years.

• We provide a good income for 1,700 dedicated and committed employees and their families.

• We are firmly in control of a professional company that will strategically reach a sales volume of $2 billion within the next ten years.

• We have a customer base numbering 65,000.

I also am the happiest father in the world, in that I have two excellent businessmen sons in management positions in the company, poised and ready to take over for me when I retire in the year 2000 at age sixty-nine.

All of this would not have been possible without the blessing of God and the support of my wonderful wife, Eva, and my six marvelous children. What more could anyone ask for than a great wife, an outstanding family and the finest company and group of employees in this entire country of ours? God has been good to me.